Leisure and Ancient Rome

JUN 08

Leisure and Ancient Rome

J. P. Toner

Polity Press

First published in 1995 by Polity Press
in association with Blackwell Publishers Ltd.
First published in paperback 1998

Editorial office:
Polity Press, 65 Bridge Street
Cambridge CB2 1UR, UK

Marketing and production:
Blackwell Publishers Ltd, 108 Cowley Road
Oxford OX4 1JF, UK

Published in the USA by
Blackwell Publishers Inc., 350 Main Street
Malden MA 02148, USA

A CIP catalogue record for this book is available from the British Library.

Library of Congress Cataloging-in-Publication Data
Toner, J. P.
    Leisure and ancient Rome / J.P. Toner.
        p.   cm.
    Includes bibliographical references and index.
    ISBN 0–7456–1432–9 (hardback : alk paper)
    ISBN 0–7456–2198–8 (pbk.)
    1. Rome—Social life and customs. 2. Leisure—Social aspects—
Rome. 3. Recreation—Social aspects—Rome. I. Title.
DG78. T655 1995
306.4'812'09376—dc20   95–16182
                                                   CIP

Typeset in 10½ on 12 pt Times by Graphicraft Typesetters Ltd, Hong Kong

Printed and bound in Great Britain by Marston Lindsay Ross International Ltd, Oxfordshire

Contents

List of Plates

Preface

I have incurred many debts of gratitude in the course of writing this book and I am pleased to have the chance to repay them, however inadequately, in this preface. For their frequent acts of kindness and generosity, my thanks go to: Neil and Melanie Crosby, Jon Gifford, David Holton, Sue Jeffreys, Chris Kelly, Rustom Khandalavala, Bruce Kiddy, John Leigh, Ashley and Jane Meggitt, Bernard and Brenda Meggitt, Nicholas Purcell, and Andrew Wilson. For their institutional assistance, my thanks to Selwyn College and the staff of the University Library. I am also grateful to Gill Motley and John Thompson of Polity Press for their enthusiastic and long-suffering support.

I would particularly like to thank Justin Meggitt, David Woodhouse, and Melanie Wright, who have all been true thoroughbreds in matters of friendly help and criticism, and Peter Garnsey, without whose expert training I would never have made the race-track, let alone completed the course.

This work is dedicated to my parents.

Texts and Abbreviations

Teubner and Oxford classical texts have been used throughout. In the interest of accessibility, I have tried to keep all translations as close as possible to those of the Loeb Classical Library. Classical texts are abbreviated in accordance with the *Oxford Latin Dictionary*, ed. P. G. W. Glare, Oxford: Clarendon Press, 1982, or, if not contained within that work, the *Oxford Greek-English Lexicon*, ed. H. G. Liddell and R. Scott, Oxford: Clarendon Press, 1968. Other titles are in accordance with the list of sources, with abbreviations, in vol. 3 of A. H. M. Jones' *The Later Roman Empire, 284–602: A Social, Economic and Administrative Survey*, pp. 394–406. The titles of periodicals and journals are abbreviated in accordance with the *Index des Périodiques Supplément à L'Année Philologique* 57, ed. P. Rosumek, Paris: Les Belles Lettres, 1982.

The following abbreviations are used:

ABull	The Art Bulletin
ANRW	Aufstieg und Niedergang der römischen Welt
CIL	Corpus Inscriptionum Latinarum
CPh	Classical Philology
CQ	Classical Quarterly
FL	Folklore
G & R	Greece and Rome
H & T	History and Theory
JbAC	Jahrbuch für Antike und Christentum
JHI	Journal of the History of Ideas
JIH	Journal of Interdisciplinary History
JLR	Journal of Leisure Research

JLS	Leisure Studies: The Journal of the Leisure Studies Association
JMH	Journal of Modern History
JPh	Journal of Philosophy
JQR	Jewish Quarterly Review
JRA	Journal of Roman Archaeology
JRS	Journal of Roman Studies
JThS	Journal of Theological Studies
P & P	Past and Present
PBSR	Papers of the British School at Rome
PLM	Poetae Latini Minores
TLS	The Times Literary Supplement

1

History, Leisure, and Ancient Rome

In his *An Enquiry Concerning Human Understanding*, David Hume asks: 'Would you know the sentiments, inclinations, and course of life of the Greeks and Romans? Study well the temper and actions of the French and English. You cannot be much mistaken in transforming to the former *most* of the observations which you have made with regard to the latter.'[1] As with the Greeks themselves, Hume's idea of history was one which revealed the eternal in the actual. But history has moved on, and, according to Schama, the search for the timeless has been replaced by the 'insoluble quandary' of the historian: 'how to live in two worlds at once; how to take the broken, mutilated remains of something or someone from the "enemy lines" of the documented past and restore it to life or give it a decent interment in our own time and place.'[2] This work is an attempt to confront that double life of an historian by using the concept of leisure to analyse Rome, whilst using the history of Rome to analyse the concept of leisure itself. It is, therefore, an inquiry into both the form of history and its epistemological foundations which is based on the practical reality of writing a history of Rome.

This work is an attempt to write what Bloch called 'une histoire plus humaine'.[3] This is an idea which rests on the belief that history is not lagging behind other disciplines. Rather, history is its own mode of thought, one which is better able to cope with the practical problems of life. Atkinson has observed:

> ... if there is a key to the understanding of history and with it historical explanation, it is that it is a study which has achieved the highest level of sophistication and professionalism, *without becoming theoretical*; without to any significant extent developing a technical vocabulary of its own; and without attempting to classify the

phenomena with which it deals in the systematic way, which is the only sure path to laws and theories and the sort of explanations offered by the sciences. There is a marked contrast between the precision and subtlety of the content of historical thinking and the somewhat homespun simplicity of its form.[4]

However, this 'more human history' hopes to achieve an understanding of Roman life and all its problems by becoming, at least in part, theoretical.[5] For the interdisciplinary influences which now affect history mean that the historian cannot escape from methodology. Nor is this necessarily a harmful development, so long as theory can be expressed in a somewhat homespun and simple way. In fact, its very simplicity makes history well suited to theorizing, in that it cuts to the heart of problems without ever losing touch with the realities from which they arise.

In that my approach seeks to understand the Romans by treating all parts of their culture equally, it is akin to a Geertzian cultural history.[6] Both approaches are informed by our egalitarian social ideals. However, whilst the use of the term 'culture' has served to reintegrate many of the different approaches to history, such a centripetal concept has also obscured ideological and class issues by assuming a uniformity in its subjects. It has imposed our ideal of equality on others by seeing equality in their cultures. The problem is that it is impossible to create a harmonious image of Roman culture because their society was fiercely hierarchical. In fact, there is no society where all its members share the same linguistic and non-linguistic practices. As Crapanzano has asked of Geertz, 'How can a whole people share a single subjectivity?'[7] Much social knowledge could be termed 'discultural' in that it is knowledge which is held by a minority of a society's members, as opposed to cultural knowledge which is generally understood. Geertz's 'webs of meaning' need to be historicized, for that will bring out a culture's disparate, inegalitarian elements. A more human history is precisely that because it does not dictate the terms of engagement with the past. It allows others to express their culture on their own terms, however abhorrent those terms might be to us.

The problem for cultural historians is that they tend to treat all evidence as coming from one ideal, homogeneous entity. The problem with traditional historians is that they see only the scattered, surface products of human life – the words and the artefacts – without looking to connect them in any fundamental way. If a deeper analysis is to be achieved, human life should be thought of as being temporally and spatially multi-levelled, with its different strata organically interconnected. The base consists of the emotive responses and the systems of ordering meaning which are common to our humanity; then there are the levels of culture and society; and finally the top plateau, on which the human personality sits, each with its own psychological structure. Every individual is influenced by the input of every level, and this creates a series of unique products: to the influence of the broader lower levels of geo-cultures (that is to say, Mediterranean culture, Chinese culture, etc.) is added that of higher, more localized, cultures, as well as specific societies and their particular constructs. The study of people therefore entails not only a study of their personal psychology, but of the many cultural, social, and mental levels which support their existence. Each individual displays his or her own influences – their hues and textures as it were – and it is the task of the historian to separate the colours of individuals into their constituent pigments. Different sections of the whole model will be closely matched – reds and blues will be the primary mix in one place, greens and yellows in another – but individuals will reveal their own subtle shadings, and it is these that allow us the opportunity to reconstruct the structures which prop up their way of life. For the differences in colour reflect not only the various levels of a culture, but its discrepancies in discourse, temperament, and behaviour as well.

As such, culture consists of a continuum between humanity and personal psychology. Culture is knowledge, for it is everything that has to be learnt as opposed to the learning processes themselves. Culture is also power, since, as Foucault has shown, knowledge is not ideal and abstract, but material and concrete; it cannot be divorced from the workings of power throughout society at all levels. The study of a culture, therefore, should be a matter of relating knowledge to power relations and structures, not of creating a unified image which naïvely papers over the social cracks. For cultures do not always have the flat, horizontal mien that our modern Western culture possesses; more often they are steeply inclined and stratified.

This image of culture represents not so much an organic unity but an organic totality. It is not a picture of Durkheimian static harmony but of a differentiated, dynamic structure in which the parts and the whole are internally related and reciprocally determine each other. All cultural parts can be seen analytically, as if even the smallest act contains a kind of social DNA which allows us to isolate specific genes and correlate them with societal features. Change comes to be seen as the organic product of constant cultural reproduction. As with an organism, culture is constantly changing in its attempts to maintain its balance; and it is well balanced only if it has achieved both homeostasis – a dynamic inner equilibrium – and a *modus vivendi* between this inner play of forces and its external environment. There is, therefore, a dynamic interplay between ideals and the changing circumstances to which they must adapt. The tensions which afflict a society can be thought of as being a function of this gap between its ideals and reality, and it is in order to bridge it that cultures build ingenious rationalizations and justifications of the *status quo*, as well as releasing pent-up stress through means as various as moralizing and the law. For cultural forces are directed towards achieving equilibrium by means of attempting to circumvent the obstacles which prevent it from achieving its ideal, harmonious state. All of a society's members, whatever their status, have to turn themselves to this task. The highly intelligent and educated may achieve it more elegantly than peasants but together their collective force provides the basis for the development of mentality.

Since homeostasis is never perfect and organisms are never isolated from their environment, change is the precondition of human life; there is no need to account for it. Yet it is possible to account for the direction and speed that change takes. The direction of influence is not only upwards, from the macro to the micro. There are different levels of both change and explanation. Changes at the top level of culture – human activity in other words – can affect the lower layers. Usually that produces only small-scale change and its influence does not penetrate far downwards, but that is not always the case. Some individual actions can have profound and long-term effects because they converge with structural and cultural forces, and this promotes their speedy transmission. At the lower cultural levels, change is more general and allows a greater range of possible responses from above. Changes are also frequently the result of outside agency, when one culture is forced to join another higher up and the sudden confluence of colour creates a strikingly different tone, or when external disaster splits cultures apart. There is, therefore, no need for an Annalistic favouring of the *longue durée*, since each of these cultural layers has an equal claim to analytical importance (although in practice, it may be discovered that any one level of input has had greater influence than another). After all, the 'deep' are not more important than the 'surface', since they are both what they are only in relation to the other. Take away the surface and what you are left with is no longer deep but shallow.

The principal concern of this model is to illuminate the relationship between ephemeral events and deep cultural forces, but it offers some flexibility as well. It allows a moving picture of growth and development to be shot, and also a still-life to be drawn, whilst simultaneously permitting an amalgam of the two to produce a more general impression of a mode of life and its enduring traits and characteristics. There can be no doubt that this model simplifies, but then that is what a model is meant to do. It is an intellectual construct that 'simplifies reality in order to emphasise the recurrent, the general and the typical, which it presents in the form of clusters of traits or attributes.'[8] There comes a time, though, when you have to stop making models and start dating them. Therefore, the main body of this work aims to produce a history of Rome which accords with this model by splitting Roman life into its constituent parts and processes.

There are, however, fundamental and practical problems which stand in the way of analysing Roman culture as outlined above. There is the practical difficulty of historical translation, that we cannot understand the Romans' conceptual world in their own terms and to attempt to do so leaves us trapped in an alien culture, prisoners to their tastes and doctrines, or as Geertz puts it, 'awash in immediacies, as well as entangled in vernacular'. To try by using only specialist tools, leaves us 'stranded in abstractions and smothered in jargon'.[9] Hence, the one-sided quantifying approach of the social sciences cannot be used. For little can be gained from the wholesale deployment of strategies and signifiers if the result is that we become deaf to the voices of the very people we wish to comprehend. Without doubt, the powerful position from which most of the surviving works from antiquity were written and their ideological content cannot be ignored (indeed, their rhetoric is at the heart of an attempt at cultural analysis), but to reduce their beliefs to power matrices and data alone is to run the risk of losing touch with the harsh immediacies of their lives. If we are to discover anything about what it meant to be Roman, it will not be enough to strip away the 'facade' and reveal the 'figures and coordinates'[10] of the 'real' structure beneath. To do so would be merely to impose our way of thinking on theirs. Therefore, if we wish to comprehend these long-extinct people, a blend of the new and the old must be created with which we can appreciate the symbolic forms they used to communicate with one another. This is an acceptance that 'history is a conversation with the dead.'[11] Hopkins considers it an advantage that 'we can do all the talking', but this would hardly seem to make for a balanced exchange. Rather, by applying our concepts it will be possible to recover the meanings which the Romans' words and actions had for the Romans themselves, as if we were looking through the windows of their perceptions into the rooms beyond, and simultaneously seeing our own reflection in the glass.

The nature of the historian's engagement with the past has to be redefined. The usefulness of historians' traditional sense of 'being there', their ability to 'feel and think as another', in short, their supposedly superior sense of historical empathy, are all thrown into doubt. It will no longer be sufficient, as if dreaming on the verandah, to 'wonder what it was like to be there'.[12] Instead, this almost divine sense of oneness with the subject is replaced by an effort to appreciate the modes of others' thoughts in the modalities of our own. It is a far more distanced relationship, and whilst sympathy, even compassion, are necessities, they are to be aimed at the investigation of the whole range of cultural expressions, not only at a more obvious group of targets.

Hence, an anthropological obsession with the mysterious and the out-landish will be of little benefit. Griffiths quotes Darnton's principle of research method: 'the best points of entry in an attempt to penetrate an alien culture can be those where it seems most opaque.'[13] But as Griffiths rightly points out, 'there is no reason to believe we are more fully in the presence of history when we encounter the bizarrely other.'[14] If there is an excuse for the practice of fastening onto the oddities of others, then it is the Johnsonian principle of writing so as to enable the reader better to enjoy life, for there can be no doubt that the weird commands more interest, and can thus initiate more thought. What seems obscure to us can be of more use when it is marginal also to the culture which is under scrutiny. To examine the edges of a society can reveal a clearer outline of its overall shape and literally define it. As Edwards observes, 'Cultural identity is constituted by its limits. Social deviants, those on its edge, define the central order.'[15] But seeing what distinguished insiders from outsiders is only one way of defining the perimeter of the culture itself. The social silhouette provided by these means needs to be supported by throwing light onto the culture's more solid masses. The practices and beliefs which maintained these boundaries have to be revealed and exam-ined, otherwise the image will remain insubstantial and its detail will stay in the dark. Yet a more accurate picture will not be obtained by concen-trating, as Griffiths would wish, on the 'finest blooms'[16] which a culture has nourished. To study the best of Roman *otium* – the art of aristocratic patronage – is indeed to observe the peaks of Roman temperament, but culture can be as wide and broad as high and low. The mundane and the central have as much claim to historical importance as the spectacular and the marginal. It is by contextualizing both that the historian will be able to understand what exactly constituted these frames of reference.

The problem we face is defining the terms of engagement with the past and the 'others' who inhabit it. This is why it is so useful to employ a concept like leisure as the tool for analysing Roman culture. For if we were to try to preserve 'leisure' as a stable category of historical analysis we would merely idealize and sterilize it. To the extent that a history of 'leisure' succeeds in concerning itself with 'leisure', it is doomed to fail as a history, unless it also includes as an essential part of its proper enterprise the task of demonstrating the historicity, conditions of emer-gence, modes of construction, and ideological contingencies of the very category of analysis that undergirds its own practice.[17] To analyse another without analysing oneself would be an act of cultural imperialism. The questions we need to ask are: 'What is the general form of our leisure?'; second, 'What was the general form of their *otium*?'; then, 'What was the form of Roman leisure, and the vehicles in which it was embodied?'[18] By using each to elucidate the others, it will be possible to create not only an interpretation of Roman free time within its overall cultural context, but perhaps also a more human history of Roman life and leisure.

Why leisure in particular? The first reason is that leisure sociologists' enthusiasm for their task does not seem to have extended into the past. The history of pre-industrial leisure remains an underdeveloped field, a third-world country to whose aid few have attempted to come, and which has languished in the aridity of positivism. There should be no doubt that the collation of detail is an essential part of the historian's task, but the history of pre-industrial leisure has often been unrelated to its wider cultural environment. For whilst accounts of the Romans' games and pastimes are two a penny, the social, political, and moral environments in which these practices occurred have been ignored.

The second is that, despite the well-established school of leisure sociology, leisure has often not been perceived as being a matter for serious research (I can bear witness to the smiles which habitually greet my subject). It might seem paradoxical to search for antiquity in a sketch drawn from seemingly non-serious leisure activities, but there is huge scope in these playful, often idealized, constructions of what life is and should be like. As with any man-made construct or institution, they express beliefs about a desired order of things, and simultaneously reflect the order as it actually stands. Furthermore, in leisure, everyday experience is ordered into events less cluttered with the demands of immediate practical purpose, and thus becomes concentrated into a form where meaning can be more powerfully articulated. They provide metacommentaries, and are undertaken in 'full awareness of the absence of the life they contrive to represent, and hence they may skilfully anticipate and compensate for the vanishing of the actual life that has empowered them.'[19]

The centrality of work and efficiency to our industrial society has also meant that leisure has come to be seen as a mere adjunct to productivity. This attitude was not prevalent in the ancient world, where *otium* competed on a far more level footing. The study of leisure, therefore, will be a helpful way for us to highlight the differences between the Romans' mentality and our own. Leisure, I would argue, also provides the best possible tool for the dissection of Roman society. Other studies of Roman life could be made – of their work, religion, family, to name only a few – some of which might conflict with the analyses which leisure offered. Leisure, though, would be the institution that revealed most of the traits of Roman life. Leisure would be the study to cover the most important areas of Roman culture. For the central themes of Roman life were most clearly connected in their leisure on account of the fact that Rome was felt to be characterized by its abundant leisure and the immorality it seemed to foster.

The study of leisure can thus offer a way into the wider life of ancient

Rome, and provide insights into the details of what it meant to be a Roman. It also reveals the cultural frictions which existed within Roman society and the attempts that were made to lessen the heat which they generated. For the use to which Roman people put their free time was the thin end of a very large cultural wedge. Ideas about leisure were some of the sturdiest of the pillars on which Roman perceptions of society and selfhood stood, and as conditions changed so new concepts of man and society were required with which to rebuild, and sometimes shore up, the old structures. Leisure represented, as in many ways it still does, the 'good life'. It offered people the chance to do what they wanted to do, and realize their hopes and potential free from the crushing constraints of everyday life. But there was no comfortable consensus about what the good life was, or about who could attain it. Leisure was not a neutral area. Strains and conflicts existed within Roman society, between the emperor, the elite, and the masses, and these found their most telling expression in anxieties over the use and misuse of free time. Leisure discourse was integral to ideas concerning the ordering of society and the worth of the individual within it. A similar view is also reflected in the etymology of our word 'leisure'. Derived from the Latin *licentia*, leisure carries connotations of licentiousness and freedom, and also the need for this behaviour to be licensed and controlled from above.

Concepts of morality, pleasure, and luxury were closely associated with these misgivings over the corrupting potential of free time. For these tensions also reflected the 'anxieties of superabundance', to borrow Schama's phrase.[20] That is to say, they revealed moral concerns about the influx of new wealth and practices which accompanied the acquisition of empire. The increase in prosperity allowed for greater and more extravagant leisure provision for a much enlarged section of the populace, and as the pleasures of the aristocratic lifestyle were made more widely available through the agency of a beneficent emperor, *otium* was seen clearly to be no longer the preserve of the rich. The new circumstances of life under an autocrat threatened the traditional qualities of *otium*, challenging them with the thrills of popular entertainment and the extravagance of imperial largesse. Leisure discourse became the vehicle for the expression of elite concerns over the transformation of Roman society, and held a double significance. On the one hand, leisure was all that was left to the elite since, with the end of the republic, they were denied their traditional position of political authority. On the other, that very leisure which had traditionally been their preserve, and to which they had retired, was increasingly encroached upon by the lower orders.

No easy correlation should be assumed between these competing moralities and definable social groups. As Roman society developed from republic to empire, the distinctions between the plebs and the elite became hazier, albeit only at the margins,[21] and their relationship changed. Different cultural levels existed both at societal and individual levels, and so whilst these rival moralities will be referred to in terms of their primary social origin – that is as belonging to either traditional elite, imperial, or popular cultures – there will be a constant awareness that these labels belong as much to the historian's tool-box as to the realities of the Roman empire. These categories were never stable: 'the Romans', 'the elite', and 'the plebs' were all groups whose composition and structure underwent constant transformation and development. In many ways, it was the partial fusion of these various levels which generated the new image of the Roman that the emperors tried to inculcate, and also allowed individuals greater scope for resistance through the selection of other modes of expression.[22]

This book does not cover an exact period, for a conceptual study cannot be marked out temporally in the same meticulous manner as a traditional history of politics. The social evolution of leisure ideas and the assignation of values to activities occurred at a near sedentary pace in comparison to the high-speed chases of public life. Attitudes towards certain forms of leisure seem barely to have changed for centuries. But these enduring concepts were put to work in fresh areas and served new functions, thereby assuring their continued development alongside the contingencies of the day. Nor can the inquiry be given free rein to race through the ages, if the concepts involved are not to be left stranded in historical generalization and unintegrated with their immediate context. It is not so much a case of our taking snapshots of events at particular moments and fixing them against the motion pictures which frame them, as the very opposite – locating the action from sets of interrelated dramas against a far more static cultural backdrop. Accordingly, for the purposes of this investigation, two time-scales have been in operation. The analysis of the political evolution of leisure has concentrated on the transition period from republic to empire, that is to say the first centuries BC and AD, with the evidence for the establishment and maintenance of an imperial image of Romanness being drawn principally from the first and early second centuries AD. However, the examination of the underlying currents of social opinion and custom has flowed on a different temporal plane. That has been allowed to meander more freely, drawing on whatever sources were to be found (mostly the period from Cicero in the first century BC to Ammianus in the fourth century AD). This may have created a farrago of convictions and prejudices, along with all their individual and local bias, but the approach has two justifications: one is the practical excuse that the ancient historian cannot afford to pass over any details that might help to build up a picture of the Roman mentality; the other is that the difficult and perplexing network of perspectives produced by this process may, in all likelihood, give an accurate record of the background hiss above which the dramas of Roman life were heard. It is to this very noise that our ears are especially well attuned. These were the bases on which Roman life was structured, the things about which they gave scarcely a second thought, but which for our understanding are crucial.[23] To put it more theoretically, when I use sources from different eras and backgrounds I am trying to use them as evidence for the structure of the lower levels of Roman culture – cutting off, as it were, the more localized upper levels of their lives to reveal the more common, enduring fundamentals beneath. For example, Christian sources can rub shoulders with pagan precisely because there were many areas of continuity between them. Many on both the left and the right will, no doubt, deplore this approach for lacking 'sophistication in reading' or the like. I can only emphasize that I am taking a top-down look at the Roman world, rather than employing their bottom-up method. By this I mean that my concern has been to create a framework of understanding for the whole of Roman culture, into which specific sources with all their axes to grind can then be situated.

A similar method is in operation in the matter of geography, and has been necessary for the same reasons. The exploration of the process of the politicization of leisure and its development within the empire, has centred on the city of Rome.[24] As the seat of government and the home of the powerful, this seemed the most obvious place to begin, the place where general attributes would be most concentrated and hence most easily accessible. Rome's unique characteristics – its immensity and its corn dole – would have affected its local form of leisure greatly, and might even have exaggerated more common traits of the Roman temperament. However, a more liberal sense of location has been required to establish these traits. Most evidence has come from Rome, from where so many of the surviving texts originated, but when other places have offered help it has not been refused. Once again, the reasons are partly pragmatic, partly methodological. Beggars cannot be choosers, but the scraps they scavenge from the scattered dustbins of history can amass into a highly effective facsimile of social realities.

The work on Rome will not produce a conclusion, nor does it seek to, but *in toto* the various chapters build up into what tries to be the 'histoire plus humaine' I have discussed in this introduction. This will have three main parts: an analysis of Rome which accords with the historical model of culture; the production of generally applicable social theory drawn from the Roman case study; and finally, the acquisition of a fuller understanding of the intellectual foundations on which such a history stands. For this is a book on leisure as well as antiquity and shows what happens when two cultures and their concepts come together.

2

Leisure

St Augustine once said that so long as he was not asked to define the
concept of time then he knew what it was, but if asked then he did not.[1]
The notion of leisure seems to have identical properties. Wilson tells us
that 'leisure is notoriously difficult to define',[2] but I think it is crucial that
prior to examining Rome we have a fuller knowledge of the concept with
which we are to try to effect our history. For whilst this book is primarily
a historical analysis of Roman culture as evidenced in its leisure, it is also
concerned with the epistemological status of that analysis. What is more
immediately significant for our project is that most leisure sociologists
have denied that the concept of leisure is even applicable to the pre-
industrial world, so if we are to progress at all we shall have first to overcome this obstacle.

Sociologists of leisure have spent long hours agonizing over its properties, but their definitions can, at heart, be split into two camps: the
qualitative and the quantitative. The primary category of the first type is
the humanistic.[3] In this view, leisure is seen as an end in itself; it is
characterized as 'essentially autotelic activity. In other words, it is chosen
primarily for its own sake.' 'Leisure is thus to be distinguished from
whatever has to be done',[4] but it cannot be tied down to any particular set
of activities. This definition, strongly influenced by the Aristotelian position,[5] views leisure as consisting of a duality of freedoms: 'freedom from
the necessity of being occupied',[6] and freedom to choose what to do.
Leisure becomes, as Goodale and Godbey see it, the 'transcendence into
the glorious, dizzying, terrible realm where one's life begins to truly
reveal who one is through the process of doing what one chooses'.[7]

Clearly, leisure in this view has more to do with an ideal way of living
than, say, the taverns and prostitutes that filled so many of Rome's back
streets. In fact, Goodale and Godbey consider that 'leisure always carries

with it the responsibility for inventing an ideal.'[8] But that a great deal of thinking about leisure remains permeated by such 'idealist conceptions' has been the basis for much criticism.[9] Once we start having to judge people's leisure against an ideal *modus vivendi*, it becomes very difficult, and probably impossible, to keep out our own prejudices about which activities and attitudes constitute that life. The ideal which tends to be formulated is one which reflects the privileged position of the acolytes of high culture.[10] For if leisure is to be judged by a degree of absolute freedom, both of choice and from obligation, it naturally leans towards those at the top of the socioeconomic pile.[11] To be free from the necessity of being occupied is a rare advantage, and 'the scope of idleness depends on the level of income.'[12] Veblen recognized this in his classic work on the 'leisure class'.[13] He saw that the elite American construction of leisure dealt with the high culture of a class who used it as a social symbol and a political tool. Their 'conspicuous consumption' and 'pecuniary emulation' reflected the expensive and exclusive idleness of a rich elite. The non-productive consumption of time characterized this type of leisure. Moreover, there was a rationalization of these practices which resulted in the denigration of productive labour.

This formulation bears a strong resemblance to the Roman elite's concept of *otium*. However, it is immediately evident that this elitist position is incompatible with a modern, more inclusive perspective. That work somehow pollutes labourers and automatically disqualifies them from participating in leisure can no longer be maintained. Consequently, there has been a move away from an aristocratic outlook towards a more quantitative approach which attempts to analyse leisure in terms of hours and minutes. This has created a sharp temporal division between work and non-work, but has had the positive effect of partially emancipating the notions of free time and leisure from economics, thereby making leisure a possibility for all but the most deprived. To most people in the modern post-industrial world such a residual definition (the measurement of leisure as time left over from work) is the most meaningful, for leisure is easily thought of as the time during which the individual is not working.[14] As working hours, that is to say employment hours, have become more exact so it is has been convenient to parcel off the rest of the day as being leisure time. However, the popular practice of merging ideas in this way has created a mess which has prevented leisure from becoming a historically useful implement. Giddens has pointed out that the study of leisure has suffered for two reasons: it has been seen as the minor and trivial opposite of work, and there has been a high degree of conceptual confusion.[15] The problems of the quantitative approach are twofold: on the one hand, it seems clear to most observers, just as it is to most leisure sociologists, that not all free time can be classed as leisure,[16] and on the other, if it is to stand as an independent academic discipline worthy of the name, leisure cannot consist only of the leftovers from work.

There seems to be, especially among the more idealistically minded, a common belief that leisure is in some sense 'free' and freely chosen. But not all agree. Berger claims that, 'no time is free of normative constraints', and even that, 'leisure may refer to precisely those activities most constrained by moral norms.'[17] In contrast to the view that it is only in leisure that we are our true selves, Rojek has attacked the consistent association of leisure with positive experiences of liberty, fulfilment, choice, and growth.[18] Instead, he tries to locate leisure forms in their specific economies of 'political and cultural regulation'. This is a neo-Marxist perspective which views leisure as the 'reward of the many who toil in domestic labour and paid employment for the profit of the few'.[19] This is, to me, extreme, even patronizing, but it does lead him to conclude:

> Leisure time and space do not merely or automatically exist in society. On the contrary, leisure time and leisure space are continuously made and remade by the actions of people. Moreover, their actions often involve basic conflicts over the meaning and uses of leisure time and leisure space.[20]

The realization that the appearance of leisure is intrinsically connected with the existence of social struggles and competing moralities is important in viewing free time in its social context. For as Parker says, 'the degree to which work and leisure are experienced, in fact and in ideology, as separate parts of life seems to be related to the degree to which the society itself is stratified, work being the lot of the masses and leisure that of the elite.'[21]

The investigation of leisure sociologists has moved on in an attempt to improve their conceptual apparatus. In particular, scholars have studied the different functions that leisure serves and its importance for social structure, interpersonal relations, and self-identity. This has resulted in an increased knowledge of the social and psychological possibilities of leisure, and also produced a new awareness of leisure as a sociological construct.[22] Leisure has come to be understood as a social fabrication which contains elements such as an antithesis to work, a perception of freedom, enjoyment, and range of choice. It is no longer seen as a unitary or residual sphere of activity, rather as a multidimensional concept.[23] Some of the ingredients which go to make leisure are to be found in work, family activities, and education; and conversely, some of the constituent parts of those constructions are often to be found in leisure. Hence, nothing is definable as leisure as such, and almost anything is definable as leisure, given a synthesis of the suggested elements. Kaplan offers a definition, after first warning that the leisure construct is 'a typical, not an average, picture against which a real activity-experience may be assessed':

> *Leisure*, we might say, *consists of relatively self-determined activity-experience that falls into one's economically free-time roles, that is seen as leisure by participants, that is psychologically pleasant in anticipation and recollection, that potentially covers the whole range of commitment and intensity, that contains characteristic norms and constraints, and that provides opportunities for recreation, personal growth, and service to others.*[24]

The lameness of this approach has left leisure limping. If the object of study is to be limited to our society, then to presume that readers know what leisure is when they see it is practical enough. They are capable of recognizing leisure as it appears in the context of their own lives. But if we are to talk about others, dead others, we must have a clearer idea of the concepts that we are using to convey meaning. This should not be seen as a call to provide lists of necessary conditions which must be fulfilled for something to acquire the title of 'leisure'. What is needed is that Wittgenstein's notion of familial resemblance be expanded within a clearer conceptual framework, to include other branches of humanity, rather than be confined to the immediate kin-group of our culture. For although leisure is an abstract term, and 'no concrete activity will necessarily exhibit all its defining characteristics in their purity',[25] that should not be used as an excuse for not attempting a definition at all, especially if the concept is to step outside the boundaries of its own culture.

Clearly, there has been considerable disagreement over what constitutes leisure. What there has been greater consensus over, which presents a problem that must be addressed, is that the concept of leisure is inapplicable to the pre-industrial era.[26] Dumazedier considers that, 'leisure has distinct characteristics, specific to the civilizations born of the industrial revolution.' In fact, he considers that 'in historical pre-industrial societies leisure did not exist.'[27] His is just another example of the widespread outlook which sees the industrial revolution as the root of all history, rather than as a historical event itself. The image thus created of the pre-industrial world is one of snug homogeneous groups, living a life of vapid simplicity, and it seems to be the result of a confusion between the terms pre-industrial and primitive. 'Can the holidays and feast-days of traditional societies', asks Dumazedier, 'be described as leisure?' He thinks not, because in pre-industrial societies 'work followed the natural cycle of seasons and days . . . its rhythm was natural, interrupted by breaks, by songs, by games and ceremonies . . . There was no clearcut division between work and rest.'[28] In his view, leisure must no longer be regulated by communally prescribed ritual obligations. Individuals must be free to choose, although their choice is socially determined, and work must be demarcated from other activities; and these conditions exist only in industrial and post-industrial societies.

In his influential work, Marrus also subscribes to this practice of sweeping over the broad plains of the pre-industrial world with a rose-tinted, and highly generalizing, view. Having supplied his definition of leisure as 'free activity, determined by individuals who make a choice independent of direct obligations of work, family, or society',[29] he explains that traditional pastimes, such as singing, folk dancing, and feasts, were too deeply rooted in custom and habit to be called leisure. They were regulated strictly by rules that approximate to a ritual and occurred within the context of some larger and strictly defined community. Since they did not take place free from direct obligation, he prefers to call them 'sociability'. For as DeGrazia explains in the same volume, 'time in the modern sense had no part of the scheme.' He explains, by way of example, that the 'shoemaker had shoes to make or repair. When he was playing cards at the alehouse he wasn't making shoes, but neither was he spending free time ... He had shoes to make, ale to drink, and cards to play, all of which he did without need of the words work and leisure.' There was no division of time or labour, like there is today.[30] Cunningham neatly refutes this argument:

> But, except in primitive societies, people have always been aware of a separation between work and leisure, and have put a high value on leisure. Leisure itself, a harvest celebration for example, may have been inextricably bound up with work, but to pretend that participants were unaware when they were working and when they were not is sheer romanticism.[31]

Marrus is prepared to accept that some leisure did exist in the pre-industrial era, but mainly amongst the aristocracy. Their leisure was 'the playing of a musical instrument, reading for pleasure, or perhaps even writing poetry'. Moreover, 'these practices did not occur in a communal context, and were not part of an intricate structure of obligation.'[32] Elitism aside, he fails to realize that these activities were, to use his terminology, just part of an aristocratic way of life – a life that was as strictly regulated by a set of rules, which approximated to ritual, as was the life of the common people.[33] Marrus believes that 'for the broad masses of Europeans, leisure became a reality only in the nineteenth century, and that its emergence was part of a more general transformation known as modernization.'[34] The only exception that he makes, rather curiously, is to confer the status of leisure on pre-industrial, lower-class card-playing. But like

aristocratic leisure, card-playing was as much influenced by social regulations and codes of conduct as ale-drinking and dancing. Many modern
forms of what we would consider leisure are also closely connected to
obligations of family, work, and society. Lower-class leisure, for example, tends to be far more family-orientated.[35] These activities are not, of
course, organized as strictly as the local feasts and festivals which were
the principal forms of pre-industrial leisure as Marrus sees it, but would
we dare call them less leisurely than middle-class free-time pursuits? The
fact that feasts and festivals were closely regulated by the community
tells us more about the relationship that existed between a society and the
forms of its leisure than about the nature of leisure itself. Otherwise, the
result is that we favour the leisure of the rich and powerful because of
the greater choice available to them, and pass over the plebs, instead of
seeing their social inferiority as being reflected in their leisure.

Utopian views of leisure as a self-determined activity are, therefore,
doubly problematic. Firstly, their idealistic stance places great emphasis
on the autonomous character of leisure and its individual expressions.
This runs a serious risk of locating leisure as an unimportant point on the
social map, an insignificant accompaniment to the serious, and more central,
world of work. Secondly, they are 'in danger of drifting towards a consumer sovereignty model, where the freedom of individuals to choose
leisure pursuits is presented as a progressive feature of modern industrial
societies in contrast to the alleged integration and bonded constraints of
the traditional communal order.'[36] Such elitist approaches are of little use
in an attempt at understanding leisure as it descends the social scale, and
even less in examining Roman culture in its diverse social forms. What
has happened is that, by seeing the industrial revolution outside history,
sociologists have come to see leisure only as an industrial product, rather
than as a phenomenon which has itself become industrialized. Thus they
try to gauge leisure on a scale of personal freedom, and take it to be an
indicator of consumer choice. This needs to be turned on its head. Increased personal freedoms and greater consumer choice, the products of
the industrial revolution, have been reflected in both leisure activities and
concepts.

3

Definitions

How, then, are we to think of leisure? It is not that all earlier theories about leisure should be rejected, rather that the issues which they raise should be reconstituted into a form which allows them to step outside the industrial world. For leisure is both a sociological concept and a social construct, one which we need to use to be able to understand, which needs to be abstracted to make it generally applicable, and then historicized to make it work. I hope to achieve this by developing a historically relevant theory of leisure; not necessarily true, but useful by reason of its applicability to the pre-industrial environment, and free of the intellectual excess-baggage of both the modern construct of leisure and the ancient notion of *otium*. The definition is this:

Leisure is a system of symbols which acts to establish a feeling of freedom and pleasure by formulating a sense of choice and desire.

It will be immediately apparent that this is broadly based on Geertz's classic definition of religion.[1] Leisure is seen as a concept definable in terms of emotive experience, a set of culturally specific symbols which produce a set of universal human feelings. As such, the definition treats the phenomenon under inspection as an institution which receives its articulation through a group of signs that are meaningful to people within their cultural context.

Once it is accepted that leisure is a social institution, it becomes impossible to state definitively the activities in which it is expressed. However, within a specific society, it does become possible to examine these patterns of signification in the distinctive forms into which that culture has shaped them. Yet there will still be many instances where a sense of leisure, albeit often fragmentary because of the presence of only a few of the leisure characteristics, will exist outside the more common forms of the cultural expression of leisure. Put theoretically, this means that the symbols which are culturally ordered to form a specific mode of leisure perception can also be experienced individually, or in hybrid combinations, with the result that the person on the receiving end of these symbols will feel an emotive response which they would classify as a partial leisure experience. We experience most of our leisure in, say, the football stadium, on the golf course, or in the pub, but other activities, which we would not normally classify as leisure, can in certain circumstances acquire some, if not all, of the attributes of leisure. Religion and the family, for example, can display many of the traits of leisure – they can produce enjoyment, can be voluntary, can be desired, can be liberating – but, in fact, are themselves social institutions which can be defined in terms of their own symbolic webs of meaning. For the individual symbols, which create separate affective reactions, can be utilized in more than one social construct, and it is for this reason that so many areas of human life seem to overlap, interconnect, and communicate with each other.

Leisure cannot be tied down to a precise period of time. Its moods and perceptions can be created, and experienced, at any point. In practice, though, leisure tends to exist in a social form which demarcates fairly distinct occasions for its occurrence. Free time can be thought of as periods in which a mood of limited freedom has been created by the formulation of a sense of future choice and possibility. But unlike leisure, free time can become a negative experience, especially when people can find nothing that they want to do. Leisure, by contrast, is something into which a perception of the act having been chosen and desired has been incorporated, and so, by its nature, is positively experienced.

Clearly, leisure has to be felt, but its sensual experience is intimately connected with the conventional social manners of its expression. This leads to an acceptance that the pursuit of enjoyment – in short, doing what one wants, likes, and finds pleasurable – is not a purely personal concern.[2] The ways in which a society offers individuals fulfilment of their desires can often initiate, and then manipulate, those desires themselves. Within a Roman context, the taverns and cook-shops which were so popular with the common people represented to many in the upper strata nothing but immorality, waste, and decadence. Conversely, the bookish pursuits of a Pliny probably for most symbolized only boredom and old-fashioned values. Thus leisure not only appears as a social construction, but it can also perform a wide variety of functions at both societal and individual levels. The degree to which these beliefs are linked explicitly to particular classes and statuses can reveal much about that society's structures and way of ordering their environment. This also means that leisure cannot be confined solely to the 'non-serious', for to engage in something seriously is merely to adopt a certain mood of participation, and that can be directed towards any activity.

However, neither the perception of freedom and enjoyment, nor the sense of choice are relative to the social position of the individual. The poor man's leisure does not mean less to him, nor is it less enjoyable and valuable – though it is certainly less expensive – than the rich man's. All leisure is created equal and is of equivalent historical importance, but it finds its expression in diverse forms which reflect the socioeconomic parameters of its environment. The very feeling that one is doing what one wants, likes, and enjoys creates a sense of choice, even if there is, in numerical terms, very little at all. This sense creates a perception of freedom, opportunity, and self-expression, which contributes to a mood of self-actualization and fulfilment. Hence, a peasant can get as much enjoyment from an evening in the one pub available as the lord and master from his array of attractions.

For the sake of clarity, it will also be useful to compare this conception of leisure to one for work.[3] Paralleling my definition of leisure, work can be thought of in this way:

Work is a system of symbols which acts to establish a feeling of restraint and effort by formulating a sense of obligation and necessity.

From this viewpoint, work is like leisure in that it is a phenomenon which, while not encompassed in any set of activities, is culturally moulded into local institutional shapes. The ways in which work is experienced are socially constructed, and what actually counts as work varies from culture to culture. Like leisure, it need not be tied down to distinct periods for it to be experienced, since some activities can carry a competing burden of symbols. One man's work can appear to another as leisure, and vice versa. There is no doubt that some forms of leisure require a great physical input, that is to say 'effort' in the purely mechanical sense, but are not felt, by some, to be laborious. Leisure activities can also acquire some of the attributes of work by becoming unenjoyable, boring, or constrained, the result of our just not being in the mood, or being forced to listen to some bore over a meal. To be sure, work can be fulfilling, even enjoyable, but these perceptions are formulated from the incorporation of leisure symbols. In other words, work can be experienced as being leisure-like, but still there will remain powerful forces of effort and obligation, of which pay is the most potent symbol. Part of the success of the Protestant work ethic was its ability to create an image of work as being fulfilling and enjoyable, and not just necessary and laborious.

The degree to which leisure and work are experienced as separate tends to coincide with the level of stratification and complexity within a society. It is only in these circumstances that work and leisure become separated into distinct systems of experience. In the most primitive of societies, where division of time and labour was far less pronounced than is now the case, it was not that these symbols were not in operation, it was that they were fused to such an extent that the categories of leisure and work, those parcels of signs, were mostly meaningless. For the perception of time is culturally constructed, and it was not until time became packaged that these independent symbol systems were formed. Different patterns of meaning can be in operation at the same time, and it is a function of our more exact way of reckoning time that they have come to be seen as mutually exclusive.

Nor is it useful, as has often been done, to think of either leisure or work as being cut off from life. The fact that some of the signs which surround everything we do and feel have been formulated into systems does not disconnect them from the central grid of life. This has been particularly true of thought concerning a concept close to the heart of leisure, that of play. The analysis of play seems to have been petrified for some time now.[4] Play has been viewed as a free activity marked out within a 'sacred' zone, and thus separated from ordinary life; also as being unproductive, uncertain, make-believe, and yet regulated. More recent research has concentrated on the therapeutic, didactic, and cathartic functions of play, and there seems to be a conceptual confusion similar to that which exists in the study of leisure. This is an important concept for the study of leisure and so a parallel definition is needed:

Play is a system of symbols which establishes a feeling of freedom and spontaneity, amusement and stimulation by formulating a sense of non-seriousness, fantasy, and chance.

Clearly, there is a close relationship between leisure and play, and it will be necessary to highlight the difference. The disparity lies in the formulation. Leisure is based on a perceptual cocktail of individual choice and decision, play on the feeling of being in another ludic world where a blend of chance, spontaneity, and creativity rule the individual. There is a dichotomy of freedoms, one based on personal control over life away from the constraints brought on by the mundane, the other based on freedom from the burden of individual responsibility. There are also distinct kinds of enjoyment: one from doing what you want, the other from having something you enjoy done to you. Play, then, is not leisure, though they are two systems of meaning which are closely related and often overlap. Games and sport represent a formalized set of symbols which often incorporate competition and skill as well as ludic elements of fantasy and chance. In sport, therefore, leisure and play merge to produce a more serious, less spontaneous event by importing a degree of strategy and control. As Caillois has shown (though not from this theoretical position) it then becomes possible to analyse particular games according to the chemistry of the elements by which they have been formulated, and furthermore, to analyse societies according to the particular elemental cocktails they prefer.

These definitions are inclusive and interpretive. That method means we do not have to judge others' leisure in accordance with actual degrees of choice and freedom in relation to us. We should not judge another's leisure as worse, or less leisurely, than ours. We should try to place those perceptions into their social context, with all its specific inequalities. For these definitions are specimens of pure theory which will have to be put to practical use for them actually to produce anything. As it is, they are the keys to the doors which stand between us and antiquity – but they are no more than that, and they can tell us nothing of the world beyond.

4

Leisure and *Otium*

According to the French historian Paul Veyne, the enigma of the ancient contempt for labour and manual work, and their 'exaltation of leisure as the *sine qua non* of a "liberal" life, the only life worthy of a man, shocks us deeply'. This is reasonable enough, but he goes on to make a most curious statement:

> And yet, if we are honest, we must admit that the key to this enigma lies within ourselves. True, we believe that work is respectable and would not dare to admit to idleness. Nevertheless, we are sensitive to claim distinctions and, admit it or not, regard workers and shop-keepers as people of relatively little importance. We would not want ourselves or our children to sink to their station, even if we are a little ashamed of harboring such sentiments.[1]

This seems to be outmodedly patrician (and to the son of a shopkeeper, as I am, rather offensive). More importantly, such a Napoleonic 'Nation of Shopkeepers' attitude is, I think, symptomatic of a residual problem in Ancient History, one which has afflicted the study of leisure. The nature of the way in which Classics has been taught has tended to draw recruits from the upper and upper-middle classes, and they in turn have tended to be content to remain in the more comfortable thought-worlds of the Roman elite.[2]

This chapter begins the process of overturning earlier analyses of *otium* by comparing it with our concept of leisure and concentrates on the relationship and tensions that existed between a conventional landed aristocracy and the mass of the population beneath them.[3] It will be argued that elite attitudes to the use of leisure, and the moral discourse through which these were expressed, were vital to the ways in which they defined themselves. Whilst it is true to say that these debates were 'concerned overwhelmingly with the behaviour of the upper classes',[4] we should not be content to leave the matter there. Just as we would no longer accept that ancient ideas about slaves and their 'natural' inferiority represent all that there is to say on the subject, preferring instead to see these thoughts as being linked to a dominant ideology, so we should no longer be content to see leisure as being neatly summed up by elite discussions of *otium*. Why, it must be asked, were the elite ardent in their desire to cut themselves off, and increasingly so? Why did they have to be everything that the masses were not? The answers to these problems will come from the contextualization of these elite texts into the total framework of Roman life by which they were supported. For the evidence we have may be the politics of the few, but it is the masses who underlie that politics. Our more inclusive notion of leisure will therefore be used to recreate the social attitudes which underpinned the elite concept of *otium*.

Otium, then as now, was an ambiguous concept which possessed numerous connotations. Some of these were the mental jumble of Roman life, part of the more common elements of their culture. For example, *otium* contained an element of doing as one pleased, in one's own good time; hence, some foods had to be allowed to cook '*otiose*',[5] whilst starving oneself to death represented a leisurely mode of suicide.[6] In contrast, to be leisurely could mean doing nothing at all: uninvested money was called idle,[7] and the industry of aqueducts could be favourably compared to the pyramids' sloth.[8]

Other facets of leisure held out the prospect of more significant benefits for all classes of people. Indeed, the promise of less labour and greater leisure has been a common goal of much utopian literature throughout the ages, and for the vast majority of people in Rome, any move towards these ends would have represented a notable alleviation of the harsh toils of their daily struggle for survival. The sense of choice, freedom, and enjoyment, which *otium* fostered within them, came to epitomize the 'good life', and, as the astrologer Manilius informs us, 'most worship possession and power, soft luxury through leisure (*otio*)', as well as the diversions of seductive music and slight labour.[9] It is only those born under the influence of the star sign Gemini who find all of life pleasant, for whom 'even work is a pleasure (*labor est etiam ipse voluptas*).'[10] Similarly, Pliny was in no doubt that he was happiest, and enjoying life to the full, when he was at his most leisurely (*otiosissimus*).[11] It is to be doubted, of course, that an aristocrat such as he would have conceded that the lower orders were capable of this deep leisure, but others of his ilk accepted that it was an object of general desire. Cicero asks:

What is so popular as leisure (*otium*)? Which is so pleasant that
both you and your ancestors and the bravest of men think that the
greatest labours ought to be undertaken in order to enjoy repose
some day, especially when accompanied by authority and dignity.[12]

Indeed, the life of leisure enjoyed by some became proverbial. Seneca
tells of the famed retirement of Vatia, which was such that, 'people used
to exclaim, "Vatia, you alone know how to live."'[13]

Otium represented the best that life had to offer, what people would
choose if they had the chance. This was especially so for those situated
nearer the chthonic realities of Roman life; they well knew the difference
between the pleasures of leisure and their 'hated toil'.[14] If Martial had had
free time to use (*disponere tempus otiosum*) and no business to attend to,
he would not have known 'the halls or mansions of men of power, nor
worrying lawsuits and the anxious forum, nor lordly ancestral busts', but
the promenades, lounges, bookshops, Campus Martius, colonnades, gardens, fresh waters, and warm baths, these would be his haunts and his
tasks.[15] Similarly, Demea, in Terence's *Adelphi*, bemoans the benefits of
his brother's life of leisure: 'He has spent all his days in leisure, given up
to society, complaisant, easy-going, affronting no one and having a smile
for everybody. He has lived for himself and spent his money on himself,
and all the world speaks well of him and loves him.'[16] Nor were the
benefits of *otium* clear only to humans. Even an animal knew that leisure
was preferable to work; and so Apuleius' ass feigns ignorance of milling
in order to be left to feed at leisure,[17] much preferring to be penned up
with nothing to do but eat choice barley and beans.[18]

Leisure was not concerned only with the best way to live. When combined with sudden death, which the Romans considered to be one of life's
supreme happinesses, it produced the finest examples of the perfect end-
ing to a Roman life. Thus, Torquatus died while helping himself to a cake
at dinner; Lucius Tuccius while drinking mead; Appius Saufeus while
sucking an egg upon returning from the bath house; Titus Hetereius ex-
pired among women, whilst two minor aristocrats passed away when with
the pantomime dancer Mysticus, the leading beauty of the day. But perhaps
the finest death was that of Ofilius Hilarus, and the most bizarre that of
an unknown fan of Felix, the Red faction's charioteer. The former, a
comedy actor, after a great public success on his birthday, held a party,
put on his mask, and ordered a hot drink – then died, a fact which went
unnoticed for some time, whilst his friends partied around him. The latter
threw himself on his hero's funeral pyre in an act of one-upmanship over
the fans of the opposing circus factions (though they later tried to play
this down by claiming that the man had fainted owing to the quantity of
cheap perfumes present at the time).[19]

The popularity of leisure represented part of a common ideological level in Roman society. However, it was not so clear cut as that. The frequent accusations of leisure misuse which we encounter in the sources reflected competing notions about how free time should be spent. This was a fundamental issue, for the temporal ordering of a society is one of its mainstays. Those who acted outside this order went against the 'natural' rhythms of the day, and by crossing such perceptual boundaries incurred the charge of immorality. The elite were keen to emphasize their own productive use of time: 'and I have been very glad to make good use of my leisure with literary work during these days which others have wasted in the idlest (*otiosissimus*) of occupations.'[20] For the 'moral minority' were convinced that others wasted their time to no purpose, and it was not their intention to waste 'precious leisure in indolence and sloth'.[21] However, not all *otium* was thought to require activity. As Gellius describes, it was possible to pass the time in meditation: 'When I have leisure from legal business, and I walk or ride for bodily exercise, I have the habit of silently meditating sometimes on trifling and insignificant questions.'[22] It was a matter of purpose. For Gellius' contemplation acted to reveal the philosophical learning of a man of high culture, but when the plebs stood idly it served only to exhibit their inability to use their free time in a constructive way. Hence, Seneca refused to regard rest and freedom from trouble as a good, 'for what is more at leisure than a worm (*quid est otiosius verme*)?'[23]

The basis for the discriminating treatment of leisure activities was the distinction between the life of leisure, a prerequisite of the elite, and the life of labour, which was the mark of a plebeian existence. From this traditional perspective, leisure was a natural and legitimate part of elite culture, whereas for labourers it was a potentially dangerous temptation and a distraction from their primary productive concerns. Leisure was an indulgence, a time-bomb of destructive possibilities, which the powerful could readily afford, but against which the plebs had to guard, or else be protected. Leisure was to be meted out in small doses and enjoyed with *temperantia* (self-control), but this was a quality which the elite thought that they alone possessed. Such a paternalistic viewpoint meant that it was seen as entirely proper to treat leisure with due regard for the status of its participants.

The paternalism of the ruling elite permeated their diverse conceptions of *otium*. It seemed clear to a man of Cicero's position that:

> in a state ruled by its best men, the citizens must necessarily be the happiest, being freed from all cares and worries, when once they have entrusted the preservation of their leisure (*otium*) to others,

whose duty it is to guard it vigilantly and never allow the people to think that their interests are being neglected by their rulers.[24]

The *otium* of this view was built on a foundation of political patronage. *Otium* offered the opportunity for people to live their lives free from the dark obligations of war, free to pursue their own aims. But it also belonged to the rhetorical justifications of elite government. Wirszubski is right when he says that Cicero's repeated use of the phrase reflected both its popularity and its ambiguity.[25] It appealed both to the populace, for its placement of, put crudely, 'leisure for all' as the aim of government, and to the elite because of its emphasis on the *dignitas* which must accompany this *otium*. In other words, freedom and opportunity were the goals, but that did not imply that the lower orders should be free to do as they wished. In fact, their inherent lack of *dignitas* suggested that their participation in *otium* would remain as limited as ever. As André says, Cicero 'a voulu définir . . . une orthodoxie de l'*otium*.'[26]

The elite's view of themselves reflected the traditional hierarchical attitudes of a landowning ruling aristocracy. Their way of thinking about work and leisure closely resembled that of Veblen's leisure class: nonproductive lifestyles and conspicuous consumption highlighted their freedom from economic necessity, as did their disdain for labour, whilst high culture and learning characterized their free time. However, that represents only half of the picture. The elite's disregard for work could only be maintained as long as they ensured that the surplus which kept them in power not only continued to be produced, but stayed in their hands as well. They attempted to produce a value-system for their agricultural workers, and coupled this with a sense of duty of their own. The surviving literature therefore exaggerates the authors' own diligence and the benefits of work, and it denigrates the idleness of the lower orders and the myriad perils which it entailed.

In general, the elite perceived that ideally their work was pursued for voluntary reasons, whereas their leisure was not aimed solely at enjoyment or diversion: for 'philosophy is not pursued for amusement or to relieve our free time of boredom (*ut dematur otio nausia*).'[27] Nor was leisure on its own an unequivocal benefit: Cicero, upon his withdrawal from public life, declared, 'I have this single boon left to me, whatever its worth, of leisure.'[28] The elite's work consisted of the voluntary performance of civic duties and the management of their assets. Their leisure entailed not only the more obvious pursuits of hunting and feasting, but also reaping the rewards of the laborious efforts of high learning. The mixture is seen clearly in Cicero: 'Therefore, give the best mental effort you can; work as hard as you can – if learning is work and not pleasure (*si discendi labor est potius quam voluptas*).'[29] Similarly, Pliny tells his friend to hand over his affairs, his *negotia*, to someone else and turn to his books: 'This is what should be both business and pleasure, work and rest (*Hoc sit negotium tuum hoc otium; hic labor haec quies*).'[30] Thus the *otium* of the ruling elite was intrinsically connected to their public life in the same way as their *labor*. It was not that they had no leisure or work, or that the two were inextricably bound together, it was more the case that there was a greater degree of overlap in the meaning of certain areas of their activity than existed for other social groups, and that this overlap was a result of their position in the social hierarchy and their relationship to the productive process.

It would, however, be misleading to exaggerate the ideal at the expense of practice. When we look at Seneca, Pliny, and Cicero we see a representation of an ideal, and, as Matthews has observed of the later empire, the Roman elite spent, on average, probably only three or four years in public office, whilst many were neither educated nor interested in literature.[31] For most of the elite, life consisted of long periods of profound free time. However, this created a new confusion in that, as powerful figures and heads of families, their lives were on constant display. In their *otium* they were constrained to act in accordance with the prestige and authority of their social position, and the dividing line between leisure and work remained unclear. This is especially apparent in a passage from Cicero:

> I took care that I should be seen personally every day. I lived in the public eye; I frequented the forum; neither my door-keeper nor sleep prevented anyone from having an audience with me. Not even when I had nothing to do did I do nothing, and what shall I say of my busy times? ... absolute leisure was a thing I never knew (*ne omnino umquam essem otiosus*). I have always thought that a sublime and noble sentiment which Marcus Cato expresses in the noble passage of his *Origins*, where he says that great and eminent men should attach as much importance to their hours of relaxation (*otii*) as to their hours of toil (*negotii*).[32]

The elite dreamed up a value-system for the free peasantry which emphasized the benefits of work. Agriculture, it was claimed, brought independence, and labour for oneself and one's family was contrasted with that which was performed for others. It was not manual labour of itself that degraded, for life in the fields could actually strengthen body and soul,[33] but the ties of dependence between producer and user. It was working to satisfy the needs of others, not to improve the self, that the elite considered debased and prostitute. Thus Seneca tells us that, 'Work is not a good thing. So what is? Hatred of work.' It was not that all work was bad, it was that work was not a good thing *per se*. Therefore, he rebukes those 'who toil to no purpose'. Work, he says, 'Fuels noble minds (*Generosos animos labor nutrit*)' so long as it is directed towards 'honourable things (*honesta*)'.[34] This amounted to a spirit of virile labour, an inner conscience, which urges men on to work: 'the very quality that endures toil and rouses itself to hard and uphill effort, is of the spirit, which says, "Why do you slacken? It is not the part of a man to fear sweat."'[35] Indeed, 'Work rouses the best (*labor optimos citat*)', or so Seneca claimed, before providing a suitable example: 'The senate is often kept busy the whole day long, when all those worthless people spend the whole time playing on the playing field, or skulking in a cook-shop, or wasting their time hanging about in some gathering.'[36]

The elite were alert to the need to maintain the existing productive order, but it was not the case that they thought that there should be no respite from labour. They held that *otium* could provide not only opportunities for personal development, but the chance for recovery as well. 'Leisure nourishes the body, and the mind feeds on it too, but too much work impairs both.'[37] For 'nature herself does not allow a man to work continuously without a break',[38] and 'timely repose heartens and nourishes strength, and valour is increased by a spell of leisure (*maior post otia virtus*).'[39] Holiday arrangements were even made for new apprentice boys in the Egyptian Fayyum.[40] The important thing was to keep leisure subordinate to work.

Whilst a clear conception existed that a certain degree of rest and recreation was necessary, even desirable, the literature is especially alert to the perils of sloth. Some considered a surfeit of empty free time to be a living death.[41] The Stoic philosopher Damasippus advised Horace to 'flee the immoral Siren, laziness (*vitanda est improba Siren desidia*)'.[42] Accordingly, Pliny is eager to earn his retirement by hard work and escape 'the charge of laziness (*inertiae crimen*)'.[43] Leisure was thought both hazardous and destructive: 'we have corrupted our souls with shady seclusion, luxury, leisure, idleness and sloth (*nos umbris, deliciis, otio, languore, desidia animum infecimus*).'[44] The temptations of leisure were thought to lead people to immorality: 'Leisure, Catullus, does you harm, you riot in your idle waste too much. Before now, leisure has ruined both kings and wealthy cities.'[45] The dangers of idleness were on hand for all to see: 'idle leisure is wont to make men hate their lives (*in odium illam sui adducere solet iners otium*).'[46] And the effects were not only psychological: 'My memory used to be swift . . . Now it has been undermined by age, and by a long period of idleness (*desidia*) – which can play havoc with young minds too.'[47] Nor were the physical effects of sloth limited to the memory. The medical writer Celsus warns that 'whilst inaction (*ignavia*) weakens the body, work strengthens it; the former brings on premature old age, the latter prolongs youth.'[48] Leisure was also the root of all indecision (*variam semper dant otia mentem*),[49] which could lead to all kinds of indolence and profligacy. One father tells us not only that he had foreseen there would be problems with his son, but that he knew the cause as well:

> I kept anticipating that he would one day break out into some vicious crime because he wasted his life in idleness (*otio*) and the flower of his youth at home in laziness (*desidem*).[50]

It was this lifestyle which had, allegedly, led the son to commit incest with his mother, and compelled the father to torture and kill him on the rack. The murder was nothing less than a social service, justified by attitudes towards leisure. For as Gellius puts it, 'a man who does not know how to use his leisure is in more trouble than the man who has work to do', since 'the idle mind does not know what it wants (*Otioso in otio animus nescit quid velit*)'.[51] Moreover, by bypassing the mind, leisure was thought to reveal people's true personality and underlying character traits:

> For it is a man's pleasures (yes, his pleasures) which tell us most about his true worth, his moral excellence, and his self-control. No one is so dissolute that his occupations lack all semblance of seriousness; it is our leisure moments which betray us (*Otio prodimur*).[52]

The elite emphasized the perils of sloth for their kind, but even greater condemnation was directed at the lazy beneath them. Soldiers were thought to be particularly at risk: 'Those pleasant and seductive lands had easily demoralized the warlike spirit of his [Lucius Sulla's] troops in their leisure periods.'[53] In a similar vein, camp duties were imposed 'sometimes from necessity, sometimes as a precaution against leisure',[54] so that 'the evils of leisure' might be 'shaken off by hard work (*otii vitia negotio discuti*).'[55] For the consequences were not confined to the soldiers, since they might 'harm their allies in consequence of the licence resulting from leisure (*otii licentiam*).'[56]

Nor were these evil effects restricted to the male sex: 'Nowadays, however, most women so abandon themselves to luxury and idleness that they do not deign to undertake even the superintendence of woolmaking.'[57] Women were thought of as being especially susceptible to the perils of free time. Velleius describes the equestrian Gaius Maecenas as hard-working, 'but when any relaxation was allowed he would almost outdo a woman in giving himself up to indolence and soft luxury.'[58] The same sentiments are to be found in Pliny's description of Quadratus' grandmother, who kept her own personal troupe of pantomime actors and

treated them with 'an indulgence unsuitable in a lady of her high position': 'she told me that as a woman, with all a woman's idle hours to fill
(*ut feminam in illo otio sexus*), she was in the habit of amusing herself by
playing draughts or watching her troupe.'[59] The results of a woman's
idling could be especially grave since, whilst 'alone and unmarried' she
would be 'wasting her youth and beauty in barren leisure'.[60] The inferior
position of women in Roman society was therefore reflected in their restricted access to leisure facilities and in their minimal degree of choice
in relation to Roman men.[61] Their domestic labour, the attitudes and
behaviour of their partners, childcare, and lack of independent income all
meant that the factors which limited their participation in the political
and social structures of society contributed to their subordinate leisure
experience.

The problem that the elite had with lower-class *otium* was that it seemed
to be characterized by laziness and short-term worthless pleasure. The
crowd of the later empire is described by Ammianus as a bunch of loafers
with too much time, and too many opportunities for leisure:

> But of the multitude of lowest condition and greatest poverty (*turba
> vero imae sortis et paupertinae*) some spend the entire night in wine-
> shops, others lurk in the shade of the theatre awnings ... or they
> quarrel with one another in their dice games, making a disgusting
> sound by drawing back their breath into their resounding nostrils,
> or, favourite of all their amusements, they stand all day, rain or
> shine, examining minutely the good points or the defects of chari-
> oteers and their horses.[62]

The elite view of pleasure was that: 'Pleasure is extinguished just when
it is most enjoyed; it has but small space, and thus quickly fills it – it
grows weary and is soon spent after its first assault.'[63] For 'virtue is
something lofty, exalted and noble, unconquerable and unwearied; pleasure is something lowly, servile, weak and perishable, whose haunt and
abode are the brothel and the tavern.'[64] The crowd, however, 'seeks all
that ebbs and flows',[65] and 'things which provoke the admiration of the
crowd are but temporary goods.'[66] The elite strove both to control and to
condemn the plebs' activities, whilst simultaneously creating an ideology
which justified their behaviour. They recognized that the elements of
freedom, choice, and non-productivity made leisure a dangerous thing for
the masses to get their hands on. Seneca exhorts his fellow senators to be
'circumspect and see how we may protect ourselves from the mob.'[67] For
it was leisure which had first made the plebs insolent.[68] Sallust considered
that the political factions and parties originated at Rome because of the

arrival of leisure,[69] whilst the Elder Pliny considered that the pyramids had been built either to keep money from the pharaohs' successors and rivals, or else to keep the common people busy (*aut ne plebs esset otiosa*).[70]

The urban rabble lacked both freedom and possessions and were assumed to desire everything around them. This made them a potential threat in a world of order and status; not only because the lower orders were felt to be easily tempted, but because they themselves could easily mislead others. This was particularly the case in leisure acts, where the sirens waiting to waylay those seeking 'proper' use of their *otium* were both numerous and especially enticing.[71] The elite were convinced that the plebs posed a threat to their high morality, since their poor example of easy and ephemeral luxury and enjoyment could tempt those in command away from the burdens of their social position. Hence, for the elite, the problems of leisure arose when free time got into the hands of lower classes who were outside their control and whom they considered morally incapable of using it properly. The plebs had to be classified and separated both in practice and in thought, and moral discourse on luxury served to justify and define.[72]

The elite expressed their concerns over their control of the plebs through moral discourse. But such moralizing also revealed concerns about the new practices which accompanied the acquisition of empire. For the increase in prosperity allowed for greater and more extravagant leisure provision for a much enlarged section of the populace, and as the pleasures of the aristocratic lifestyle were made more widely available through the agency of a beneficent emperor, *otium* was seen clearly to be no longer the preserve of the rich. The new circumstances of life under an autocrat threatened the traditional qualities of *otium*, challenging them with the thrills of popular entertainment and the extravagance of imperial largesse. Leisure discourse became the vehicle for the expression of elite concerns over the transformation of Roman society, and held a double significance: on the one hand, leisure was all that was left to the elite since, with the end of the republic, they were denied their traditional position of political authority; on the other, that very leisure which had traditionally been their preserve, and to which they had retired, was increasingly encroached upon by the lower orders.

What this analysis tells us is that *otium* and *labor* were judged differently from our conceptions of leisure and work. *Otium* was judged in accordance with Roman society's moral hierarchization. For if it is the case that the degree to which leisure and work are experienced as separate parts of life is related to the degree to which the society itself is stratified, then it is also true that the manner of their separation is related to the form of the society's stratification. Differences of status and rank played a more important part than is now the case because Roman society had an obsession with these qualities,[73] and the oppressive hierarchy which it created carefully delineated between areas of *labor* and *otium*. The line between them was drawn differently, compared with now, and the content of the experience implied by them varied according to social position. But by examining the differing conceptions of leisure it has also become clear that it was the elite, and not necessarily other social groups, who understood *otium* in this way, as a phenomenon related to social position. The practices of other groups, which are as good a record of culture as any literary text, are evidence of alternative notions of leisure. The frequent attacks contained in the literary sources on others' leisure activities, on their misuse of leisure, also attest to such alternative values and were a function of the strong vertical divisions of Roman society.

Our experience of the phenomena of leisure and work has been tied to our increased temporal stratification and industrialization. This has been related to increased horizontal divisions in society, articulated through the attempt to develop neutral modes of evaluation designed to measure merit rather than morality. Roman categories were not linked to industrial urges for increased productivity and growth. We should not, however, think that we now experience work and leisure more deeply than they did. We have merely parcelled off leisure and work as separate areas of time as a prelude to measuring their efficiency and productivity. This has heavily influenced our understanding, just as Roman ideas about moral worth affected theirs. Temporal division has also produced a conflation of many of the meanings of work and leisure, for in an industrial culture it is not entirely desirable to separate the meanings of work and leisure. The productive process requires that work be seen, in part, as a fulfilling, even enjoyable, piece of time, which then comes to be packaged as employment, and this fundamentally affects our perception of the differences between work and leisure. The result is a concept which reflects our principal cultural concerns. It is also a reversal of the general preindustrial hierarchy of values, work now having a superiority over leisure.

It could be argued that the meanings of work and leisure were experienced more distinctly in Roman society as a whole since for the non-elite there was little overlap between these areas. In their pre-industrial society, work for the vast majority was a grim necessity eased by the interludes of leisure. *Otium* came first in the conceptual order, *negotium* (business) second. By contrast, work is now seen as the basis of our personal fulfilment, and leisure a problem period to be filled productively. In Rome, it was only the masses' leisure which posed a problem, and then only for elite control. The elite were the ones who headed a hierarchy based on a productive process of agriculture and slavery, and it was in their interest to keep their peasants and slaves under their charge and working. But the elite's position, both in the productive process, and at the top of highly differentiated society, resulted in their having a conception of work and leisure not unlike that which exists today.

The aim of the next sections is to look at the activities which fit with our definition of leisure in order to get a better understanding of Roman culture and history in its entirety. For these are acts which the elite would not have termed *otium* since they lacked moral worth. The following chapter begins this analysis by looking at the area where a cross-social consensus most clearly existed – the imperial games. That is not to say that there were no conflicts in these activities. In fact, the analysis of these frictions will act as a prelude to the subsequent chapters where I try to dig progressively deeper into Roman culture and examine its underlying fault-lines and developments.

5

Blood, Sweat, and Charioteers: The Imperial Games

'Sport is truth' said Howard Wilkinson, the manager of Leeds United football club, when asked what it was that made soccer so appealing. Footballers love such aphorisms, yet at the same time (albeit unknowingly) a Geertzian analytical standpoint is being articulated. As in the Balinese cockfight,[1] the emotional explosions of sport occur in realms in which many of the most powerful and intrinsic themes of society are focused with an acute intensity, and that allows a clearer impression of them to be made than is possible in many other more diffuse areas of existence. For it is winning and losing that is the crux of sport – how to achieve success, how to respond to it in celebration, and how to react to failure and the defeated – and the results of this confrontation can provide us with an in-depth commentary on Roman life.

The exaggeration of the gladiatorial combats was noted by Gellius:

> For, to a gladiator ready to fight, the fortune of battle offers the alternative, either to kill, if he should conquer, or to die, if he should yield. But the life of men in general is not restricted by such unfair or inevitable necessities that one must be first to commit an injury in order to avoid suffering injury.[2]

What he did not notice was that this hyperbole drew on the mundane for its effect. The aim of this chapter, therefore, is to examine the gladiatorial combats, the animal hunts, the horse-racing in the circus, and the assorted athletic contests which took place in the stadium, by locating them within their everyday context. It is, of course, obvious to say that each of these activities had its own special meanings for a Roman audience, but, I would argue, they display a generic similarity: each one represented aspects of competition. Moreover, their popularity increased dramatically

with the advent of the empire, and this fact was causally connected to
assets, inherent within them, which made them ideally suited to the purpose of disseminating the imperial ideological system. Hence, it was by
its games that the empire came to be known, both contemporaneously and
through the ages.[3]

The place of the games in the scheme of leisure was broadly cross-
social and cross-gender. Their popularity is well attested: they were, 'That
kind of spectacle to which every sort of people crowd in the greatest
numbers, and in which the masses find the greatest delight.'[4] Children
played at gladiators,[5] adolescents were addicted to them, and they provided the staple stopgap of everyday conversation. Indeed, the desire
for games was such that it led the people of the town of Pollentia to hold
the chief centurion's dead body to ransom in the forum until they had
extorted money from his heirs for a gladiatorial show.[6] The degree of
intense excitement and fanaticism in a crowd watching the horse-racing
in the later empire is well described by Friedländer:

> The long rows of rising seats were thronged with a moving mass of
> men, moved by one passion, almost a mania. Near the close of a
> race suspense, anxiety, fury, joy, savagery burst forth. Their eyes
> ever fixed on the chariots, they clapped and shrieked with all their
> lungs, sprang up, bent over, waved handkerchiefs, incited their fa-
> vourites, stretched out their arms as though they could reach the
> course, gnashed their teeth, groaned, threatened, exulted, triumphed,
> or swore. The winning chariot aroused a thunderous applause – and
> loud curses from the losers – re-echoed over the deserted streets of
> Rome, announcing to those who stayed at home the end of the race,
> and struck the ear of the traveller, when Rome had vanished from
> sight.[7]

The excitement was such that one man was moved 'to wrap up his head
while a horse which he favoured was running; and when, contrary to
expectations, the horse won, he required sponges to recover from his
fainting fit.'[8] Even magicians were consulted for gambling purposes, and
to counteract any such enchantment the horses had bells hung on them.[9]
In such a sharply stratified society there was a need for these safe areas
of equalization, and 'the enthusiastic participation by spectators, rich and
poor, raised and then released collective tensions, in a society which
traditionally idealised impassivity (*gravitas*).'[10]

The gladiators came to exert their own pull on Roman society. For
many women, they were sex symbols.[11] Moreover, the links between sex
and the competitive games penetrated deeper than the opportunities they
provided for mixing and ogling. Sex took on a gladiatorial symbolism. It

was described as 'Venus' gladiatorial games'.[12] The gladiatorial contests acquired an explicit sexual symbolism. Faustina, the wife of the emperor Antoninus, once saw some gladiators go by and was inflamed with love for one of them. She later confessed to her husband, who killed the gladiator and had Faustina bathe in his blood before bedding her. This allayed her passion, but their son, Commodus, was born a gladiator, and 'not really a prince'.[13] Were a poor man to dream that he fought as a gladiator that was thought auspicious as it signified marriage.[14] The dream-interpreter, Artemidorus, elaborates on the significance of gladiatorial dreams:

> I have often observed that this dream indicates that a man will marry a woman whose character corresponds to the type of weapons that he dreams he is using or to the type of opponent against whom he is fighting . . . For example, if a man fights a Thracian, he will marry a wife who is rich, crafty, and fond of being first. She will be rich because the Thracian's body is entirely covered by his armour; crafty, because his sword is not straight; and fond of being first, because this fighter employs the advancing technique.[15]

To dream of a retiarius, who fought with a net and trident, signified a poor and wanton wife, 'a woman who roams about consorting very freely with anyone who wants her'. But like the dream-interpreter Antipater, we should be careful about over-exaggerating the sexual link between dreams and gladiators: he told a man 'who once dreamt that he had intercourse with a piece of iron that he would be condemned to fight in a gladiatorial contest. The dream did not however come true in this way. Instead, the dreamer's penis was cut off.'[16]

This brings us to the heart of the problems which face the historian of the Roman games: what are we to make of such a mentality and culture, and how was it that the games played such a crucial role in the imperial ideology? What were the mechanisms by which a new identity was created, and from where did that image get its all too raw material? To begin with there is the deeper historical problem of adapting the distinctive flavours of this, for us, unrefined existence to suit our own very different conceptual palate. For it is clear that the games were central in Roman life, but just as apparent that we find them highly problematic. In this respect they represent a very different dilemma from that which will be encountered in studying the baths, where the moral difficulties lay solely on the Roman side of the fence. When it comes to animals, for example, few societies have developed a degree of sensibility sufficient to condemn the torture and killing of animals for amusement: the Spanish still torment bulls, and the Balinese hold cockfights. In our society, the exploitation of animals is considered justifiable, if not actually commendable, only in the mass production of the factory farm – a process which probably inflicts far more suffering (if, indeed, it is possible to measure such things) on many more animals than the Roman hunts ever could. Because of our industrial leanings we accept the animals' suffering as a necessary product of work, but denounce it as a product of leisure. The enjoyment which others get out of this kind of entertainment also seems to tell us something especially significant about their mentality and their culture: after all, what are the Spanish if not bullfighters? What kind of society is it, then, where crowds of people enjoy physical contests where blood flows, and how can we understand it?

The examples of the cruelty and the strangeness of the Roman spectacle are plentiful. Having arrived in the amphitheatre the animals were hunted (see plate 1), made to fight each other, and let loose on men, whilst some less dangerous animals were only exhibited. They were often decorated to increase their splendour: bulls could be white-washed, gilded with gold, and covered in silk. Psychedelic sheep, their fleeces dyed scarlet and purple, also appeared. Many animals were trained before entering the arena. Alternating with the exhibition of these tame performing animals there were fights between still wild ones: a bull might take on a bear, or a rhino an elephant, the combatants being driven on by whips and hot irons until one had savaged the other. They were also matched against skilled huntsmen and their dogs, until, chased to exhaustion by the hounds, the animals fell to the hunters' spears and arrows. Yet not all the contests between man and beast were so biased towards the humans, for another of the spectacles of the amphitheatre consisted in the execution of criminals tied to a stake and left to be mauled, or else lightly and insufficiently armed so that the entertainment might be prolonged. Torn apart, these victims provided an opportunity for curious physicians to inspect their entrails.[17] Some of these executions were literally staged, the condemned becoming the stars in the performance of their own death. They appeared in elaborate tunics embroidered with gold and purple onto a specially constructed platform, whereupon the tunics burst spontaneously into flames.[18] Scenes from history, mythology, and literature were also enacted: one man's arm was held over a fire to represent Mucius Scaevola;[19] the castration of Atys was reproduced, as was the living pyre of Hercules on Mount Oeta; and the mythological union between Pasiphae and the bull became a reality.[20] Every effort was made to meet the expectations of a crowd which was accustomed to the bizarre, monstrous, and exciting, and most seem to have been unconcerned.

Such stylization implies approval; and such cruelty tends to provoke polemic: 'by far the nastiest blood sport ever invented', suggests Grant, and adds that, 'the two most quantitatively destructive institutions in History are Nazism and the Roman Gladiators . . . No amount of explanation can mitigate the savagery.'[21] Similarly, 'the Romans were a bloodthirsty people. Their empire had been won by the victories of the citizen army, and slaughter was second nature to them. So in times of peace their thirst for blood had to be slaked somewhere, and it was to the great contests in gladiatorial arenas such as the Colosseum at Rome that they looked for satisfaction.'[22] Pearson considers that the games are evidence of a 'mass lobotomy' and show a lack of 'popular initiative'.[23] But it is worth noting 'just how sophisticated and pervasive a cultural institution the amphitheatre was. It will now be less easy to dismiss the games held in amphitheatres as symptomatic of Roman cruelty.'[24] Nor can they be adequately understood as a function of the 'social psychology of the crowd, which helps relieve the individual of responsibility, and in the psychological mechanisms by which some spectators identify more readily with the victory of the aggressor than with the sufferings of the vanquished.'[25] So what were the reasons for the Romans' love of gladiators? 'Slavery and the steep stratification of society must have helped.'[26] Also, 'Rome was a cruel society. Brutality was built into its culture, in private life as well as in public shows.'[27] A more satisfactory explanation is still required, for, as Welch says, 'the games were ordinary and required no justification. But their very ordinariness to the Romans makes them well worth re-evaluating.'[28] Yet Welch is wrong to say that it is the games' ordinariness that makes them worth reassessment. The games were never ordinary, except in terms of their own form; they were specialized highlights of Roman culture which came to represent being Roman itself. The question which has to be addressed is how such forms of violence acquired this unproblematic central role; in other words, why physical violence was an acceptable medium for the message, and what exactly that message was.

Violence grows out of the social and cultural order and so can only be understood in a social and cultural context. It need not be pathological, it can be part of a normal social process. To us, violence has negative moral implications, but for the Romans it did not. Violence, whether we like it or not, is a common form of collective or individual expression. In fact, violence was not a by-product, or a disagreeable instrument, it was the empire itself. It represented an unambiguous statement of power, which effectively dramatized the importance of key social ideas, and these goals were themselves a sufficient condition for acts of violence to be performed. Its visibility and universality also made it an excellent means of mass communication. It might seem strange that violence was an obsession in an ordered society but it reflected the force that maintained the order itself. Violence, therefore, fulfilled both an instrumental and an expressive function, and it focused attention onto the image of the body and its accompanying code of morality.

Stylized violence was the medium by which the meanings of the games were expressed. The question of what made the games so important can only be answered by putting them in their context so that we too might get their message. The games were appropriate for the conditions of the new imperial order because they drew on traits, themes, and developments that were highly significant to the Roman way of life – the need to have honour and to avoid shame, the need to display publicly one's manliness, the need to act properly in the public sphere of life – all of which came together, articulated through the symbolic use of violence, so that Romans might better understand and more clearly express their own relationship to their way of life. Hence, the cultural significance of the gladiators can best be understood if they are interpreted as acts which both encapsulated and succinctly summarized the important structural opposition of nature and culture which underlay the idea of what it meant to be civilized or truly human as expressed in terms of Roman thought. More specifically, they communicated what it meant to be a Roman male. The games appear as an interpretive act, a Roman male reading of the Roman male experience.[29] They were an expressive form which reflected shared assumptions about masculinity and gave these assumptions a concrete reality. But they were also an attempt to use these assumptions for social and political ends, and by drawing on the well of common understanding the early emperors hoped to water the green shoots of imperial ideology. For the Roman empire did not consist only of buildings and land, it was also an empire of the mind.

In the imperial view of culture, as expressed in the games, it was self-control and style that mattered, not violence. The manner of death and the display of bravery counted, and these were highlighted by the proximity of death. The image of death became the national spectacle, but the brutality was not the focus for the individual fan. Instead, the process of death became the focal point, and its function was more expressive and communicative than utilitarian. What counted was the ability, itself an expression of *virtus* (bravery/manliness/virtue), to master oneself, and one's body; to master the slightest movement when face to face with death. 'There is an old adage about gladiators – that they plan their fight in the ring; as they watch intently, something in their adversary's glance, some movement of his hand, even some slight bending of his body, gives a warning.'[30] A myriad shadows of character were thought to be revealed in the conduct of the combatants, conduct which to our untrained eyes would have seemed like no more than an endless repetition of savagery. Similarly, in a gladiatorial fight, 'before closing a number of strokes are made that seem not to be intended to inflict a wound but to be done for the sake of appearance (*ad speciem valere videatur*).'[31] But the ability to control was necessary for far more than appearance's sake: in Gaius' school of 20,000 gladiators the only two who could stop themselves blinking when in danger were invincible, since they neither missed any of their opponents' moves nor gave anything away themselves.[32]

Not all gladiators had reached the same high degree of technique. In general, there were two classes of fighters: the old pros and the young lambs to the slaughter. Whilst it probably was true that, 'a gladiator counts it a disgrace to be matched with an inferior, and knows that to win without danger is to win without glory',[33] it was also the case that this is what often happened, with the predictable outcome. These mismatches actually offered an excellent illustration of the benefits of proper technique, and the contrasting failings of lack of training. As Quintilian says, when describing the usually more vigorous untrained speaker:

> Even a gladiator who plunges into the fight with no skill at arms to help him, and a wrestler who puts forth the whole strength of his body the moment he has got a hold, is acclaimed by faulty critics for his outstanding vigour, although it is of frequent occurrence in such cases for the latter to be overthrown by his own strength and for the former to find the fury of his onslaught parried by his adversary with a simple turn of the wrist.[34]

Such reckless valour was itself an exhibition of *virtus*, but for victory to be gained, the body had to be controlled and that *virtus* properly directed. For with gladiators, 'skill is their protection, anger their undoing.'[35] And for both gladiator and soldier alike, 'it is the keen and ready intelligence, endowed with sharpness and resourcefulness that secures men against defeat.'[36]

This studied control and meticulous comportment gave the games, just as it gave oratory, an undeniable style and elegance:

> For as we observe that boxers, and gladiators not much less, do not make any motion, either in cautious parrying or vigorous thrusting, which does not have a certain grace (*palaestram*), so that whatever is useful for the combat is also attractive (*venustum*) to look upon, so the orator does not strike a heavy blow unless the thrust has been properly directed, nor can he avoid the attack safely unless even in yielding he knows what is becoming.[37]

The proper conventions had to be observed, especially in death. The gladiator had to die in the correct position – chest out, leaning to the right, head drooping, half-seated on his weapons. It was the dying swan of the

Roman world; but instead of rich romanticism, it represented a cool, impersonal, and formalized way of death. It was a tight-lipped ideal which harboured no guilt or horror for the victor, and the spectators were extremely critical of any performance that did not come up to the mark. The gladiators learned how to die even as they learnt how to fight: 'Wasn't it enough that by daily practice for combat for so long a time I learned how to die?'[38] They were ordered to 'accept the stroke (*ferrum recipe*)' in the correct fashion.[39] The people called out for a defeated gladiator to expose his breast to receive a final blow. He must not flinch or draw back from the sword; rather, he had to receive the blow 'with his whole body', as Cicero put it, whilst the victor was expected to dispatch him efficiently.[40]

The training which gladiators underwent could turn the most desperate criminal into a model of Romanness:

> Look at gladiators, who are either ruined men (*perditi homines*) or barbarians, what blows they endure! See how men, who have been well trained, prefer to receive a blow than basely (*turpiter*) avoid it! How frequently it is made evident that there is nothing put higher than giving satisfaction to their owner or to the people! Even when weakened with wounds they send word to their owners to ascertain their pleasure: if they have given satisfaction to them they are content to fall. What gladiator of ordinary merit has ever uttered a groan or changed countenance? Who of them has disgraced himself, I will not say upon his feet, but in his fall? Who after falling has drawn in his neck when ordered to suffer the fatal stroke? Such is the force of training, practice and habit.[41]

A mutant form of such bravery could also be revealed in suicide committed to avoid the arena: a German animal hunter (*bestiarius*) went to the loo before the fight and choked himself to death on the sponge stick;[42] a gladiator broke his neck in the wheel of the cart taking him to the spectacle;[43] a barbarian in a mock sea-battle (*naumachia*) killed himself with his spear saying, 'why should I be armed and yet wait for death to come?'[44] But generally, the cowardice of criminals merely confirmed to the audience that they deserved to die. For in gladiatorial combats, 'where the fate of the lowest classes of mankind is concerned, it is natural in us to dislike the quaking suppliant who craves permission to live, whilst we are anxious to save the courageous and spirited who hotly fling themselves at death.'[45] The crowd were only likely to save the loser if he had fought properly.

Death was necessary because its proximity brought the finest exhibitions of *virtus*:

> For death, when it stands near us, gives even to inexperienced men
> the courage not to seek to avoid the inevitable. So the gladiator,
> who throughout the fight has been no matter how fainthearted, of-
> fers his throat to his opponent and directs the wavering blade to the
> vital spot.[46]

Consequently, the point of death became the climax of the fight since it
accentuated, and in cases revealed, the true character and *virtus* of the
fighters: 'Among gladiators the worst position for a victor is to have to
fight a dying opponent. You should fear no adversary more than one who
cannot live, but can kill . . . When his chance of release is removed, a
gladiator will pursue naked the opponent he had fled under arms.'[47] Similarly (and this invited reflection), wild animals went into a strange uncontrolled frenzy in their dying moment: 'Madness is most violent at the
point of death, and its last despair drives a mind to fury. Some beasts snap
at the shaft that hits them, and rush on despite their wounds at the author
of their death.'[48]

Excitement came from the game itself, the victory, and, most importantly, the way it was done. The killing of the gladiator was unimportant
in itself – what were gladiators if not worthless? – and the climax of the
games became only really enjoyable as the fulfilment of a sufficiently
long period of fore-pleasure. The agonistic type of contest emphasized
and then prolonged the climax, the moment of decision and victory, as the
most crucial part of the contest, more momentous than the game itself.
The crowd were not a bloodthirsty mob. They were the most urbane
sophisticates in the world. The Roman public did not come to see blood-
shed, they came to see, without apology, a professional performance.
Theirs was a gaze, not of any observer, but of a spectator supported and
justified by an institution.[49] It was a highly selective gaze that 'could and
should grasp colours, variations, tiny anomalies.'[50] As such it was part of
a visualization of social experience, which not only generated and promoted a new universal way of seeing, but was more universal precisely
because of its visual qualities.

All of these points about the gladiatorial fights are neatly encapsulated
in *The Case of the Ransomed Gladiator*.[51] This text is a rhetorical exercise concerning the law that a father may disown and renounce his son for
just cause, and it relates the situation where a poor man and a rich man
were enemies, but their sons friends. The rich man's son was kidnapped
and sold to a gladiatorial school by pirates. The poor man's son went to
rescue him, fought in his place, and died. On his return, the rich man's
son had promised to help the poor man, did so, and was promptly cut off
by his own father. As part of his defence, the rich man's son describes the
gladiatorial contest where his friend died, using the fight to emphasize

every detail of his friend's *virtus*. His friend, a poor novice, was unevenly matched with a veteran, but he did not give up:

> It is a terrible shame that his courage and fervour were not em-
> ployed in the army, in military combat, where real courage is not
> circumscribed by any fencing etiquette. With what vigour did he
> rush out into the fray, enraged against his opponent as though he
> were still mine! But every assault was deftly set aside with the skill
> of a veteran gladiator.

He would have escaped death, but 'the gladiator did not want him to live. Therefore, now offering his bared body to his opponent's blows ... he died standing up.'[52] 'He received the sword blow facing straight ahead ... Neither a criminal nor down on his luck, he entered the arena. Gentlemen, when did you ever hear of such a thing? He became a gladiator because of his virtue!'[53]

What was at stake was simply the ability to win in style. Racing pro-vided a similar opportunity to triumph through skill and flair (see plate 2). The excitement of racing was based on gambling,[54] the obstacles to be overcome, the skill required, the unforeseen vicissitudes which tested the character of the horses and their training, as well as the agility and brav-ery of the drivers. The penalties for lack of skill could be severe: 'as an untrained charioteer is dragged from his chariot, trampled, lacerated, crushed' is one of Cicero's similes.[55] The horses were themselves sym-bolic of rebelliousness and arrogance, and so added to the difficulties of control.[56] Success in a chariot race, therefore, often depended solely upon the driver's skill. At Constantinople, a winner could even be challenged to swap horses and repeat the victory, thus proving that success was the result of merit. Races were most often won in the closing stages by holding up the horses for a late surge, and this required a knowledge of strategy, and the nerve to carry it out. Races had little to do with speed, and more to do with the tactics involved in just crossing the line first. The image from *Ben Hur* is misleading, for, in reality, the horses were held up for most of the race and came with a late run – more in the manner of modern-day trotting. The elder Pliny describes the strategies involved in a chariot race: a charioteer of the White faction was thrown at the start, 'and his team took the lead and kept it by obstructing their rivals, jostling them aside and doing everything against them that they would have had to do with a most skilful charioteer in control.'[57] The first century AD epic poet Silius Italicus also describes a chariot race which supports this im-age, one which was supposedly held at Scipio's victory games after the Punic wars.[58] Four four-horse chariots (*quadrigae*) were racing, and Cyrnus got off to a flying start, leaving the rest behind. The crowd roared with applause, thinking that with such a start their favourite had as good as won. 'But those who looked deeper and had more experience of the race course, blamed the driver for putting forth all his strength at the beginning: from a distance they uttered various portents, that he was tiring out his team with his efforts and keeping no reserves of power.' 'Put down your whip and tighten your reins', they cried. 'But, alas, he did not listen; on he sped, without sparing the horses, forgetting how much ground had still to be covered.' The others were held up, Cyrnus ran out of puff, tried to block by swerving, but was soon left behind. He was 'learning too late the wisdom of controlling his pace'.

The animal hunts (*venationes*) gave out a comparable message. They were meticulous reconstructions of the trials of the animal world. 'People like racing and enjoy stage shows, but nothing attracts them as much as men fighting animals; escape from the beasts seems impossible, yet through sheer intelligence the men succeed.'[59] Town and country were brought into confrontation in a specially constructed arena. This was a perfect form for defining the Roman human qualities, since the animals from the country contrasted with the civilized values of the Roman. For a fundamental distinction existed between urban and rural. In the new terms of the city of Rome, urban space was human space in that it was an ordered, man-made environment, which was controlled and sustained by human will. The city was a place from where nature had been expelled. By contrast, the countryside was sub-human space, in that it was subject to the forces of nature. Hence, to be fully human in the urban environment was to be fully in control.

The hunts were spectacles in which men killing and being killed by animals generated emotional responses which were powerful enough to convey the sense of being human in Roman society. The docility and intelligence of elephants made them almost too human, too Roman. Elephants expressed Roman virtues – size, splendour, and discipline – and when a large number were killed at Pompey's games the crowd were so indignant that they nearly turned against him.[60] The audience did not become dehumanized in the hunts but the *victims* did, as part of a process which restricted humanity to an exclusive club. For the hunts expressed the values central to the way in which people were expected to behave and regulate their relations with one another. As such, the games were in strong contrast to the old hunts of the countryside for they were part of a new urbanized culture which had banished nature from its precincts by creating a public male space, a place for men to assert themselves.

The games reflected upon not only the nature of mankind, but the nature of manliness (*virtus*). The ideal of manliness is central to the male image, and in Rome, it became closely linked to sport, physical toughness, and prowess. It was also portrayed as a corrective to many of the prevailing social problems. The encouragement given to 'manly' pursuits (and an implicit concomitant call to suitable 'womanly occupations') was a function of the mounting concern felt about the conditions and welfare, both physical and psychological, of a highly urbanized plebeian culture where traditional ties had weakened. It established itself as an internal moral code. Athletes and gladiators made dynamic, physical statements for a clearly defined purpose: victory in competition which was both quantitatively and qualitatively determined. Their achievements were proof that men had not become womanly and that the social order would not come apart as a result of the changes which had occurred. Manliness came to be the matter of acquiring the habit of winning, and doing so in style.

The male body was set up as the symbol for controlled style. The gladiators had great care taken over their bodies: physicians oversaw their diet;[61] distinguished surgeons healed their wounds;[62] *unctores* massaged them;[63] and, less pleasantly, the *lanistae* whipped them into shape. They were the apexes in a physical culture which emphasized body care for all classes. Sport put the focus on the body and its attributes (though with varying degrees of physical input): strength, skill, endurance, speed, grace, style, and shape; but all of these attributes had to be controlled. Gladiators became proverbial for their physical control: Gellius even tells the story of a certain savage gladiator who used to laugh when his wounds were probed by the doctors.[64] The extent of gladiators' reputation for physical control even meant that their blood was popular as a cure for fits of epilepsy, as if by imbibing their life-spirit the patient might also acquire their composure.[65] The body was mobilized in the regimen of games in order to provide part of a new image of increased normality. The body was also well-suited for this purpose on account of its universality. The emperor himself acquired an idealized, athleticized figure to which all could aspire (see plate 7). For imperial culture attempted to structure and satisfy individual needs so that people enthusiastically disciplined themselves, and the body's use in art and leisure was related to its transformation into an ideological emblem. Hence, 'the portraiture of gladiators has been the highest interest in art for many generations now.'[66]

Virtus and its counterpart *fortuna* were considered to be the great principles governing human affairs: *virtus* being rational and certain, *fortuna* irrational and unpredictable.[67] *Virtus* was a term 'heavy with moral significance for Roman writers',[68] and whilst *nobilis* or *novus* sharply divided Romans at birth, both were in firm agreement as to the ends and aims of *virtus*. *Nobilitas* was not part of *virtus*, since *virtus* was obtained by personal deeds, and so both it and the fame and honour won were personal.[69] The well-born were, however, assumed to possess by inheritance the appropriate character and sentiments of *virtus*, but whether this was in fact the case would be revealed in their public and competitive

acts. It was *virtus* that distinguished men from beasts and secured favour
from the gods.[70] Conversely, the gifts of fortune, though pleasant, even
desirable, were nevertheless dangerous since they tended to corrupt. They
were awarded and removed without regard to *virtus*, and so were evanes-
cent and deluding.[71] Fortune was blind, and capricious chance, against
whose machinations no man was able to provide, could rob even the
virtuous man of the just rewards of his merits. 'For all the gifts of Fortune, as they are bestowed by her, so are they easily withdrawn.'[72] However fickle, though, the favour of fortune did imply the blessing of the
gods; hence, the man who had both fortune and *virtus* was unstoppable.
Virtus was portrayed as the ancestral foundation of the Roman state,[73] and
for men to struggle over *virtus* and to compete for *gloria* was not merely
natural but a mark of felicity.[74] *Virtus* consisted of winning by one's
deeds an undying glory. Fame and honour were the rewards, and even to
seek to win them by brave deeds was considered to be an act of *virtus*.
To do so by chance was not: 'the man who thinks himself fortified and
guarded by good fortune (*felicitas*) rather than education, steps along
slippery paths and struggles with an unstable and insecure life.'[75] Nor was
talent by itself, nor hard graft, sufficient: 'the best wrestler is not one who
is thoroughly acquainted with all the postures and grips of the art, which
he will seldom use against an adversary, but he who has well and carefully trained himself in one or two of them, and waits eagerly for the
opportunity to use them.'[76] What mattered was the ability to mobilize
one's virile power into striking at the right moment, even if that required
agonizing moments of self-restraint. Hence, fortune was seen as secondary to *virtus*, and so was compelled to come to the aid of those who had
acquired moral superiority through their bravery; 'Fortune favours the
brave (*Fortes fortuna adiuvat*)', as the old proverb said.[77]

Roman manliness, as expressed in the arena, exalted self-possession
over emotional outpouring, since it was, quite self-consciously, a virile
and masculine culture: austere, muscular, and inflexible. The games re-
minded the Romans that their superiority was conditional upon their *virtus*,
whilst their *virtus* itself was based upon their pride. A public sense of
masculine dignity existed, something which had to be expressed openly
so that popular estimation might be won. As such, the games were based
less on an internal guilt mechanism, and more on a public shame culture.
In such a society, the man who felt no shame was thought to retain no
sense of value; and to break the law was to incur a public guilt, which was
liable to a public punishment. An audience was required to remind both
the proud and the shamed of their position in the world and so ensure that
the proper standards of behaviour were reached.

Honour was vital to this public sphere of male Roman life, representing
as it did a person's value in his own and his society's eyes. It created

status, since the 'honour system' established people's identity as dependent on their possessing the relevant virtues. Honour, therefore, referred to an ideal type of person since it provided a model for social conduct and the entitlement to a certain level of treatment in return. In order to acquire this ideal persona, the correct lifestyle was essential. Honour was a public code and in this kind of public shame culture, to have honour was to have private integrity – wholeness and incorruptibility – but the correctness of this morality was open for all to see. Such a person publicly acted according to certain honour-code evaluations and values: he was able to control his desires, and to know how to be in control was to know one's public value. Conversely, to lose control was to lose honour, integrity, and status, since in doing so one put private lust first, over and above society.[78] When conflict did occur, honour, because of its close connection to the physical person, found its ultimate vindication in violence. Physical courage was thus an essential element which could enable a person to undergo a necessary ordeal or a trial of strength. Cyprian's dismissal of the games as 'mere questions of honour (*favores in honoribus*)' can be seen to miss the point.[79] Seneca was nearer to the mark: 'We are stirred at times with pleasure if a youth of steady courage meets with his spear an onrushing wild beast, if unterrified he sustains the charge of a lion; and the more honourable (*honestior*) the youth that does it, the more pleasing this spectacle becomes.'[80]

This was a culture in which men were expected to be vigorously competitive in defence of their masculine self-image – a competitiveness which was discharged through the idiom of honour and reputation. Gender roles meant that men were on stage in public life and were expected to act in accordance with the proper standards of comportment. Their scrota were up for scrutiny, and they had to show that they had balls.[81] Victory gave prestige, status, and vindication; defeat brought insult, ridicule, and loss of reputation. Just as in everyday life people judged each other's behaviour in accordance with rules of honour, status, and prestige, so they responded likewise in the arena, for the crowd provided a vocal commentary on the fighter's masculinity and reputation. In the arena, the audience could contemplate a spectacle of highly competitive maleness in a stylized and ritual form where the potentially dangerous effects of violence were cut off from daily life. It was an institutionalized conflict in which the fighter's manner was the primary concern, not the fate of the victim. But the communal gaze meant that if the gladiator failed then it dishonoured both him and the whole community. Their interest in violence only extended to the manner in which a fighter responded to injury. The combatants were expected to show proper self-control in the face of pain, suffering, and death. In this way, the appropriate state for a true man was ritually dramatized, and the losers were, in effect, emasculated.

No cultural relationship existed between the audience and the victims. Yet for the audience this was not only a civilized spectacle; it was the most perfect form for defining the human condition in that it epitomized their notions of beauty, style, and antithesis, notions which were based on the contrast between the winner and loser. The games symbolized the Roman struggle and victory; they were a re-enactment, and a rehearsal, of what Romans had to do, feel, and be, if their success was to continue.[82] Similarly, as a punishment the games drew their psychological force from the bloody depths of Roman culture. Through the use of myth, executions provided a punitive parable, and through death, the victim was brought into the Roman community by being forced to show *virtus*. The condemned had shamed Roman society and by their death society's honour was saved. In the final analysis, the games were the logical outcome of an ideology which progressively dehumanized its adversaries and became incapable of seeing any middle ground between total triumph and utter defeat.

Competitive games created a cultural paradigm for the empire. They were based upon a blending of the opposite and somewhat complementary attitudes of competition and chance.[83] Competition stressed the ability to overcome obstacles and opponents in order to achieve victory, while chance threatened to render the outcome quite independent of those taking part. But they both obeyed the same law: the creation for the competitors of the conditions of pure equality denied them in real life (though not, of course, actually handicapping the contestants so as to create genuine equality). The games attempted to substitute a perfect situation of opportunity for the seemingly insurmountable disparities of everyday life. In the amphitheatre, competition ruled and celebrated the order which had enabled Rome to be so successful; it celebrated Rome's power over others, and its own power structure. In the circus, chance and skill were more equal partners; and for the masses this satisfied a need for equalization, whilst for the nobles it celebrated the luck which had allowed them to be born with a silver spoon in their mouths. The fundamental principle was for the charioteers to overcome chance by their own virile skill and bravery. *Virtus* had to overcome *fortuna*, but it was the interplay of *fortuna* that made the games exciting and provided the opportunity for real *virtus* to be displayed. Thus the games were a medium whereby common understandings about the nature of social existence could be developed and stated in a condensed, striking form, notably the ideal that ordered struggle, in which some are destined to win and others to lose, was a normal and inescapable feature of social life.

The form of play in a society is intimately connected with the overall power structure. The charioteers and gladiators summed up widespread ideals: the importance of victory in competition, and the principle of

social mobility (albeit ephemeral for the competitors themselves, especially the gladiators) and equality through merit or chance. They were
cross-social heroes, and their athletic world of power, speed, and pain was
an expression of the masculine ideals of Roman culture. Their power
was articulate and self-created, obtained via personal achievements; but it
was also based on prestige and elite patronage.[84] The public competitor,
therefore, represented a power derived both from the anomalous power of
some members of society based solely on prestige, high culture and elitism, and also from the defined and articulate power represented by the
developing imperial bureaucracy, which had been obtained through legitimate and meritorious means. As such, the competitor's power was drawn
from his being near the heart of things; he was connected with an arena
in which themes central to Roman society joined with its leading structures. He symbolized the conflict between articulate and anomalous power
as change and stability battled for supremacy in a traditional society.

The Roman 'revolution' had given birth to a new kind of political
order. The republic had been killed by its inability to create representative
institutions through which the state could exercise its authority, and into
the vacuum left by its collapse poured the contending (though not mutually exclusive) influences of tradition, despotism, Greek culture, and
change. By themselves, none of these supplied a ready-made solution to
the problem of where and in what form Roman society was heading. For
the empire needed to find a new common destiny, to stigmatize the recent
past, and to inaugurate the future, and there were three sources for this
creation: the past and tradition, the present success, and the re-enactment
of the heroic struggle which had brought that success. Therefore, from
ingredients drawn from their cultural depths the Romans set out to create
a fresh identity. The result was that the future generations were to experience, vicariously, the conquest and delights of victory, and a fantastical
representation of social relations was produced to reflect a return of the
golden age.

It would be easy to assume that the games summed up Roman life. The
games have undoubtedly provided a clear analysis of some of the key
elements of Roman culture, but we should not fall into the trap of seeing
them as representing Roman culture as a whole. To do so would be to
take the emperors' propaganda at face value, to see the Roman world as
they wanted it to be seen.

There were problems with the games, and these stemmed from elite
concerns about the people's misuse of time: time which the elite no
longer controlled as they used to – or as they ideally and romantically
thought they had in the traditional past. The surviving references which
purport to condemn the cruelty of the games have less to do with any

transcendent humanity, and rather more to do with social conflict. When Cicero wondered what pleasure a cultivated man could have in seeing a huge animal tear apart a weak man, or a splendid beast pierced with a spear, he meant that such displays were pandering to the lower classes' vulgarity.[85] Similarly, he justified the cruelty of the original gladiatorial fights on the grounds that they provided a most effective training in the endurance of pain and death when such a training was required for military purposes. It was only in his own day, when they had become mere popular entertainment, that, 'A gladiatorial show is apt to seem cruel and brutal to some eyes, and I incline to think that it is so, as now conducted.'[86] Again, there is Seneca's famous passage:

> All the previous fighting had been merciful by comparison. Now finesse is set aside, and we have pure unadulterated murder ... In the morning, men are thrown to lions and bears. At mid-day they are thrown to the spectators themselves. No sooner has a man killed, than they shout for him to kill another, or to be killed. The final victor is kept on for some other slaughter. In the end every fighter dies ... And all this goes on while the arena is half-empty. You may object that the victims committed robbery or were murderers. So what? Even if they deserved to suffer, what's your compulsion to watch their sufferings? 'Kill him,' they shout, 'Beat him, burn him.' Why is he too timid to fight? Why is he so frightened to kill? Why so reluctant to die? They have to whip him to make him accept his wounds.[87]

This does not show that the Romans weren't all bad, that Seneca was a good chap; it describes an elite man's view of the games as a place of pleb degeneracy, and so exaggerates the negative aspects of the games: 'The sentiment expressed something of Seneca's scorn for the crowd.'[88] He chose to describe the low point of the games, when they went downmarket at the quiet midday section; for it was then that the point of death, the lowest common denominator, became the whole exercise, that style was discarded, and carnage ensued. For at that time, style, grace, *virtus*, honour, and skill, all focused by death, had gone, and only death remained. Seneca said afterwards that he felt 'more callous and less human', but that had as much to do with his revulsion at the habits and crudity of the lowest of the plebs than any sympathy he felt for the sufferer. In any case, as Wistrand points out, Seneca's famous condemnation was not of a gladiatorial combat but the executions of criminals.[89]

The moral doubts which the elite possessed reflected their concerns about the debilitating effects on the lower orders of such time-wasting, for 'nothing is so damaging to good character (*bonis moribus*) as the habit of lounging at the games.'[90] Nobody objected to the shows' cruelty, only to the crowd's immorality. That immorality also seemed to corrupt members of the elite. Nobles volunteered for the games and were extremely popular with the crowd. 'In such a steeply stratified society, it seemed outrageous for men of high status to throw away privilege, to declass themselves, even if "in this way they achieved death instead of dishonour" (Dio 56.25).' So why did they do it? 'It is difficult to know why senators and knights performed as gladiators. I suspect what attracted them was the opportunity to display their military prowess, their courage and their skill, plus the desire for victory, and the shouts of the crowd. At the risk of death, it was their last chance to play soldiers in front of a large audience.'[91] More significantly, they reveal a changing culture. Noble volunteers exposed a narrowing of the gap between the elite and the popular cultures. Previously, it would have been literally inconceivable for a noble to appear in a public performance since their *virtus* was inherently linked to their social position. But by the heyday of the empire appearing as a gladiator had become a logical step for those of the elite who sought popular acclaim; and only the moralists were left to condemn it, in accordance with their own reactionary agenda.

There were also many problems associated with the introduction of Greek athletics and the gym, on account of the fact that they symbolized the perils associated with the Romans' burgeoning wealth and worldliness. At first sight, athletes seem to have been privileged by elite patronage beyond their public popularity. More than other entertainments, they were chosen to illustrate points in prose, possibly because the Greek athletics appealed most to the elite literate classes, rather than the more populist games.[92] Augustus, for example, loved watching boxers – particularly those of Latin birth, Suetonius explains almost by way of explanation and apology.[93] Athletes also never incurred legal *infamia* for their actions, which suggests that they were closer to the dominant morality than gladiators, who were considered the basest of men.[94] But athletes were, especially in the early empire, morally problematic. Their nudity marked them out as potentially degenerate. They were thought effeminate, frivolous, stupid, sweaty, greedy, fat, uneducated, oily, and dirty. They were infamous for their indulgence in sleep and food, and this was owing to the fact that their excessive concern for the body caused moral disquiet.[95] Athletics only became more acceptable later when the import of Greek culture ceased to be so sensitive an issue, when Roman culture grew calluses over what had been soft spots in its skin and came to terms with its success.

The moralists, who provide so many of our sources, retained the right to arbitrate the claims to honour in accordance with their own values, and so need not reflect contemporary opinion. They reflected the traditional culture and morality, systems which had weakened under the weight of historical change. The political authorities also claimed to represent the moral values of the society which they governed; but to imply a consensus would accept that claim. For by the time of the empire different social groups had acquired different systems of evaluation. The old structures of honour and manly control had lost their former cross-social dominance. New conditions had arisen which required a more inclusive set of social ideals. In the games, therefore, the emperors were attempting to market the old elite ideals in a radically new packaging with the purpose of enticing the lower classes into, and then training them in, some semblance of aristocratic values; for just as they were to share elite pleasures, so they were to share their morals. Through the universal media of the body and violence, they drew on common cultural themes and collective mythology in an attempt to produce a social consensus. The games were a popularization of traditional elite leisure and culture. They represented the fusing of popular and traditional elite cultures, and as such were an imperial reinterpretation of lower-class leisure and aristocratic military training and hunting. And just as the purpose of elite philosophy was to inculcate *virtus*, moral quality, so the games were to act as mass philosophy.[96]

The games reflected a reaction to a social hierarchy in transformation. The elite's relationship with those whom they ruled had changed, and the cultural gap between the two had narrowed. The influx of wealth and the accompanying growth in popular culture had demanded a relaxation of traditional ties and their replacement with more horizontal modes of measurement based on the principles of competitive merit. As such the games represented the powerful's idealized view of social relations and individual identity, and provide us with a one-sided image of Roman culture fashioned for the purposes of social control. It is this process of social transition to which the games bear witness. But this process also created tensions, and it was in the baths that these tensions were most apparent.

6

The Baths

The elder Pliny attributed the success of the physician Asclepiades' system of hydropathic treatment to the fact that it appealed to 'humanity's greedy love of baths'.[1] Whatever the underlying reason might be, the popularity of baths amongst modern academics continues to swell, and almost matches the enthusiasm with which the Romans themselves participated in this activity. Most recent studies have concentrated on the basic issues of the introduction of baths into Italy, their typology, and their place in the wider social structure; and we now have a fairly clear picture in these areas.[2] Here, I shall attempt to say something about the baths as places where social tensions welled up to the surface of Roman life, and as places where underlying social developments were clearly visible.

The trip to the dip took, for all classes, a prominent place in their scheme of leisure. It was not for nothing that many poets preferred to 'haunt lonely places and shun the baths'.[3] Bathing was regarded as being as vital as eating, drinking, sex, and laughter. 'Unlike the theatres, amphitheatres and circuses with which they are usually classed, baths were not just places of occasional entertainment but an integral part of daily life.'[4] 'Baths were found throughout the Roman empire, and the major role they played in everyday life is indicated both by the number of baths which have been found and by the amount of literary and epigraphical source material referring to them.'[5] 'For the Roman they were one of the essential elements of the civilised life, one which could be used as a symbol of the romanisation of conquered barbarians.'[6] The baths were multifaceted – both private and public, and also commercial – and multifunctional as well – for meeting, cleansing, exercise, health, relaxation, education, talking, eating, ostentation, and awe, for actor and spectator alike. 'We bathe for warmth, health, cleanliness or pleasure,' as Clement of Alexandria explained.[7] Whereas in Greece, bathing was an adjunct to gymnastics – brief, cold, and invigorating – in Rome, more emphasis was placed on leisure and relaxation, refreshment and resultant well-being. Terence's image summed up the baths' qualities: 'Perfumed and comfortable after a bath, your mind at ease (*otiosum ab animo*)'.[8] The greatest fatigue was measured by the fact that, 'all the baths in the world will never rid me of this tiredness.'[9]

As a result of their popularity, considerable prestige was involved in the construction of baths, and this justified the vast cost. The imperial *thermae* 'represent an enormous expenditure of resources by the emperor, magnificent symbols of legitimate power turned to the public good.'[10] 'These baths were showpieces, and to use them must have been to participate in a spectacle; the principal characters must always have been the rich, who went to be seen, and the rest, who went to gape as much as to bathe, living the life of the rich vicariously for a brief moment', willing extras in a monumental epic.[11] The imperial baths were huge recreational facilities for the populace to enjoy the pleasures of the aristocratic villa: parks, streams, baths, promenades, exercise, and sport. *Thermae* also offered an array of peripheral services including food, drink, laundries, and prostitution, as well as being cultural centres for music, sculpture, art, and literature. Scobie questions the benefit of spacious public facilities and buildings reflecting *maiestas imperii* (imperial power) to a poor casual worker; he argues that baths offered temporary alleviation but not a genuine substitute for the slum conditions which dominated most of the poor's life.[12] This is partly true, but it ignores the fact that the *thermae* were a paradigm of the attractions which animated, enlivened, and invigorated mere existence, and for the poor, to escape from some foul hovel or mean apartment to the baths for an afternoon must have been a joy. Leisure in the baths became a way of displaying civilized Roman attitudes. This was carried out in the context of imperial generosity, and the baths became fundamental to the expression and establishment of a new imperial imagery and authority. But baths reflected the social structure in a less dramatic way than the circus and amphitheatre. As such, baths were vehicles for social relations and the means of the transmission and diffusion of imperial ideology.

Thus far this analysis seems unproblematic. But a difficulty arises in that the baths were not simply or straightforwardly popular. They were problematic in two ways: in a straightforwardly conventional moral sense, and also in a more complicated cultural sense. Many Romans disapproved of bathing, or so they claimed, and in the eyes of the moralists, cleanliness was next to decadence. It was in the baths that pleasure, the opposite of virtue, was found.[13] Galen saw the growing custom of the daily bath, even among farmers, as a sign of spreading effeminacy.[14] Seneca saw it as a decline in morality; for in the good old days only the arms and legs were washed every day, baths being taken at weekly intervals.[15] Similarly, Columella did not approve of slaves bathing frequently as it softened them for work.[16] The baths were places where excess seemed prone to occur: people drank heavily, then either slept it off or went for a vomit and a freshen-up so as to start over again.[17] Some only went there in the first instance in order to 'raise a thirst'.[18] By the end of the second century, it was the mark of an undisciplined military unit that at noon its officers were all to be found at the baths.[19] In Antioch, the people were temporarily excluded from the baths because of the enormities committed there.[20] The contradictory double-image of the baths as both boon and vice was also reflected in Jewish thought: once, three Rabbis were sitting talking, and the first, Rabbi Judah, began, 'How splendid are the works of this people (the Romans)! They have built market-places, baths and bridges.' The second, Rabbi Yose, said nothing, whilst the third, Rabbi Simeon, countered by saying that, 'Everything they have done they have made for themselves: market-places, for whores; baths, to wallow in; bridges, to levy tolls.'[21]

Baths were portrayed as places of immorality and disruption, and as such, they seemed to threaten not only the individual body, but the citizen body which had made Rome great. It was believed that baths taken to excess, far from being healthy, could actually weaken the body. 'The continued use of baths undermines a man's strength, weakening the muscle of his body,' as Clement of Alexandria stated,[22] and those who bathed 'enfeebled and polluted themselves.'[23] Likewise, the historian Livy, describing troops wintering at Capua in the Punic wars, tells that, 'those whom no severe hardship had conquered were ruined by excess of comfort and immoderate pleasures ... for sleep and wine, feasts and harlots, and baths and idleness, which habit made daily more seductive, so weakened their bodies and spirits that it was their past victories rather than their present strength which thereafter protected them.'[24] The use of heated water, though pleasing, could soften the body in precisely the same way as it did in the boiling of meat; and, moreover, induced a simultaneous tenderizing of the character and its morals. Nor was it only men who could have physical change induced by a surfeit of bathing: a woman could take on manly attributes. Juvenal condemns a patrician woman who goes to the penny (i.e. male) baths in the evening, works out with weights, flogs people, drinks heavily, and then offers to Silvanus, the god of wild land worshipped exclusively by men.[25]

The baths were thought to be hot and steamy in every sense. 'The subject that attracted the greatest public censure was the alleged immoral and sexual indiscretions associated with the baths.'[26] Even a supposedly morally upright man might be left upright in an altogether different manner when among the temptations to be seen at the baths. Martial describes a typical old-fashioned Roman: 'though no one's duller in dress, his morals sport a different colour . . . We bathe together, and his line of vision keeps below waist-level, he devours ocularly the boys under the showers, and his lips twitch at the sight of a luscious member.'[27] Seneca talks of one Hostius Quadra, who scoured the baths for especially well-endowed men, then took them back to his house, where he used distorting mirrors to enlarge his prize catch still further, before watching obscene acts being performed on himself.[28] Martial describes the problems associated with the lecherous in the baths: 'You eye me, Philomusus, when I bathe, and continually enquire why I have with me such well-developed, smooth-cheeked boys. I will answer your question in plain terms: Philomusus, they assault meddlers.'[29] The baths were also problematic for those wishing to conceal their good fortune: Caelia hid her slave's private parts by a fibula whenever he accompanied his mistress to the baths – for modesty's sake, she said, but, according to Martial, to hide her slave's noble proportions from the envious eyes of other women.[30]

It was not only sexual body misuse that occurred in the baths. Depilation and other 'effeminate' adornment also served to mark out the baths as places which contributed to the immorality which threatened Rome's survival. According to Juvenal, 'a hairy body and arms stiff with bristles, give promise of a manly soul', but not all hankered after this image. The infamous boy-emperor, Heliogabalus, used depilatory ointment on himself, and also shaved his minions' groins, using the razor with his own hand, with which he would then shave his beard;[31] none of Juvenal's slaves were, or so he claimed, noisy frequenters of baths, presenting their armpits to be cleared of hair.[32] Most notorious of all, it was common knowledge that depilation was practised by catamites, who were wont to remove the hair from both their private parts and their buttocks.[33]

Moralists considered the baths a dangerous threat, but the baths were central to Roman life and culture. How is this to be explained? The answer lies in the analysis of the reasons which lay behind the fears of the baths' potential for encouraging immoral behaviour. Yegül is right to say that 'the objection to bathing on ethical grounds reflects the beliefs and convictions of its exponents and the overall moral atmosphere of the period as much as it expresses a judgement on the baths themselves. Often, the subject is used only as a vehicle to express views on larger issues and requires consideration of the full context for a fair assessment.'[34] This can be expanded, for baths were the location where several socially and culturally sensitive issues converged: the transformation from republic to empire; the influx of foreigners, wealth, and luxury; rapid urbanization; and the growth in the power of popular culture. Some of these areas of tension were sited nearer the surfaces of Roman life, others lay embedded more deeply, but all were interconnected and created a mesh through which Romans experienced the baths. Baths, therefore, represented the point about which many social and cultural tensions were articulated, and it is the job of the cultural historian to explain what it was about the bathing location that made it suitable for such a pivotal role.

Moralists' doubts, and the emperors' anxieties which caused them to spend so lavishly in the provision of baths, reflected the ambiguous nature of baths as a mediator of tensions between rulers and ruled. For the baths were places of equalization in a sharply stratified society. All Romans knew their place, and status divisions were not vague class terms, as is now the case, but were more precisely defined in law, more closely linked to political rights, and far more pervasive. Each declared his wealth in public and so publicly defined his status. Political institutions also reflected the formal stratification of Roman society. The baths, however, were places to which people went to relax and where a concomitant relaxation of social rules took place. The baths represented a hole in the ozone layer of the social hierarchy. They were the weak spots in a system which normally protected its members from what it saw as the harmful rays of equality. It was the working-out of this tension between condign equality and inherited prestige that characterized many aspects of Roman life during the early empire.

Leisure in places such as the baths was the social space in which people felt free from the dictates of the outer world and able to assert and develop their 'real' identity. However, this freedom could cut both ways. It not only gave opportunity for development, it also threatened to undermine existing social identities. The baths, therefore, posed a twin dilemma. The *nouveaux riches* went to excess in the baths because they saw both a need to defend their newly-won social gains against devaluation in the leisure environment, and an opportunity to inflate their standing still further by means of conspicuous consumption. Wealthy parvenus arrived with retinues in order to demonstrate their power and recently acquired status.[35] Seneca mocked the man surrounded by his entourage, carried from the baths back to his sedan chair,[36] as did Juvenal when attacking Tongilius' mob of muddy retainers and his outsize oil-flask of rhinoceros horn.[37] Clement of Alexandria criticized those who brought slaves to the baths, since they underlined social differences there, where everyone was supposed to be equal.[38] Ammianus Marcellinus, writing about fourth-century Rome, describes how the aristocracy went to take the waters accompanied by huge retinues.[39] These attempts at status retention reflected elite and personal concerns over the loss of face that a trip to the baths might engender. They were entering a place where undercurrents of status tension flowed both deep and strong.

The ambiguous nature of leisure spent in the baths because of its potential for self-expression and change was reinforced by the temporary nudity of the participants. The baths 'provided one of the major opportunities for exposing the naked and seminaked body in public',[40] and, as Dyson tells us, 'Given the nature of the bathing process, social distinctions and hierarchies were bound to break down.'[41] Those of superior status could be undermined by any inferior qualities of their physiques. Likewise, any man could become the focus of attention on account of the size of his penis: 'If from the baths you hear a round of applause, Maron's giant prick is bound to be the cause,' as Martial puts it.[42] Plutarch 'says that it was Greek influence that caused the Romans to bathe naked', and that bathing was originally done privately.[43] Whatever its origin, nudity in the baths presented an opportunity for status concerns centred on the body to be most clearly expressed, whilst it was also in the baths that these tensions were most apparent.

The nudity of the baths meant that they were a place of potential embarrassment. The discredited were up for ridicule, and the discreditable had to guard against the same happening to them if their own stigma were to be revealed.[44] For example, Augustus' mother supposedly acquired a birthmark before getting pregnant, and so stopped going to the baths.[45] Some Romanized Jews wore fibulas in order to conceal their circumcision.[46] Martial describes a woman called Thais, who smelled so bad that, at the baths, she covered herself in a depilatory or wrinkle cream so as to conceal the odour. Martial also tells of a certain Fabianus, who used to mock those afflicted with hernias – until he himself ruptured. It is not surprising that the sick used to enter the baths while still wearing their clothes.[47]

It was one of the paradoxes of the wealthy's trips to the baths that they came to be regarded as an opportunity for extravagance in dress.[48] Clothing, along with food and shelter, is one of the primary requirements of mankind, but it does not only meet utilitarian needs, it also supplies various social and emotional demands. The study of clothing is not just the study of man in relation to the material world. 'Clothing is very much a social artefact – a form of communication.'[49] Capable of carrying manifold meanings, clothing reflects values and lifestyles, a social body-surface which superimposes on the wearer a super-personality, the dress possessing the properties of the state inherent within it. One of the most essential functions of clothing is that of differentiation: to indicate social status and prestige, and increase (or be thought to increase) the wearer's attractiveness. Since dress is a fundamental social habit, the public wearing of garments often comes under the regulation of law. In Rome, the official dress of each class was strictly regulated,[50] and in such an environment it is not surprising that the nudity of the baths was especially problematic.

Nudity can be thought of as an 'unclothed intermedial state', and na-kedness as 'a state of being undressed which causes shame, disrespect, and harmful results in one's social surroundings'.[51] These occasions of legitimate nudity are marginal areas in which a person might pass, albeit temporarily, from one social status to another. An unclothed person is in a 'liminal situation', which can possess either a positive or negative social function, for in such places, people exist 'devoid of ordinary social status; he or she becomes a kind of human *tabula rasa* able to assume some new status or state he has not previously held. Such a potent, unclothed state is dangerous in the sense that it is pregnant with possibilities and may be readily influenced towards the different directions of all kinds of new states.'[52] It is a moral holiday. For when clothing is the norm, short-term, legitimate nudity acquires increased value and is the most violent nega-tion possible of the clothed state; and a violent change in the course of the 'natural' order of things is made more possible by a violent change of dress. Nudity achieves a medial condition and thereby paves the way for potential transformation. It is the situation where people are most open to change and new ideas.

These twin notions of the unclothed state, the one to be praised, the other condemned, were also at play in Roman society. Traditional Roman rhetoric was often commended for its plain (*nudus*) state; Caesar's writ-ings are compared to 'nude figures, straight and beautiful; stripped of all ornament of style as if they had laid aside a garment'.[53] Conversely, the nakedness of immoral emperors was characteristic of their debauched lives. For being undressed was one of the occasions when the Romans thought 'true' character was revealed: 'When you wish to enquire into a man's true worth, and to know what manner of man he is, look at him when he is naked; make him lay aside his inherited estate, his titles, and the other deceptions of fortune.'[54] It was not surprising, in fact it was particularly revealing, that Nero had planned to emulate the exploits of Hercules by killing a lion (which had been specially trained to be harm-less) in the arena whilst naked before all the people.[55] Two moral stances were in operation: the first applauded the nudity of statues and athletes because of the display of *virtus*, body control, and traditional simplicity; the second censured the nakedness of degenerates since its sole purpose was to aid their pursuit of pleasure, lust, and excess, and so became symbolic of the wealth worries which afflicted Roman culture. In the baths, therefore, nudity did not eradicate prejudice, snobbery, class or status but it made them momentarily critical and problematic because it was difficult to tell which moral stance was to be adopted.

The levelling forces which were present in the baths contributed both to their popularity and to their notoriety. When dress had been discarded, status became difficult to define and could reveal itself only in body, voice, conduct, and attitude. But the body was not simply a self-sufficient mechanism. It represented a place of social conflict and was 'the site and focus of a whole variety of problems and conflicts'.[56] It was in the baths that these body conflicts were brought out into the public sphere. The ideal of the *'mens sana in corpore sano'*[57] battled with excessive pleasures of the flesh on account of the fact that in the baths the potential for losing control was great. An oft-quoted saying neatly captures the dilemma: 'Baths, wine, and women corrupt our bodies – but they make life worth living.'[58]

In the traditional elite view, the body represented an ideological uniform which expressed superiority in terms of a hierarchy based upon nature itself. Medicine and philosophy linked closely, and medicine was thus expected to propose a 'voluntary and rational structure of conduct' concerned with total health rather than cures and remedies.[59] Medicine offered a way of living based on attention to the body and its activities, and the environments in which they occurred. 'Between the individual and his environs, one imagined a whole web of interfaces such that a certain disposition, a certain event, a certain change in things would induce morbid effects in the body. Conversely, a certain weak constitution of the body would be favourably or unfavourably affected by such and such a circumstance.' This was a 'differential valuation of the environment with regard to the body, and a positing of the body as a fragile entity in relation to its surroundings.' Different rooms were considered suitable for different illnesses and also for different times of the year, month, and day.[60] The bath environment became an integral part of this correct regimen of life.[61] For 'this preoccupation with the environment, with places and times, called for a constant attention to oneself, to the state one was in and to the acts that one performed.'[62] Otherwise, the heat and vital spirit which were the 'imponderable elements in the make-up of the male . . . unless actively mobilized, might cool, leading even a man to approach the state of a woman' and become womanish.[63] 'It was never enough to be male: a man had to strive to be "virile". He had to learn to exclude from his character and from the poise and temper of his body all telltale traces of "softness" that might betray, in him, the half-formed state of a woman.' For things were never as they seemed: 'the physical appearance and the reputed character of eunuchs acted as constant reminders that the male body was a fearsomely plastic thing.'[64] Juvenal describes the danger: 'Look at that specimen – you could spot him a mile off, everyone knows him – displaying his well-endowed person at the baths. Priapus might well be jealous. And yet he's a eunuch.'[65]

The elite Roman body was not only private property.[66] 'The maintenance of exacting codes of deportment was no trivial issue'; it expressed the '"gentle violence" of a studiously self-controlled and benevolent style of rule'.[67] The 'notables ... watched each other with hard, clear eyes. They noted a man's walk. They reacted to the rhythms of his speech. They listened attentively to the telltale resonance of his voice. Any of these might betray the ominous loss of a hot, high-spirited momentum, a flagging of the clearcut self-restraint, and a relaxing of the taut elegance of voice and gesture that made a man a man, the unruffled master of a subject world.'[68] As Dupont says, 'un corps corrumpu est souvent l'effet d'une corruption de l'âme, la cupidité rend pâle et efféminé, l'avarice fait l'homme dur, sec, et constipé, les débauchés exhalent des odeurs et des humeurs nauséabondes.'[69] This physiognomic outlook held that 'if you watch them, all acts are always significant, and you can gauge character by even the most trifling signs. The lecherous man is revealed by his gait, by a movement of the hand, sometimes by a single answer, by touching his head with a finger, by the shifting of his eye. The scamp is shown up by his laugh; the madman by his face and general appearance.'[70] Even to talk or move wrongly was to show one's deviancy and immorality. The bather had to decide whether to try to maintain his proper comportment and attention to the self: 'Oh, I shan't be having any dinner when I get home,' he might say, and hope to be believed.[71]

The traditional elite view of the body was of an object to be controlled as meticulously as the lower classes over which they ruled. But it was no longer their society which made the rules: new conditions permitted a different image of man, one which was less controlled and more popular. Moreover, this freedom to indulge in the physical riches provided by the empire was most obvious in leisure contexts. Tensions resulted because new, less controlled images of masculinity contrasted with the old-style toughness which had won the imperial wealth in the first place. The body became a focus around which some of these problems were negotiated for two reasons: those with traditional moral concerns saw internal and external threats (both societal and individual) as being causally connected; and secondly, the body represented the central medium of the new imperial programme because of its universal and inclusive nature. Two sets of moralities were in conflict and both found their fullest expression in the physical sphere. The baths were where this conflict was most apparent and it is for this reason that so many of the surviving descriptions of Roman immorality occur in the baths. Accusations of body misuse in the baths reflected tensions in a social situation, whilst these tensions were neatly encapsulated in the context of the bathing establishment. The extent to which these practices actually occurred is largely irrelevant because the accusation itself functioned as a trope of moral discourse. It served to highlight the differences which existed between traditional definitions of what constituted moral behaviour and what most people were actually doing in the imperial period. This conflict is seen in Quintilian's discussion on usage (*consuetudo*), in which he states that it is not to be defined as merely the practice of the majority: 'The practices of depilation, of dressing the hair in tiers, or of drinking to excess in the baths, although they have thrust their way into society, cannot claim the support of usage, since there is something to blame in all of them.'[72]

The change in image from the traditional stereotype of the man of control and *gravitas* was the consequence of a change in social conditions which had caused the old conception to become redundant. The new image was built not only through the use of 'others', that is to say the negative pigeonholing of outsiders, but also through the manipulation of more positive internal images. In the baths a process of cultural construction was under way and the image which was forged was less restrained, and less confined to the traditional elite. The creation of an identity was one of the primary aims of the imperial programme because without it the empire could never hope to differentiate itself from preceding republican turmoil or from those whom it had conquered. As for the early modern Dutch, to be clean, leisurely, and healthy was an affirmation of separateness.[73] To bathe was to differentiate and to exclude, and bathing was a custom by which the Romans came to recognize their common identity. To be properly clean, and benefit from being both leisurely and healthy, came to be the mark of a Roman. Yet this had less to do with quantifiable degrees of hygiene, and rather more to do with psychological perceptions of the environment. Unlike the Dutch, they were not washing away the impurities of the flesh and filthy lucre, they were celebrating the good fortune and virtue which had gleaned them so rich a harvest. If they went over the top in their revelry, that was a matter for moral concern, but, if used properly, the influx of wealth was now portrayed as something which could actually work to the benefit of the citizenry.

The centrality of the baths to ideas of morality meant that they became an axis about which delicate issues could be turned. It was also the case that, as the imperial system became established, moral anxieties often came to be concentrated on the personage of the emperor himself. In the imperial baths, these two lines of thought came together. Hence, in the surviving biographies of the emperors in Suetonius and the *Scriptores Historiae Augustae* a double helix of the moral system was in operation. Certain bath-house actions came to be attributed to emperors in accordance with the moral fingerprint being taken rather than historical fact. In two parallel but contraflowing processes, the 'good' emperors spiral upwards along the standard lines of building or restoring baths, providing free entry or oil, forbidding mixed bathing, and bathing themselves in cold water with the ordinary folk; and the 'bad' emperors corkscrew down into the depths of immorality because of their bathing frequently in hot, perfumed, mixed-sex baths, and their indulging in every new twist of excess.[74]

The introduction of the great imperial baths was problematic because the acceptance of public bathing required a transformation in moral attitudes. This transformation sprang from the change from republic to empire, and the subsequent change in the nature of the dialogue between the government and its people. Yegül notes that, 'the generations hypercritical toward the increasing material comforts of life, and of the baths in particular, belonged to the early decades of the empire. Cicero, of the late republic, had no quarrels with the modest bathing establishments of his day. In the second half of the first century, Martial, Statius, and the younger Pliny accepted the public baths as legitimate and quite in line with the luxuries offered by the imperial system.'[75] The later acceptance of imperial wealth was a result of the fact that by the latter half of the first century the change from republic to empire no longer presented a moral dilemma, since it was an upheaval which was well in the past. This transformation in attitudes towards the baths is seen clearly in Artemidorus' comment on how the baths should be interpreted in dreams, one which reflected both their more positive attributes and their inherent dangers:

> Long ago it was reasonable for the baths to be considered unlucky, since men did not wash regularly and did not have so many baths. Rather, they washed themselves when they returned from a campaign or when they left off some strenuous activity. (Thus, the bath and the act of bathing were, to them, a reminder of toil or battle.)
>
> In our time, though, some people do not eat unless they have taken a bath beforehand. Others, moreover, also bathe after they have eaten. Then they wash when they are about to take supper. Therefore, in our day, the bath is nothing but a road to luxury. And thus washing in baths that are beautiful, bright, and moderately heated, is auspicious. It signifies wealth and success in business for the healthy and health for the sick. For healthy men wash themselves even when it is unnecessary.[76]

But despite the fact that some attitudes had changed, other tensions remained and continued to find their expression in 'bathing discourse'. Physical immorality, for example, was still condemned because it represented the wealth-induced character-softening which threatened Rome's very survival.

The reasons for the success of the baths, and for the emperors' being so fond of them, were also the reasons for their moral ambiguity. They were places where new conditions were most obvious and tensions most openly debated. Concerns about the baths reflected their status as places of double mediation: between rulers and ruled, and between the old and the new. The emperors used the cultural currency available to them to create new benefits which were relevant to the changing society in which they lived, and whilst the literary sources which we possess are often hostile, they reflect a more traditional elite ideology. The baths themselves were evidence of a new interpretation of the relationship between the government and its people, and confirmation that this was expressed in a new type of civic social space. They are the extant record of those for whom written history belonged to another cultural world. The baths embodied elaborate acts of self-congratulation, by which the Romans both rewarded themselves for their success and also created a new kind of political world – the product of an imperfect union of popular culture and traditional elitism.

7

Goodbye to *Gravitas*: Popular Culture and Leisure

The notion of 'popular culture' has a long tradition in mainstream history, but it has failed as yet to have any significant impact on the study of the ancient world. Ginzburg has shown that you do not have to have lower-class authored texts to write a history of popular culture, so there is every chance that the concept will be a useful way of looking at the Roman plebs and their leisure.[1] To begin with, though, we must examine what is meant by the term popular culture. Beik takes the practical stance: 'I use the term "popular culture" as a convenient way of lumping together the collective forms of thinking and acting of the bulk of the nonelite population.'[2] Burke agrees: 'As for popular culture, it is perhaps best defined initially in a negative way as unofficial culture, the culture of the non-elite, the "subordinate classes" as Gramsci called them.'[3] For most historians, the concept of popular culture has consisted of the study of the particular activities associated with the lower orders. As such, it was what the elite 'failed to get'.[4] This seems straightforward enough, but it fails to take into account the other dimension of popular: that which is cross-socially common. For if there is one aspect about popular culture which is immediately apparent, it is that its appeal is spread widely over the social hierarchy. Ginzburg, after discussing the confusion which exists in the concept of popular culture,[5] notes that, 'it should be clear . . . why the term "popular culture," which is unsatisfactory in some cases, is preferable to "collective mentality." A concept of class structure, even if conceived in general terms, is still a big advance over classlessness.' But, he adds by way of qualification, 'This is not to assert the existence of a homogeneous culture common to both peasants and urban artisans . . . The intention here is simply to suggest an area of research within which specific analyses similar to the present one will have to be conducted.'[6] As Chartier concludes: 'What is needed is a historical approach not unlike that of sociologists when they try to identify cultural types not from a group of objects supposedly characteristic of a particular group but rather from the relation each group has with shared objects, knowledge, or practices.'[7]

How are we to think of popular culture? If we imagined a perfectly ordered society, we would find that society would map onto its culture exactly. By this, I mean that the people of a particular social level would have a clearly defined, homogeneous set of beliefs and practices. So in a hierarchical society, the elite's culture would be separated from that of the lower class and vice versa, whereas in a purely egalitarian society, since there would be only one social level, there would be only one level of culture, which everyone shared (although this does not mean that everyone would be the same, only that no knowledge would be privileged over another). This is, of course, an ideal. In any real social situation, culture does not fit neatly with its society. Lower-class culture spills over into the other classes and vice versa. Thus the study of popular culture is the study of two different levels of life. The first is the culture of the lower orders – their taverns, tenets, and values; the other is that of the unofficial subordinate culture and represents the underprivileged aspects of life – in the case of Rome one which involved pleasure, excess, loss of control, a closing of the gap between the genders, and a greater acceptance of chance in human affairs. For popular culture is not only the knowledge of the subordinates but also the subordinate knowledge within the culture as a whole. The fact that society and culture are out of sync in this way creates stresses and fault lines. The degree of mismatch is greatest in periods of social upheaval, such as the end of Rome's republic, and it is here that we have the best opportunity of seeing a culture coming to terms with a changing social structure. Therefore, when sources reveal social tensions, these can be used to establish the exact nature of a society's structural weaknesses.

In ideal terms (and these were the terms in which the elite moralists claimed to see the world) traditional Roman society in its purest form would have had a clear divide; for in such a perfectly ordered society, the plebs would think, want, and do as plebs should, and likewise the elite. In reality, matters could never be so clearly defined. An unofficial culture existed cross-socially, though necessarily mainly amongst the mass of the ruled. Moreover, as the relationship between the rulers and the ruled became increasingly strained, the whole culture of the subordinate classes came to be seen as unofficial and threatening. As such, the plebs and the popular can never really be separated, since a causal connection was perceived between any unofficial act and the profit which the subordinate classes stood to gain from this weakening of the social order. This became particularly important in the late republic, when Roman society was being dramatically transformed by the acquisition of empire. The traditional social order was forced to adapt, and this created cultural problems in that beliefs and practices which had been subordinate came to possess a more dominant cultural role. Culture was forced to accommodate a new social order, and as a result, there was a battle between the deepest cultural forces at work in their existence. There was a struggle for the popular, and this was expressed in the moral and legal discourse of the Roman elite.

The 'common people' still had cultural practices of their own; and these ideas, beliefs, and world-views were not the incoherent crumbs which had fallen off the table of elite culture. Unofficial values also existed and these seemed to act as lowest common denominators in that they attracted people of all statuses. It was when these two factors came together that the condemnation was greatest. In other words, some activities on their own were less threatening in that they were no longer entirely associated with popular culture. Gambling, for example, epitomized the faults of the popular levels of culture, but was a cross-social activity. It was a part of popular culture in only an incomplete sense, since it was not a non-elite practice alone. It did not pose an inherent threat to the social order, only to dominant cultural sensibilities. Some other activities of the plebs disgusted the elite without ever meriting the most stringent censure because they were not seen to represent alternative values. Taverns, however, explicitly expressed both the popular and the plebeian, and as a consequence were more vehemently despised by the moralists. Similarly, condemnation of gambling was fiercest when it was the non-elite placing bets, or the elite in a non-elite manner. Popular culture cannot, of course, be summed up by a set of activities, but by starting with their analysis I hope to draw out the popular values inherent within them and then relate these back to their social context. The aim of this chapter, therefore, is to examine the taverns, theatres, carnivals, and other assorted activities which constituted much of the popular culture of Rome, and analyse both the competing outlooks which they represented and also the problems which this competition created in a rapidly changing society.

Dr Johnson was of the opinion that, 'the true felicity of human life is a tavern', but a visit to one of Rome's inns might have changed his mind. Not only did they reek,[8] but the quality of the food on offer, especially of the meat, may also have been doubtful. At best, dish of the day might have been tripe, at worst it was lamb's lips or sow's genitals.[9] They were also patronized by less welcome guests: for the elder Pliny explains that everything grows in the sea, 'even the creatures found in the inns in summer time – those that plague us with a quick jump or those that hide chiefly in the hair'.[10] But despite these discomforts, the taverns were the primary locus for the everyday leisure of the mass of the Roman populace.[11]

To us, the popular activities under scrutiny here seem harmless enough. Yet bars were denounced vehemently. Cook-shops (*popinae*) had connotations of gambling, prostitution, and all vices.[12] They were a union of all kinds of debauchery: 'pleasure is lowly, servile, weak and perishable, whose haunt and abode are the brothels and taverns.'[13] Their clientele were portrayed as the scum of the earth: 'Citizens of every class, freedmen, slaves, slaves of all kinds – robbers and runaways, beaten, bond, or debtor slaves. Anyone with the price is welcome. Dark little nooks all over the place, eating, drinking, the same as a *popina*.'[14] Similarly, Juvenal describes an Ostian *popina* full of cut-throats, sailors, thieves, runaway slaves, hangmen, coffin-makers, or some drunken eunuch priest.[15] It was obvious to all why innkeepers were psychologically associated with affliction: 'An innkeeper portends death for the sick. For he resembles death in that he receives everyone. But for all other men, he foretells afflictions and distress, movements and trips. And the reason is obvious. What need is there, then, to explain something so clear?'[16] Innkeepers (*caupones*) were portrayed as lacking morals and even as murderous thieves, whilst their legal status was lowered like that of the actor's.[17] Knowledge of bars was a standard piece of rhetorical abuse.[18] The bars also differentiated the elite from the lower classes: 'Just as I do not care to live in a place of torture, neither do I care to live among *popinae*.'[19] Socrates, an elite hero, supposedly used to boast that he had never 'peeped into a tavern or seen a large crowd.'[20]

Actors faced a similar barrage of criticism and were legally penalized for their profession.[21] They were thought to be morally deficient: 'Actors and players who mount the stage are obviously not to be believed by anyone, since they play parts.'[22] Theatrical characteristics were effeminacy of gesture and posture, and a wanton desire for public display: 'a man who would scarcely lift his tunic in public for the necessities of nature, will take it off in the circus to make an exhibition of himself.'[23] This decadence led to political transgression: 'there is no actor, more frivolous and vicious than the rest, who does not claim to have been his (Catiline's) almost constant companion.'[24] It was such a routine character slur that a man had taken part in the gang rape of a mime actress that Cicero did not even try to deny it, but just brushed it aside as a folly of youth.[25]

The Roman theatre was primarily a popular activity associated with the lower classes, whereas in Greece it was neither of these, but was politically central and centralizing. Wistrand observes that, 'in a perspective of social control, the theatre was clearly counter-productive: it taught the wrong things, including idleness, inactivity, corruption and softness, all sorts of indecency; it was frequently associated with riots and strife, and it lacked strictness and dignity.'[26] The main objection to the theatre was 'its lack of *severitas* and *gravitas*'.[27] But the stage enjoyed a customary licence,[28] and this enabled it to fill the role of interface between rulers and ruled.

Such a spirit of licence also pervaded the festivals during which the theatre was held. The most famous of these was the Saturnalia when the tunic replaced the toga, extra wine was allotted for the household,[29] and gambling was permitted.[30] Lucian's description of Cronus as Saturnalian king sums up the fun: 'what I do is drink and be drunk, shout, play games and dice, sing stark naked, clap and shake, and sometimes even get pushed head-first into cold water with my face smeared with soot.'[31] The Saturnalia were a 'licensed restoration of the Golden Age at which the social order was toppled'.[32] There were other festivals, and they were also character-ized by a temporary increase in freedom. Ovid refers to the popular fes-tival of Anna Perenna, held on the Ides of March, when as many cups were drunk as years of further life desired. In this festival, sexual licence also increased, and pairs of lovers lay on the grass amid the singing and dancing.[33] However, these festivals were not condemned by the elite or thought to be morally corrupting.

If we are to explain such vitriolic abuse and also such tolerance it will be necessary to examine the perceived values which were thought by moralists to underlie the activities of popular culture. To begin with, the plebs were thought to be in a state of total ill-health. The supposed de-cline of their moral health was a constant source of invective:

> And what of the plebs? They follow fortune as always, and detest the victims, the failures. If a little Etruscan luck had rubbed off on Sejanus, if the doddering emperor had been struck down out of the blue, this identical rabble would now be proclaiming that carcase an equal successor to Augustus. But nowadays, with no vote to sell, their motto is 'couldn't care less'. Time was when their plebiscite elected generals, heads of state, commanders of legions; but now they've pulled in their horns, there's only two things that concern them: bread and circuses.[34]

Lucan agreed with Juvenal in thinking that the mob consisted of idlers, the dregs of every nation.[35] These sentiments have continued into the modern world. In his notes to his edition of Juvenal, Hardy puts it bluntly: 'The distribution of corn and the attractions of the games had long been drawing to Rome a host of idlers and loungers, ready for any disturbance, willing to do anything but work for their own support.' 'Rome was in all probability fearfully overcrowded by a population ... which ... was pampered and caressed by the emperor himself, who, to please and oc-cupy them, was forced not only to extend the corn-distribution, but also to increase the number of festivals and holidays and shows, already far too numerous.'[36]

In the eyes of the elite, the lower classes were characterized by their stupidity, laziness, and time-wasting. In the theatre, the populace 'careless and unable to distinguish between truth and falsehood, shouted loud the usual flattery, as it had been taught to do.'[37] Even if they noticed mistakes in delivery they had no inkling why it was a mistake: 'for the whole audience will hoot at one false quantity. Not that the multitude knows anything of feet, or has any understanding of rhythm; and when displeased they do not realize why or with what they are displeased.'[38] They spent their time idling in wasted leisure: the man who wants to follow oratory will not 'spend his time, like so many, in the theatre or the Campus Martius, in dicing or in gossip, nor the hours wasted in sleep or long drawn banqueting, but in listening to the geometrician and the music teacher.'[39] 'Most sit about in public places, gossiping and wasting time',[40] and such great numbers seemed to have this kind of 'restless laziness',[41] that the Romans came to be seen as a nation of *ardeliones*, ever idly busy, ever profitlessly out of breath, useless busybodies, a nuisance to themselves, and a bore to others.[42] Their talk centred on the city's leisure: 'the uproar of the city, the crowding, the theatre, the races, the statues of the drivers, the names of the horses, and the conversations about these matters. The craze for horses is really great, you know, and men with a name for earnestness have caught it in great numbers.'[43] Their desire for racing was seen as mindless (*neglegentias*).[44] Ammianus also describes the fourth-century crowd: 'some spend the whole night in wineshops, others lurk in theatre awnings . . . or they quarrel with one another in their dice games (*aut pugnaciter aleis certant*) . . . or, favourite of all, to stand all day, rain or shine, talking in detail about the relative merits of the charioteers and their horses.'[45] They became one of the anti-wonders of the world: 'It is most remarkable to see an innumerable crowd of plebs, their minds filled with a kind of eagerness, hanging on the result of the chariot races. These and similar things prevent anything memorable or serious being done in Rome.'[46]

The popular also stood accused of a lack of seriousness: 'For an extraordinary law springs from the fickle temper of the mob, and is very little suited to our dignity, very little to this our order (*Nam extraordinarium imperium populare atque ventosum est, minime nostrae gravitatis, minime huius ordinis*).'[47] Similarly, Cicero is eager not to be thought to be displaying *levitas* by his subject matter: 'I beg you not to think that any spirit of levity has led me to fall into an unusual method of speaking, if I talk about poets, actors, and plays in the course of a trial.'[48] For 'men unduly elated by delight are rightly adjudged weak and worthless (*nimis elata laetitia iure iudicantur leves*).'[49] Gellius gives us an accurate definition:

'I observe that *levitas* is now generally used to denote inconsistency and fickleness (*inconstantia et mutabilitate*) . . . but those men of early days who spoke properly and purely applied the term *leves* to those whom we now commonly call worthless and meriting no esteem (*viles et nullo honore dignos*).'[50]

This contrasted with the traditional ideal of the man of *gravitas* at the heart of which lay the paternalism and patronage of a rural aristocracy, expressed in a virile shame culture. Pride in honour, and shame at its loss, were primary in the emotional economy. The elite were exhorted to maintain a grip on their emotions: 'obey nature but maintain *gravitas* (*naturae obsequi gravitate servata*).' For 'there is a proper conduct even in grief (*est aliquis et dolendi decor*). This should be cultivated by the wise man; even in tears, just as in other matters also, there is a certain sufficiency; it is with the unwise that sorrows, like joys, gush over.'[51] To take some pleasure was thought acceptable, even natural, but 'there is a great difference between slackening and removing your bond.'[52] The traditional man of *gravitas* was epitomized by Cato, who by his presence alone stopped people at the Floralia asking for jokes from the naked prostitutes.[53] Similarly, M. Crassus, grandfather of the triumvir, reputedly laughed only once in his life.[54] But such a degree of control could pose expressional problems: Quintilian states that whilst the epic poet Antimachus deserves praise for the vigour, dignity and height of his language (*vis et gravitas et minime vulgare eloquendi genus*), 'he is deficient in emotional power, charm, and arrangement of matter, and totally devoid of real art (*et adfectibus et iucunditate et dispositione et omnino arte deficitur*).'[55]

It was clear that the lower classes had not even a pretension to the traditional image of self-control. Nowhere was this more apparent than in the popular: 'For when Cicero wished to indicate a kind of extreme sordidness in the life and conduct of Mark Antony, that he lurked in a tavern, that he drank deep until evening, and that he travelled with his face covered so as not to be recognized . . . he said, "Just see the *levitas* of the man." '[56] Inns were decorated with frivolous and lewd pictures: in the Ostian inn of *Via della Calcara*, the mottoes of the 'Seven Sages of Antiquity' were adapted to read: 'To shit well, Solon used to rub his belly'; 'Thales advises the constipated to push hard'; and 'the subtle Chilon taught the art of farting silently.'[57] *Levitas* also characterized the frivolity of women and the young.[58] Apuleius describes how a bunch of robbers held a debauched banquet and 'played raucously, sang deafeningly, and joked abusively, and in every other respect behaved like those half-beasts, the lapiths and centaurs.'[59] The non-elite were seen as the missing link between elite order and the sensual chaos of the animal world. Their taverns were symptomatic of this lust for pleasure, and it is no surprise to see the word *ganea* meaning both an eating-house and, by extension, luxury in general.[60] Moreover, the elite could be dragged down into a spirit of *'levitas popularis'*, a 'style of comportment characterized by personal accessibility to the people and a willingness to share in their amusements'.[61]

The popular pleasures acted on a shorter timescale: 'Set forth the wine and the dice! Away with him who heeds the morrow! Death, plucking the ear, cries, "Live, because I'm coming!" (*pone merum et talos. pereat, qui crastina curat. mors aurem vellens "vivite" ait, "venio")*.'[62] Such lack of thought for the morrow was epitomized by the lower classes' supposed belief in luck, which was especially noticeable in their passion for gambling (see plate 3).[63] Fortune became conceptually linked to the plebs in that both were considered to show *levitas*: 'Fortune is a goddess who admits by her unsteady wheel her own fickleness *(levitas)*', 'She is less stable than any leaf, than any breeze',[64] and is 'steadfast only in her own inconsistency *(tantum constans in levitate sua)*'.[65]

The popular culture was also noted for its mistreatment of the body through excessive indulgence. This could corrupt the young elite who strayed into its path: Apuleius describes a young man of distinguished birth, 'whose wealth fully matched his nobility. But he was given to the pleasures of the tavern, and spent his time in whoring and daytime drinking. Through this he had fallen into the evil company of thieves.'[66] Once defiled, the body's degeneration took greater hold on the morals, so that it was no surprise that Catiline's followers had learned 'to dance naked at banquets'.[67]

The elite saw the lower orders as a violent and uncontrolled threat. According to Ammianus, a description of Rome is of 'dissensions, taverns, and other similar vulgarities *(vilitates)*'.[68] This was also the view of the earlier elite: 'What difficulty is there in stirring up craftsmen and shopkeepers, and all the dregs of the city?'[69] The plebs were fickle, shifting, and lovers of each new sedition.[70] They had no concept of friendship *(amicitia)*, for 'The common herd value friendships by their profit.'[71] Instead, they spent their time in squabbling: 'You will see the crowd (at the spectacles) quarrel, jealous husbands against gallants.'[72] These arguments, unlike the philosophical discussions of the elite, frequently spilled over into violence. This could be entertaining, for Augustus liked to watch boxing, not only professionals, but 'the common untrained townspeople that fought rough and tumble and without skill in the narrow streets *(sed et catervarios oppidanos inter angustias vicorum pugnantis temere ac sine arte)*'.[73] But generally, they were noisy and troublesome.[74] Sometimes fights were the result of drink,[75] sometimes gambling,[76] but whatever the cause, it was clear to the elite that they were frequent,[77] and connected both to pervasive street crime[78] and the taverns which spawned them (see plates 4 and 5).[79]

To what extent were these observations true? The evidence is fragmentary but it does not support the elite image of a spoiled, fickle, and irresponsible mob. From a modern work-oriented point of view, there is a tendency to see work, especially formal work, as being fundamentally important to people's lives, since without it we have a diminished sense of identity. The social fact of unemployment becomes transformed into a universally observable mental and moral decline into apathy, apolitical attitudes, and aimlessness.[80] To a large degree, the Roman elite's perceptions coincided with these observations, but they were the result, not of a work-centred outlook, but of different work and leisure patterns among the lower classes, and hostility between the classes. For their stereotypical view of the lower orders was as much ideologically determined as based upon observation, although on a surface level it was not an unreasonable description; it was the nature of free time in Roman society to drive people out of doors. Thus Rome was full of underemployed people just hanging around in public places. They passed their time in the parks and piazzas,[81] on public walkways and in the baths,[82] and in temples.[83] They met in bookshops and libraries,[84] in the barber's,[85] and even lay in wait for their acquaintances in the public latrines.[86] This was the public face of not working, and it is probable that this view of the workless plebs as lounging about looking aimless, as listless and apathetic, and in a demoralized condition was therefore to some extent factually grounded. This is what their environment of underemployment and poverty must have looked like. To the elite they had no worth, money, or status; they controlled no labour power save their own; and they were worse than a slave in that they had not even the security of food and lodging; they seemed scarcely better than slaves because they relied on patronage, on selling themselves into dependence for casual work, whilst their free time could never be a positive leisure because of social and economic restraints.

Regular paid employment was not the norm. Within the city of Rome the urban plebs could rely on a corn dole, occasional doles of meat and oil, subsidized corn sales, as well as patronage links to provide a basis for living. The degree to which they earned money and actually sought work is highly problematic,[87] but the wide range of jobs attested in extant sources – shopkeepers, traders, skilled and semi-skilled craftsmen, stevedores, transport workers, and builders – suggests that there was a large and relatively sophisticated labour market. Also, Cato states that in the country the landowners always needed a plentiful supply of wage labour to supplement a permanent servile labour force on the slave estates.[88] In a situation such as this where there was a pool of unskilled labour and a demand for it, it would be surprising if no, or little, use of wage labour occurred. Usage might have been spasmodic, casual, and marginal but it may also have been widespread.

For the plebs whose status as casual labourers meant that their work was intermittent, it was likely that routines were always flexible. Much of the apparent aimlessness of underemployed pleb life was due to the fact that unskilled men often looked for work and spent their time in an unskilled and aimless way. Luck would frequently be thought to dominate the casual labour market, and in reality probably did so, relying as it did on the favour of shopkeepers and the charge-hands at the ports and building sites; and this accounts for the fatalistic attitude which writers like Juvenal detected.[89] But that they were fatalistic did not stop them from seeking work or passing their free time; they merely looked purposeless whilst doing it. Furthermore, this unrewarding way of spending work and leisure made people tired and that tiredness was easily mistaken for apathy. If the plebs seem to have been unable to find substitutes for casual work it was because of poverty, not demoralization. In a society where work was less central than in our own, there was also less social or psychological need for the creation of alternative 'work' such as the modern practice of D. I. Y. and hobbies. It was leisure which provided the identity of the Romans; they 'found themselves' in the baths, and they satisfied their intellectual interest in racing-talk, betting, and gambling.

In part, therefore, the attitudes of the elite can be explained as the product of different lifestyles; but they were also the result of different values. It was not that the elite could not see that people could legitimately hold other beliefs: 'On the other hand, many actions are seemly according to our code which the Greeks look upon as shameful. For instance, what Roman would blush to take his wife to a dinner party?'[90] But the elite could not accept any alternative which threatened their own social order. What, then, were the different values of the lower classes, and how did these differ from those of the elite? The hostility aimed at taverns was based on the elite Roman concept of what honourable people could do in public. For the elite, social life was mainly conducted at home, the entertainment provided by domestic or hired performers. Elite public life consisted of government and its display. Hence, their distaste for taverns and *popinae* arose because they represented the taking of pleasure in a public place, when it was personal control which should have been on show. A sure sign of Nero's immorality was that he learnt to drive a chariot and held a trial show in his gardens in front of his slaves and the dregs of the populace (*sordidam plebem*).[91] He even let the plebs watch his exercises in the campus.

Such a transformation of what some thought to be acceptable in public was the result of the massive urbanization which had occurred in Rome. 'The poor tended to live in garrets or in rooms behind a shop or tavern. These spaces were used for little more than sleeping. Most other activities were carried out on the streets or in the various public facilities.'[92] The poor's living conditions were so bad that taverns offered an escape and also a means of obtaining food, for often they had no cooking facilities. The elite contempt for public display was largely a function of their economic ability to enjoy themselves in private, and so was an extravagance which the poor could ill afford. Urbanization necessitated a high density of dwellings, and this produced intense social activity and close human contact which became highly valued as constituents of the best plebeian life. The taverns became key points of social gathering: the centre for leisure, criticism, and information: 'It is the brothel and the greasy (*uncta*) *popina* that stir in you a longing for the city.'[93] The city life of the urban plebs demanded a new, more public, manner of socializing, and this conflicted with the home-based leisure of traditional culture.

For the non-elite, therefore, taverns and piazzas became the arena in which their public life took place. 'You see many groups of them gathered in the fora, crossroads, streets, and their other meeting places, engaged in quarrelsome arguments with one another, some (as usual) defending this, others that.'[94] These arguments, carried out in the plebeian patois,[95] did have a certain etiquette; they were not just the prelude to drunken brawls: 'Among them the old are influential because of their long experience, and they often swear by their hoary hair and wrinkles that the state cannot exist if in the coming race the charioteer whom each favours is not first to rush forth from the barriers.'[96] By offering a place for these debates, the public leisure of the taverns became central to the everyday politics of the lower classes. It was also for this reason that the elite were so hostile to the lower classes' use of leisure, for many guilds used taverns as meeting-places and fronts for political activity, and 'if people assemble for a common purpose, whatever name we give them and for whatever reason, they soon turn into a political club.'[97]

It was clear to the elite that what the lower orders thought it was acceptable for a man to do differed from their own idea. But that does not mean that the lower orders were without their own image, nor that there was no overlap. It was, I would suggest, largely in the modes of expression that the difference between them lay. Both were public expressions of a patriarchal male image, but the expression of the non-elite involved a greater public expressive release, which the elite condemned as *levitas*. To begin with, it must be realized that masculinity is neither measurable nor a timeless universal concept. It is only possible to talk of masculinities: the culturally specific ways of expressing maleness.[98] Manhood is the approved way of being an adult male in any given society: not a biological state, but an elusive image built up through cultural sanctions, ritual, and trials of skill and endurance. It is a problematic state which is often questioned in a public and dramatic way, and in Rome, it was something acquired by winning small battles honourably. Men were deeply committed to an image of manliness because it was part of their personal honour and reputation, but it was closely bound up with aggressiveness and potency. Male honour was a domestic duty, a sacrifice for the family; the male was to impregnate, provide for, protect, be brave, whereas to be dependent on another was reprehensible. Male and female worlds were strictly demarcated, and it was wrong for men to hang around at home. They were expected to spend their free time outside, back-slapping in public places, for they could not give the impression of being under the spell of the home or women. To be a man, therefore, was to run risks, to stand up in danger, for the collective good, and violence was part of that culture's normal behaviour. Slights to a man's honour and image demanded a physical public recompense,[99] but whereas the elite gained compensation in the austere atmosphere of the law courts, the plebs' restitution depended on their own ability to defend themselves in public. As such, the frequent tavern fights attested to in the sources were not symptomatic of a lower-class malaise or love of disorder, but rather the very opposite, since they reveal the extent to which they were prepared to protect their image. It was in the degree of emotional expression thought acceptable in public that the classes differed. For both the elite and those beneath them, to be masculine required not only self-reliance and self-control, but control over other people and resources. The plebs expressed their masculinity in taverns, in standard masculine pastimes of gambling, arguing about sport, and competitive drinking, whereas the elite debated in the senate and carried out the offices of public life. It was the controlling power of the elite which allowed them to expel their emotions from this public sphere, but that also resulted in their perception of the plebs as having values which threatened their own.

Taverns were protopolitical centres which incorporated specific attitudes to consumption, generosity, honour, and leisure. They were good for lower-class culture because, with their food and drink, they acted as the focus for popular communal activity.[100] They represented semi-public economic areas, privately owned, but open to the public, and the creation and control of these areas were issues central to and arising from urbanization. The growing diversity in public drinking-places paralleled an increasing stratification of urban society and popular recreation. Taverns served crucial urban functions: they sold food and drink, and they sold space and the freedom to use it within certain constraints, both of which were especially important for the spaceless urban poor. Music and dancing also served to emphasize and enhance the openness and accessibility of a tavern by highlighting its public quality. Public consumption gave opportunities to mix openly with friends alfresco, and as such, taverns were neutral terrain in which to engage in the public reproduction of social relations. They were a public space for local politics, gossip, and contests of honour and status. As Dyson says of brothel patrons' graffiti, they reveal a 'community of low-life types whose social life centered on the brothel in much the same way that the social life of the elite was focused on the curia or the basilica'.[101]

Drink was central to the entertainment and recreation of the poor, but it brought with it a social hangover.[102] For whilst public drinking brought men together for leisure and business, it also caused alarm among the elite because of concerns about excess. Drink was seen as an indicator of the state of social health, and the drunkenness of taverns was the metaphor of a consistent and recurring critique of lower-class culture by the elite. It seemed to summarize their prodigality, time-wasting, idleness, and immorality. Hence, public consumption constituted a battlefield of conflicting cultures. The elite condemned the taverns and the public drinking, leisure, and sociability associated with them. Taverns were seen as a moral contagion, a place for clandestine meetings, a place for deviants and deviancy, outsiders, and foreigners. Also, there was a fear of violent and criminal behaviour arising from such decadence. Taverns became a symbol of debauchery and misery and gave focus to elite hostility towards the lower orders by helping to define a dangerous class. For just as taverns played an integral part in the lives of the lower orders, so they also played a major part in the elite's conception of that culture.

The sociable uses of taverns have been concealed by the tradition of elite censure. But elite and popular conceptions were separated less by disagreement over the reality of what went on in taverns than by radically opposing assessments of the implications of tavern culture. What was for the magistrates (*aediles*) the centre of disorder, dissolution, and debauchery, was for the populace a space in which to create a public theatre for its culture. Drink-related violence and crime characterized taverns in the eyes of the elite, but this ignored the overwhelmingly peaceful uses of taverns that allowed daily friendship and relaxation. To be sure, violence was part of the tavern culture, but it was infrequent and discriminate, rather than commonly criminal. The real significance of the violence lies in the nature of the disputes which took place there. The elite perceived them as irrational and random, but they were the discords of the lower-class honour system, when no real alternative means of redress was available. For within a patriarchal framework, taverns gave the lower orders a stage on which to insist on their self-respect and the respect of others, and to fight to defend it. The dubious status of the innkeeper reflects his status both as an elite symbol of popular decadence and as an arbiter of disputes. The lower orders did consume publicly with less restraint (or, at least, less pretence of restraint) than the elite, and such consumption might seem incongruous to their income, but their mentality was different. Public consumption was their investment in identity and communal networks of aid and obligation. It was a social capital.

These social tensions increased because of the rise of the popular, the rise of *levitas*.[103] This does not mean that the Romans suddenly became infected with frivolity, but that the set of practices and attitudes – the culture – which had traditionally been described as *leves* acquired a more serious cultural role. The old popular culture was now incorporated into official 'serious' culture as the old official culture, epitomized by *gravitas*, became partially redundant in the face of empire and wealth. The pursuit of pleasure became more respectable as the traditional community standards weakened under the pressure of prosperity and urbanization. A new tendency arose for people influenced by popular culture to place their own pleasures and needs above the obligations of the community. Moreover, these people liked to take their pleasures in a less controlled way: noisily, effusively, and in public. Traditional culture had maintained a strong boundary between the elite aristocracy and those beneath them, but in the face of incredible wealth, old standards of self-restraint and simplicity were no longer by themselves sufficient. The old-fashioned self-control was being threatened by the spirit of levity which characterized the non-elite. For the increase in prosperity had not only loosened the bonds of the lower classes, it also freed the elite from some of the restraints of their traditional white man's burden. This meant that they were free to enjoy their wealth, and in order to find the means by which to do so they had to look to the popular.

The emergence of popular heroes is evidence of the growth of this new mass society. Charioteers, gladiators, actors, (and later holy men), all came to epitomize the new importance of the popular culture. These icons became strong cross-social forces. Located on the borders of the *ancien régime*, whose power was based on prestige, and the new society, whose power rested on definable merit, popular heroes became the arbiters of Roman culture. They were the axes around which conflicts revolved, and it was to them that Romans turned for the settlement of their disputes. A new interface was created between the traditional elite and the popular, but this also created moral concerns about what such a weakening of boundaries meant for traditional identities.

There were a number of responses to the rise of the popular and its different values. The elite's moralizing was one. For these new modes of practice conflicted with the traditional dominant morality. In early Rome, *levitas* had been clearly marked off from normal life; hence, seats were not put in the theatres because it was feared that it might tempt people to pass whole days in indolence (*ignavia*).[104] But what traditionally had been confined to festival periods was now spilling over into everyday life: 'every dinner party is loud with foul songs.'[105] The moralists responded to this narrowing of the cultural gap between the elite and the popular by lamenting a lost age:

I understand that yesterday's morals and strenuous manner of living are out of tune with our present extravagance and devotion to pleasure (*Intellego luxuriae et deliciis nostris pristinum morem virilemque vitam disciplinae*). For, even as Marcus Varro complained in the days of our grandfathers, all of us who are heads of families (*patres familiae*) have quit the sickle and the plough and have crept within the city-walls; and we ply our hands in the circuses and theatres rather than in the grainfields and vineyards; and we gaze in astonished admiration at the posturings of effeminate males (*gestus effeminatorum*), because they counterfeit by their womanish motions a sex which nature has denied to men, and deceive the eyes of spectators. And presently, then, that we may come to our gluttonous feasts in proper fettle, we steam out our daily indigestion in sweat-baths, and by drying out the moisture of our bodies we arouse a thirst; we spend our nights in licentiousness and drunkenness (*libidinibus et ebrietatibus*), our days in gaming or in sleeping, and account ourselves blessed by fortune in that 'we behold neither the rising of the sun nor its setting'. The consequence is that ill health attends so slothful (*socordem*) a manner of living: for the bodies of our young men are so flabby and enervated that death seems likely to make no change in them.[106]

Nor was this just empty rhetoric, for in the moralists' eyes the allurements of pleasure and leisure threatened the state with destruction.[107] The popular was perceived as the lowest common denominator, what appealed to all, but to the moralists it seemed to appeal at a base level.

A more direct response by the traditional dominant morality was to pass laws directed against the popular. Guilds met in taverns, got drunk, and then became bold, irresponsible, and prone to conspiracy and public unrest.[108] Hence, Augustus dissolved all *collegia* except the ancient and legitimate ones.[109] Claudius also disbanded the *collegia*, but went further: 'Moreover, seeing that there was no use in forbidding the populace to do certain things unless their daily life should be reformed, he abolished the taverns where they were wont to gather and drink and commanded that no boiled meat or hot water should be sold.'[110] The emperors who reacted strictly to guilds were usually ruthless with the taverns, for to control the taverns was to control the guilds.

But regulations concerning the cook-shops and taverns went further than was required by the need to maintain political control. Along with other sumptuary legislation, they were enacted over the whole of the late republic and early empire. The dictator Sulla had set the ball rolling by limiting the elite's expenditure on banquets.[111] The proto-emperor, Julius Caesar, kept up the attack on luxury: 'In particular he enforced the law against extravagance, setting watchmen in various parts of the market, to seize and bring to him dainties which were exposed for sale in violation of the law.'[112] Both Mark Antony and Augustus issued sumptuary edicts aimed at curbing the excesses of the table.[113] Tiberius turned the assault onto the popular, and restricted cook-shops and *ganea* so that not even pastries could be exposed for sale.[114] Claudius' ban was based on cooked meats and hot water.[115] Caligula imposed a tax on all eatables sold in any part of the city,[116] and 'although Nero spent practically all his life in taverns, he forbade others to sell in taverns anything boiled save vegetables and pea-soup.'[117] Similarly, Vespasian, since 'his own style of living was very far from costly and he spent no more than was absolutely necessary', allowed, 'even in the taverns, nothing cooked to be sold except pulse'.[118]

To some extent, economic reasons of supply shortage underlay this legislative activity, so that they can be seen as an attempt at price control. But even if the motives were partly economic that does not explain why the emperors chose to pick on the taverns. Also, the laws seem to have been largely ignored. Even tenants of Claudius' estates were violating the law forbidding the selling of cooked victuals, and Claudius is also said to have banished a senator who fined his tenants for ignoring this ban. It might be wondered whether restrictive laws made taverns less appealing, but the continued growth in popular entertainment testifies to the fact that it could withstand the hostility of both moralizers and magistrates. The only evidence for success comes from the *Panegyric* written by the Younger Pliny for the emperor Trajan. According to this, the mimes were successfully suppressed through public respect for the emperor, not terror, and the restrictions were seen as a 'public benefit and not an enforced necessity'.[119] Leaving aside the validity of this claim, Pliny does go on to reveal the real motivation for these laws: to teach the 'vulgar crowd' a 'lesson from its rulers'.[120]

The law was not a point of common consensus. The point of such laws was to symbolize the moral superiority of the traditional element of culture, and vilify the values of the popular. As such, they did not depend on enforcement for effect, for even when the law was broken, it was clear that it was the traditional culture which set the standards. The need for these laws intensified as social change threatened that traditional culture. Hence, the laws acted as an index of social tension between the popular and the traditional in Roman culture. They were part of a social confrontation between traditional morality and the new popular mentality, which refused to accept conventional values. But even if it is accepted that the law served such a symbolic role, it will still be necessary to explain why the elite directed their concern at taverns and actors. According to Edwards, low official status of actors was both a recognition of, and an attempt to control, their disruptive potential. They were socially central yet morally problematic, and actors posed a threat because they could not be defined. They could become persons of any status, transcend all codes of dress, and even their gender was uncertain. All of which is true, but is still true today when actors' status has never been higher. To some extent, it was because theatres were places where the tensions between the popular and the elite were most obvious. But it was also because their role as intermediaries was intimately connected to the transition from republic to empire. They acquired an increasingly political position during this period as the traditional methods of communication between rulers and ruled broke down. Hence, these highly paid sex symbols exemplified the advancing popular culture which was posing a threat to the traditional social order.[121] Similarly, taverns were legislated against because they epitomized the popular.

In part, elite legislation was a response to the political threat which taverns were thought to pose, but bans on certain pub food also revealed ambivalence towards commodities the consumption of which was associated with unproductive, and potentially subversive, forms of social behaviour.[122] Roman conceptions of food represent a set of attitudes very difficult to analyse. Certain foods had strange moral overtones: 'Quintus Metellus, in the Jugurthine War, when discipline had similarly lapsed, restored it by a like severity, while in addition he had forbidden the soldiers to use meat, except when baked or boiled.' As the Loeb commentator notes: 'The point of the prohibition is not obvious to the modern sense.'[123] But perhaps some understanding can be achieved. In traditional society, it had been the elite's lot to eat meat regularly; for it is generally people with power and in control who are allowed to enjoy its strength-giving properties:[124] 'If Aristippus could be content to dine on greens, he would not want to live with princes.'[125] Likewise, Horace's untroubled life free from ambition was one of 'greens and flour', and a dinner of 'leeks and peas and fritters'.[126] In contrast, it was for the plebs to eat grain, and they were supplied with sufficient luxury by vegetables and pulse. It was not that meat was only for the elite, it was just not for the poor on a daily or dainty basis. Luxury, like leisure, was related to status, and was to be distributed accordingly. Therefore, meat, vegetables, and pulse did not have a universal cross-social meaning. Vegetables were associated with frugality among the elite and, being poor food, were generally considered *infra dig.* – though still luxury enough for the poor.[127] An emperor's personality could thus be revealed by his diet: Didius Julianus was so frugal that, 'even when there was no religious reason, he was content to dine on cabbages and beans without meat.'[128] Conversely, Maximinus ate 40 lbs of meat a day and 'wholly abstained from vegetables.'[129]

In traditional society, when the plebs had been permitted to eat meat, it was either during officially sanctioned holidays or the result of religious sacrifice, and both these institutions were firmly embedded in traditional culture. By the principate, both meat and vegetables were commonly available. 'Curius used to raise spring greens (*oluscula*) on a little allotment, and bring them in himself to cook on his modest hearthfire. But today the scruffiest chain-gang ditcher disdains such fare, is nostalgic for the smell of tripe in some hot and crowded cook-shop. Once, as a special treat on feast-days, they'd bring down a side of salt pork from its rack, or a flitch of bacon for some relative's birthday, and maybe a little fresh meat if they'd run to a sacrifice.'[130] Luxurious distinctions got to such an extent that, 'even among vegetables' some kinds had no place on 'the poor's tables (*pauperis mensa*)'.[131] Moralists harked back to the earlier ideal state of affairs, for although vegetables had become common, they still chose to see them as luxurious in accordance with their reactionary outlook. For at that time, 'the lower classes got their market-supplies from a garden – how much more harmless their fare was then!'[132]

Certain foods came to symbolize decadence in a direct relationship of representation. So pigs, because of their wide variety of cuts, became . synonymous both with luxurious excess and cook-shops.[133] Similarly, hot water was associated with the drink with which it was mixed, and the subsequent excess and loss of control. It was in the tavern that these foods were prominently on display, and this threatened the elite's sense of control. Their response was sumptuary legislation aimed at curbing consumption of this type.[134] In traditional society the lower classes' food had been supplied by elite-dominated institutions, but taverns were a supply outside this framework.[135] They took consumption out of elite hands, and as such they were symbolic of a new popular waste. Moreover, taverns were tied to a different, and increasingly competing, morality and lifestyle. They represented a different concept of what was acceptable in public, and so attempted to redefine public life. The elite had the money to take their pleasures indoors, out of public view, but the pleasures of the tavern threatened to entice them out of their traditional home life into the new popular way of life. Exotic foods, even the daily opportunity to buy meat, were likely to beguile men from home cooking and plain morality. For an orderly, regular, and balanced dietary regime was connected with a morally wholesome and thriving family life.

Taverns reflected a growing pressure from lower-class demand which was pushing leisure in directions which many in authority deplored. Also, its practice was associated with a threatening, disorderly, and immoral ideology. As such, taverns were a leisure with negative links, and the emperors acted to purify them, so as not to let their new public leisure be contaminated with the rank smell of the *popina*. Yet eventually the authorities came to tolerate the new forms of leisure because it saw them as

fundamentally safe. Popular leisure ceased to threaten the dominant hegemony, because of its partial integration within a new official culture. It
is for this reason that anti-tavern legislation ends with Vespasian, for by
then the imperial system was fully established. Later, the emperors were
even to supply meat to the lower orders. This was for two reasons: firstly,
because this aspect of popular culture was no longer seen as such a threat,
and secondly, it served to bring the plebs back into an elite supply system
and so further bind them to the centre.[136]

The emperors legislated against luxury as part of a plan for social and
moral reform, which involved restricting taverns but compensating with
baths and games in a process of public amelioration. Their restrictions
were integral to the imperial effort to create another social order. The
imperial response to the development of the popular was not just a question of domination; it was of hegemony. It was based on the notion that
leisure might be used as an instrument of class conciliation. Hence, leisure became legitimate for the mass of the people precisely because it was
shorn of other associations, and in particular of radical political associations. But although the imperial response represented a popularization of
elite culture for the purposes of enticing the plebs into hegemony, on a
cultural level a process of gentrification of popular culture had occurred
which stood outside the elite's control. For just as the emperors developed
ways in which the lower classes might partake of the fruits of empire, so
traditional Roman society had to find methods by which it could safely
consume its surfeit. The elite had, in part, to abandon its old-fashioned
gravitas in favour of more greedy popular pleasures, and this hurt their
traditional moral sensibilities.

The emperors' new centrality within society meant that they became
the focus for the discussion of these social problems. It is for this reason
that so much emphasis in the imperial biographies is placed on their
pleasure and their leisure. They were used to pose the question of how
Roman society was to display its wealth in a manner suited to the Romans' frugal past. Contrast Heliogabalus and Severus Alexander: the one
preferred to have perverts placed next to him at banquets,[137] and liked to
touch them up; held summer banquets in various colours on every day;[138]
gave out large banquet gifts of anything from eunuchs to 1000 gold pieces
or 100 lbs of silver;[139] and often brought four-horse chariots into banquets.[140] The other gave banquets with friends treated as equals,[141] modest
banquets with no gold plate,[142] in good taste,[143] and with no dramatic
entertainments.[144]

The imperial response lessened the political tensions which existed in
Roman society, but it did not altogether eradicate them. Moreover, with
the establishment of an autocratic system, the expression of these concerns became a matter of great delicacy. It was in their humour, their use

of *levitas*, that the Romans accomplished this task. I shall not try to propose a theory of humour, for 'all who tried to teach anything like a theory or art of laughter proved themselves so conspicuously silly that their very silliness is the only laughable thing about them.'[145] It will be enough to say that humour relies on ambiguity, for whilst jokers attack, they depend on shared values to operate.[146] But it should also be pointed out that humour is closely related to leisure in that it produces a similar effect of enjoyment and pleasure, and it was this strong link which made it such an excellent medium for the expression of tensions. For as leisure discourse had become the mode of communication between the ruler and the ruled, humour offered an alternative channel which operated on the neighbouring frequency.

Traditionally, Roman humour had been used for social control. Roman wit was aimed at the ugly and deviant: Ovid's son-in-law, Fidus Cornelius, burst into tears when called a 'plucked ostrich' by Corbulo in the senate.[147] In Martial, all Rome's deviants are paraded: the one-eyed, the bandy-legged, the facially deformed, the toothless, the lanky, the bald, and the malodorous.[148] These freaks were outside normal boundaries, as if foreigners, and humour was used to establish firm borders of exclusion. A joking relationship was created which reflected wider social roles. Under strict codes of comportment, humour provided a standard means of communication between the elite and their slaves: Columella was friendlier and more familiar with country slaves for 'when I perceived that their unending toil was lightened by such friendliness on the part of the master, I would even jest with them at times and allow them to jest more freely, too.'[149] Humour worked upwards, too: Phaedrus claims that fables were invented to enable slaves to say what they thought under the cover of humour to escape punishment.[150] Seneca was not, therefore, insulted by the waggery of slaves, because the perpetrator 'is incapable of being contemptuous'. In fact, 'the more contemptible and even ridiculous any slave is, the more freedom of tongue he has.'[151] Which worked both ways, of course; for the greater the *levitas* displayed, the greater the indication of worthlessness.

Traditional *levitas* played with the concepts by which the Romans conducted themselves in periods of seriousness. In the festivals, the world was briefly subverted to allow the chance to rehearse the categories by which society lived for the rest of the year. Hence, carnivals were not just safety valves, they perpetrated certain values of the traditional community. It is for this reason that the surviving literature is soft on the licence of the carnivals, because their temporary excess not only reinforced the values of traditional culture, but did so as part of the old-fashioned joking relationship.

The rise of *levitas* meant that its old usage could no longer be maintained in any exclusive fashion. The old joking relationship had partially broken down as social categories themselves had changed. Its new importance meant that political humour came to reflect the tensions that existed between the emperors and those whom they governed, and was also the means by which these problems were articulated. Political dissent was expressed in humour: secret ballots in the senate led to abuses, for Pliny complains that some voting papers at recent elections had jokes and obscenities scribbled on them, and 'The result was farce fit only for the vulgar stage.'[152] But such political humour could draw a harsh reaction: Augustus issued edicts against anonymous jests and political lampoons.[153] Some were condemned under Severus for jesting about the emperor.[154] Nero, however, was very patient with curses, lampoons, and the abuse of the people. There was even a satirical song on his *domus aurea*.[155]

Political jokes resisted the increasing bureaucracy and standardization, and were a powerful transmitter of the popular mood in a society where no officially sanctioned outlet existed. However, they served only to reflect the powerlessness of the tellers, without actually changing anything.[156] The emperors became the centre for humour, indicating the totalitarian nature of their rule. They also tried to return humour to its traditional role by making it a part of the populist imperial image. Macrobius records how 'Augustus was fond of a joke, but he did not forget the respect due to his high ranks, and he showed a proper regard for decency.'[157] He then goes on to list some of Augustus' jokes, and they reveal the image of the paternal benevolent ruler – generous, but wise in his generosity. For example, a seedy-looking Greek used to try to get Augustus' attention by offering him complementary epigrams. Augustus once offered him one instead. The Greek read it and then gave Augustus a few pence. He laughed and gave him 100,000 *HS*.[158] It was a sign of Claudius' oddity that when his sister died he appointed a season of public mourning during which it was a capital offence to laugh.[159] By contrast, the emperor Vespasian's humour was such that 'He did not cease his jokes even when in apprehension of death and in extreme danger.'[160] But it was only in personal matters that he took so light an attitude – unlike Heliogabalus, whose jokes crossed all known boundaries: he kept lions and leopards as pets and let them loose on his friends at night; he used to invite eight fat men to dinner and laugh at them trying to fit on the same couch; and sometimes he laughed so loud in the theatre that no one else could be heard by the audience.[161]

The deep-seated transformations of Roman society were voiced in the growth of *levitas* as a means of cultural expression. *Levitas* now expressed not only the conflicts of the new politics, but also the anxieties of influx, and this was especially clear in satire. Satire reflected an elite

response to, and attempt to cope with, the influx of wealth and the subsequent weakening of the strength of the retaining walls of their social
structure. The values of the carnival had become separated from the traditional framework which they had helped support, and had become a
more autonomous expression of the popular. As such, satire reflected the
concerns over moral values, less certain social boundaries, and the increase in popular pleasure. Satire was the truly Roman humour, since it
was based on attacking base morals, luxury, and decline. It attempted to
delineate the nation, or at least to appear to do so. Satire also expressed
the conflict between legitimate but opposing societal objectives. For the
Romans were faced with two sets of moral requirements: the need for
simplicity, and the necessities of empire, and it was satire that reduced
anxiety about their failure to observe these mutually exclusive norms.

For moralists might thunder but there was no escape from the great
invasion of riches which had occupied Rome.[162] The rewards of empire
had been substantial, but that wealth, which was a reassuring sign of
success and divine favour, also acted on contemporary consciences as a
moral agitator. Without it the state collapsed; with it it could fall through
softness. Nor was this only a problem for the elite: moralists made no
social distinctions in their attacks on degenerate deportment. Their assumption was that abundance was a common, if unevenly distributed,
patrimony, and that the lower classes just as much as the elite needed
warning of the dangers of luxury and excess before they incurred the
ineluctable penalties of vice. Therefore, methods were needed by which
wealth could be used in ways compatible with the austere tradition of the
republic. It was through the elaboration and prescription of a set of beliefs
that could distinguish between vice and modesty, permissible comfort and
dangerous luxury, that the elite Romans sought to conquer their plenty.
The ability to control excess by a phalanx of traditional tenets became a
standard refrain, a topos of cultural, not material, reality. It was never
enough to consume conspicuously, one had *not* to consume conspicuously, also. A golden mean was established between abstinence and excess, and this was achieved by fusing *levitas* with *gravitas*, the popular
with the elite. But over time the differentiation of luxury and necessity
suffered an attrition which wore down these self-imposed boundaries.
Inhibitions about the exotic gave way to the need for ever more rarefied
and exquisite decorative effects. As a consequence, only the reactionary
moralists were left to complain, to act as prophetic correctives to the
consuming passions of the Romans.

The function of such an espousal of traditional values developed alongside Roman society. Cato's morality was an expression of a unified elite
culture, that is to say, where a small aristocracy recognized a common set
of values, an elite culture which was sharply marked off from the popular

culture. During the late republic, these values had to be mobilized to meet the challenge of the new wealth and the popular morals which it encouraged. However, like Canute, they could not hold back the tide of riches that swept over Roman society. A new dominant morality emerged, one which pragmatically accepted the demands of empire, but also dictated that the penalty for wealth was public disavowal through the medium of moral discourse. In reality, of course, not all meals were sumptuous banquets, and not all banquets were salacious orgies, but you would not know that from reading the texts. This morality reworked the previous moralities into one more appropriate for a richer, more urbane, society. It succeeded because it allowed a variety of interpretations: the more traditionally minded could still condemn the popular, the more populist could enjoy the benefits of wealth, but both reactions were comfortably contained within the membrane of imperial culture. As such, moralists reflected both the traditional reactionary mentality and a wider cultural response to the new prosperity and its concomitant tensions. This double act found its apotheosis in the imperial mentality. It was left for 'stern old men to denounce those revels', but those very men were enjoying the delights of their success to the full: even the austere critic, Seneca, owned 500 citrus wood tables, had a fortune of 300 million *HS*, and was a pederast. It was not that Seneca was a mere hypocrite; for his times, he was a moral conservative. But conditions had changed since the elder Cato, and his brand of tradition no longer represented the dominant morality; it was now competing with more popular outlooks, not in the market-place, but in the taverns and the games.

The problem for the Romans was how to be rich yet simple, powerful but humble. Success left them looking over their shoulders; or rather, looking into their hearts, for wealth was the enemy within, the fifth column in the besieged Roman character. Yet this moral duplicity did not confuse Romans in their everyday life because the peculiar coexistence of apparently opposite value systems was what they came to expect from their culture. It gave them room to manoeuvre between vice and restraint without ever having to opt for one in any final way. By definition their dilemma was insoluble, but we should not see their attempt at making these contradictions more complementary as two-faced hypocrisy. Under the empire they discovered a *modus vivendi* and a *modus operandi*; a working arrangement was established between the contending influences on their life which allowed them the opportunity to go about the business of daily life without suffering a moral paralysis. To be sure, they had to keep one eye on their excess, and relieve their tensions by projecting them into moral tirade, law, and satire, but their concerns were never sufficient to make them lose faith in their own good fortune. Their power and wealth could not be given back so they had to be accommodated, and this left them two options: to suffer a debilitating anxiety attack, or to offset their hubris by a penitential moralizing which sacrificed to the traditional values. For the Romans, this was Hobson's choice. Their success had been virtuously won, they deserved their pleasures, and so they took them.

8

Gambling

It is the business of winning and losing that is the eternal dilemma of sport, and in our attempt at communication with an ancient culture, the pay-offs of this confrontation afford us an X-ray of Roman life stripped to the bones.[1] As in the imperial games, many of the most deeply in-grained motifs of Roman society were concentrated into the emotional explosions of their gambling. This condensed nature meant that a whole range of feelings was experienced simultaneously, such as was not pos-sible in everyday life, where these themes were more scattered. And just as it spoke to the Romans, so it can give us a clearer description also. But the message that we shall receive will be of a different nature to the one which the imperial games gave us: it will be a message which relays some of the profound structural tensions in Roman culture.

First, it will be useful to define more carefully just what it is that is being talked about.[2] Gambling is one of the forms of leisure,[3] and as with leisure more generally, the fact that it is usually fairly simple to isolate the particular cultural forms of gambling has meant that its constitution has tended to be assumed rather than argued. This has prevented a more detailed analysis of the relation of culturally specific forms of gambling to their social context. Using an interpretive formula, therefore, the fol-lowing can be thought of as a definition:

Gambling is a symbolic system which acts to establish a mood of freedom and excitement by formulating competing senses of control and chance.

To see the element of control in a definition about gambling may be surprising, but it is only at first glance that gambling seems to be related solely to chance. For it is not the case that gamblers throw themselves to the vagaries of chance, it is more that they place themselves in a special relationship with their social environment by challenging the boundaries which normally demarcate their existence. The degree to which certain individuals and groups are prepared to test these socially constructed mechanisms for self-control, not to mention their social status itself, by making the outcome of a chance event consequential can tell us much about those people's relationship to their social context; and the degree to which the elements of chance and control are balanced in the broad range of a culture's forms of gambling can reveal wider cultural attitudes. The application of the term 'gambling' to an activity comes to be seen as a function of that culture's attitudes not only towards chance but also the relationship of chance to the structures of control. Gambling, therefore, is not simply concerned with trusting to luck as opposed to taking planned and calculated risks; it is concerned with the type of risk undertaken, by whom, and in what fashion.

Gambling held a continuous fascination for Romans right across the social scale.[4] To some, it was a vice among the rich, one which caused them to gamble the night away in front of their ancestors' august statues. Huge fortunes were won and lost while freezing slaves lay forgotten, or so Juvenal would have us believe.[5] At the other end of the social scale, labourers diced when the weather was bad enough to stop them working,[6] and schoolchildren bunked off lessons to play surreptitiously.[7] It was the last pleasure left to old men,[8] and for the smart prostitute to attract good clients she had to be able to keep her head at the table.[9] All these people took their lead from the emperors. Augustus played frequently, though only for pleasure, whereas Nero's minimum stake was 400,000 *HS*.[10] Such was Claudius' interest that he fixed a gaming-table to the side of his coach to enable him to play on the move without the pieces being thrown into the air; and, as a man of letters, he wrote a book on games of chance, turning his passion into literature.[11] Significantly, it was only the philosophically inclined emperor, Marcus Aurelius, who professed his indifference.[12]

Not only did Romans of all classes gamble and game, but they did so in many varied forms and locations. Gaming-tables were scratched into pavements in porticoes, basilicas, and any flat public surface: these gambling graffiti have been found on the pavements of the Forum Romanum, the Basilica Julia, the Colosseum, the entrance to the temple of Venus and Rome, and even in the house of the Vestal Virgins.[13] They were also particularly abundant in barracks. Within the household, gambling usually followed a meal, and parties relaxed with dice.[14] Taverns were also one of the primary loci of popular gambling. Many of these establishments allowed clients to plug into the electricity of aleatory excitement by offering gaming rooms where bets could be laid and knuckle-bones rolled.

Most taverns have been found to have *tabulae lusoriae* and may well have been frequented as much for the gaming facility which they offered as for any specialities in food or wine.[15]

The *tabula lusoria* was used for a game of *terni lapilli*, in which three counters were moved into strategic positions. Often, the boards themselves were arranged into appropriate or ironic sayings:

SPERNE   LUCRUM
VERSAT   MENTES
INSANA   CUPIDO

'Reject wealth, insane greed flips minds.'[16] Or:

VENARI   LAVARI
LUDERE   RIDERE
OCCEST   VIVERE

'Hunting, bathing, gaming, laughing – that's living.'[17]

There were many other forms of gaming. The simple end of the range consisted of casting lots,[18] *micatio*, or just odds or evens.[19] A sheer chance event was not only the most basic form, it was the quickest machinery for a gambler to repeat the bet. *Duodecim scripta*, similar to modern backgammon, had more complex rules but was still largely chance-based and hence was banned.[20] At the top of the range came *latrunculi*. No dice were used in this tactical game of phalanxes and blockers, and it seems to have attracted an intellectual following analogous to that of modern chess.[21]

Dice and knuckle-bones, however, were the principal media for gambling. Knuckle-bones, *tali*, are small bones found in the leg of most quadrupeds between the shin and the ankle, and each has four faces: 1 = the plain side, known as *canis* (dog), 3 = the convex, 4 = the concave, and 6 = the twisted, known as *senio*. They were thrown in fours onto a gaming-table by hand or cup, and, most probably, operated within a pool system. That is the case in the surviving example, where the throwers placed 16 *HS* into the pool if they got three dogs or a six, and the winner scooped the pot on the throw of Venus (one of each face).[22] Dice, *tesserae*, were thrown in threes in a game of hazard for generally higher stakes,[23] and to ensure a good throw it was usual when rolling to invoke a divinity or a lover's name. Dice could also be lobbed into the neck of a jar in the game of *tropa*, the first to succeed winning the pooled stake money.[24]

Not only adults chanced their luck. Children wagered on cockfighting, and this was considered a juvenile entertainment (see plate 6).[25] The young also played at nuts.[26] This could be played in three ways: by attempting to knock a pyramid of four nuts over with a fifth; by throwing them into a triangle marked onto the ground and with compartments of different scores; and by projecting them into a jar in the same fashion as the game of *tropa*. As these activities were banned except during the Saturnalia, nuts were also known as *Saturnaliciae*,[27] and were often exchanged as presents or carried about the person for general use. Nuts appeared at weddings as well, the groom tossing handfuls to the young men assembled outside the nuptial chamber as if casting aside the follies of youth. Probably as a result of their use for gambling, good luck was attributed to nuts for their supposed ability to repel the evil eye, and hence corpses were often buried in possession of them.

The games and the races also provided gambling opportunities (see plate 9). A large and organized betting industry now exists – bookmakers, totalizers, shops, and pools – but there is no evidence for anything of this kind at Rome. The prospective punter for a gladiatorial show was able to study street adverts, programmes, and even graffiti in order to assess each fighter's ability, based upon his record, trainer, and gladiatorial stable.[28] At the circus, race-cards and placards advertised the horses and their drivers, and betting was, by all accounts, common. However, the stakes may mostly have been small, and the satirists deplore the losses of the gaming-table, not the racecourse. Despite, or maybe because of, the small size of the bets, interest was spread across a large section of the populace. The pervasiveness of racing-talk, betting, and gambling was widely noted, and people of all statuses were interested in the names of both horses and riders. In everyday conversation, chariot races and gladiatorial fights were all the rage,[29] and in the days preceding the festival, talk turned on nothing but bets.[30] The pedigrees and records of horses, many of which raced for several years, were widely known. Lucian even refers to 'hippomania'.[31]

Once in the circus, the punter would bet on one of the four racing colours – blues, greens, reds, or whites – not on the horse or driver.[32] However, the colours were not considered equal; instead the blues and the greens enjoyed a pre-eminence which went back to their earliest existence.[33] The partisan fanaticism of the later empire seems merely to have been the institutionalization of existing factions and tendencies. The colours were also recognized as partners, blue and red against green and white,[34] and some races were run in which they joined as a team, one obstructing the opposition to leave the field clear for his team-mate. Cameron suggests that the blues' and greens' 'greater popularity and power was a phenomenon as old as the empire itself, of social significance only in so far as it may be inevitable that a highly competitive sport will divide a compact population into two rather than four primary groups.' However, he does not explain the continued existence of separate, smaller factions, autonomous until the late empire. London soccer in the seventies offered a comparable picture: four clubs – Arsenal, Spurs, West Ham, and Chelsea – dominated the whole of London football, but the extra power and influence of the first two did not eclipse the support of the latter. Nor were they coupled in any way.

An explanation of the early existence of linking can be found in a study of their betting practices. Bets seem to have been made mostly informally: Trimalchio at dinner made a bet with his cook on the result of the first race of the next meeting,[35] whilst in the circus itself spectators would wager with their neighbours. Juvenal talks of young men going to the circus and making 'rash bets (*audax sponsio*)',[36] and the phrase suggests that bets were made on the spur of the moment rather than as a calculated investment based on a cool study of the form. But that a bet was made on the spur of the moment does not necessarily mean that it was rash, only that a minimum of information was required to make it intelligent. All that the punters needed to know was whether they wanted to back the blues or the greens. For in a system with no bookmakers, the odds laid, for the purposes of maximum simplicity and practicality, would mostly have been even money; and the way to achieve this was by pairing the two more successful factions with the lesser ones. The fans had additional information to take into account – the name of the horse, its pedigree, gate number, trainer, and charioteer – but all of this was secondary; it only told the punters whether they wanted to bet at all. If a team was considered a 'good thing', then, in this scenario, there would have been fewer of the opposing colours' supporters prepared to bet. Only the people in the know could take into account secondary information, and then lay proper odds. Yet there is no evidence that they did, and for most people, simply by backing their own colour that was coupled with another for betting purposes, they would break even. Epigraphic evidence supports this.[37] Diocles, a red-faction charioteer, won 205 victories over the blues, 216 over the greens, and 81 over the whites. If we assume that the reds were performing comparably to the whites,[38] figures for the total number of each team's victories would read: 14% red, 14% white, 35% blue, and 37% green, equalling a coupled ratio of 49:51. Trimalchio's bet with his cook was therefore a sensible one since, having no secondary information, they would, on average, both win on virtually the same number of occasions.

These figures would have resulted in average odds of approximately 6/1 for red and white, 2/1 for green and blue, producing a pool of 95%; but a bookmaking system would have produced the lesser odds of 4/1 and 6/4, a pool of 120% resulting in a rake-off for the bookmaker of 16.66%.[39] Naturally, these odds would change for each race according to the secondary information, a highly complicated process for the average punter. Even for the cognoscenti, therefore, the pairing of factions allowed a simple betting medium, for only two odds needed to be calculated. For example, a fancied team of the blue or red factions might be offered at 1/2, whilst his less fancied opponents were offered at a corresponding 2/1, thus creating a 100% pool. Put simply, in this example that would have required that a blue or red supporter bet two sesterces to every one of the green or white fan. The existence of paired races can also be explained only by assuming that the factions shared the prize money in these contests in which they were coupled for competitive purposes, whereas normally they were joined only for the practical reason of making betting easily intelligible and practical. Gambling, it is clear, was not just part of the 'emotional glue' which brought the crowd together,[40] it also divided them into factions, and thus framed and shaped the context of the event itself.

A day at the races was a nice day out, doing what you wanted in an invigorating atmosphere of rivalry and shared excitement. Having a flutter added to the fun by making the outcome of the day's entertainment potentially consequential. In general, the consequentiality of gambling – what winning allows and losing prevents the player later to do – is far more manageable than that of real-life chance-taking, but it is the staking of money which makes it consequential at all. In all Roman gambling, the staking of money made the outcome of a throw or an event significant because of the very importance of money within Roman society. The staking of money served as the method of inducing the correct seriousness in the attitude of the players towards the event. After all, it was half-hearted play that ruined it, even more so than cheating. The size of each wager in relation to individuals' social position and wealth reflected the degree to which they were prepared to risk their control over their lives, and the size of the moralists' concerns reflected the degree to which that gamble was perceived as a threat to the *status quo*.

For gambling was not only a financial matter, it was closely tied to Roman concerns over status. The size of the bet enhanced and reflected the non-material gains which were on the line – esteem, honour, dignity, respect, and status. As in the Balinese cockfight, money caused the Roman status hierarchy to be transposed into the body of the bet in a game of interchanging prestige. The risks of gambling were undertaken primarily for the purposes of entertainment, but the record of performance also built into a direct expression of the gambler's make-up and provided a basis for status additional to socioeconomic position. The self was voluntarily subjected to examination, not through impulsiveness, irrationality, or greed, but because of the possibility of affecting reputation.[41] Few really lost in this status war, but the small losses of face incurred with each defeat accumulated into the rewards of the sharp pleasures of victory. The gamblers of Rome were, as in their other forms of leisure, attempting to accommodate themselves to their place in the social order, and in doing so provided a metacommentary on the social matrix.

Clearly, gambling was both popular and significant, but its practitioners were mentioned in the same breath as adulterers and other '*impuri*'.[42] It was said that 'the cleverer the gambler, the greater the wickedness.'[43] The evil of gambling was associated with threats to the state; Catiline's co-conspirators are described as *aleatores*, and as plotting amidst banquets and whores and gambling and drinking.[44] Caesar also treated the republic as if it were a stake to be won by the casting of a dice.[45] The aleatory activities of 'immoral' emperors offered examples of their degeneracy. Commodus pretended that he was going to Africa in order to raise funds, then spent them on banquets and gambling.[46] Domitian was criticized for loving to play dice even in the morning, and Caligula, equally inappropriately, not only played dice when the court was in mourning for his sister, but he cheated as well.[47]

This condemnation was partly the result of social conflicts in Roman life. Gambling confirmed the traditional elite in their view that the lower orders were incapable of using their time intelligently or morally without supervision.[48] Their own philosophy enabled them to play without losing control: thus Theodoric II, 'if the throw is lucky he says nothing; if unlucky, he smiles; in neither case does he lose his temper.'[49] Similarly, Augustus, although a frequent and keen dicer, restricted himself to post-prandial games in which he was generous to his guests, donating the stakes and refunding the winnings.[50] But the pervasive racing-talk was not just another example of the plebs' idleness, their inability to use their free time properly; it represented a politically safe topic of conversation for which the *acta diurna*, the official 'news sheet', provided information. The stereotyping of gambling as irrational was irrelevant to the small-scale, regular type of betting which may of itself have represented only a small part of the gambler's income.[51] Obviously, it is impossible to recreate figures for the Roman world in respect of betting as a percentage of income, but in a sense they would be meaningless in any case. For only the addict really loses (or the chronically unlucky), particularly in a system where it seems likely that no bookmakers were taking their cut. In the circus, the punter had every chance of breaking even, whilst in a gambling group of socioeconomic equals, money is merely circulated in a system of surrogate saving. Uncertainty was controlled, skill and care were exercised in the management of money, and returns were regular and occasionally significant, thus returning previous losses in one wind-fall. Moreover, the winners acquired social standing and respect by proving, albeit temporarily until the next defeat, their judgement and good fortune.

Nor was betting an expression of a vague belief in luck. Instead, for all people, it offered an intellectual activity in which the minimizing of chance was part of the skill and satisfaction. Games of skill such as *micatio, terni lapilli, latrunculi, duodecim scripta*, and even hazard gave callisthenics to the brain, and the decision-making process offered a relief from the routines and control of everyday life.[52] For the paternalistic attitude of the ruling elite to the plebs denied them the ability to make their own decisions. In their gambling, the plebs showed themselves that this was not the case, whilst simultaneously compensating for the lack of control they had over their lives. According to Galen, many devoted as much zeal to dice as earnest men did to science, and showed Stoic endurance in this pleasure-seeking.[53] The Circus Maximus became the plebs' temple, home, meeting-place, and source of hope (*templum et habitaculum et contio et cupitorum spes omnis*).[54] As McKibbin has noted, gambling's appeal was straightforward: it was popularly sanctioned, it permitted genuine intellectual activity, and it induced thrilling excitement. It allowed physical and emotional excitement when comparative poverty deprived many of other stimulation. Tertullian describes how, 'The people rush to the spectacle with frantic enthusiasm, a disorderly mob, blind and already in a fury of anxiety about their bets.'[55] In a city where underemployment was endemic, the function of gambling became one of diversion. Gambling was a popular way of passing the time, and, as such, was mostly very distant from the caricatures that the moralists painted.[56]

Gambling, therefore, was innocent of the charges of idleness, stupidity, and superstition, but it was still the object of both moral and legal condemnation. It is well known to the modern middle class that gambling is a mug's game, best left to idling aristocrats and the uneducated lower classes. It has also often been seen as a social problem because it affronts the prudent and long-term mental environment which middle-class organizations wish to encourage and perpetuate. It would, of course, be anachronistic to see a middle-class element in Roman life, but what can be seen is a comparable cultural conflict between the dominant moral structures and popular practice.

In Latin literature the actual word *alea* is a *rara avis* indeed. '*Iacta alea est*' was not the commonplace it is now, it had shock value, and that effect was founded upon attitudes to chance and merit.[57] For the ways in which a society apportions blame or praise to these forces reflects the deep-rooted manner in which power is allocated within it. It reveals that society's fundamental ordering. The rarity of the word *alea* reflected the fact that it was a traditionally minded elite who wrote the texts which are our sources. To the elite, *alea* represented reckless submission to fortune. For example, farming on infertile land was 'nothing more than a gamble, in which the farmer's life and property are at stake'.[58] Occasionally, other social factors could allay such dangers: 'Parents had to be given a certain authority (*aliqua potestas*) so that they might be more content to run the risk (*aleam*)', for 'In the rearing of children nothing is left to the choice of those who rear them – it is wholly a matter of hope.'[59] But the fact remained that *alea* was a matter of chance, not order, and this was threatening in a traditional society. The elite claimed that, 'it is a rooted principle of the wise to avoid blind hazards (*vitare fortuita*).'[60] 'For not only is Fortune blind herself, but as a rule she even blinds those whom she has embraced.'[61] Moreover, they contended, even Fortune was 'moulded for each man by his manners (*suis ea cuique fingitur moribus*)', so that personal morality should be thought of as intervening in luck.[62] *Alea* conflicted not only with the traditional morality, since it wobbled the social ladder, but also with the imperial order because it counteracted their propagation of the spirit of *virtus*. For *alea* was usually the result of greed, an unnatural desire for profit, and was indulged in with no regard to *virtus*, honour, or merit.

To be a gambler was considered to be a sign of lacking control. Gambling was portrayed as a madness which brought with it a concomitant disorder. A slave with gambling tendencies was considered to have a mental defect, though not one which the vendor had to declare.[63] However, if a buyer returned a slave, any deterioration, including defects of character such as gambling, which had developed subsequent to the original purchase, had to be made good.[64] Similarly, the early Christians rejected the 'insane frenzy' of gambling.[65] Gambling, for the moralists, represented not only a loss of control, but a voluntary loss. In gambling, 'recklessness and luck (*temeritas et casus*)' prevailed over 'reflection and judgement (*ratio nec consilium*)'.[66] The reckless youth could lose his patrimony, and thus disrupt the social order. The ultimate gamblers, the Germans according to Tacitus, were the prime examples of this loss of control:

> Gambling, one may be surprised to find, they practise in all seriousness in their sober hours (*inter seria*), with such recklessness in winning or losing that, when all else has failed, they stake personal liberty on that last and final throw: the loser faces voluntary slavery.[67]

This outlook saw gambling as a moral pathology which threatened to destroy the individual's character and sense of personal responsibility and become a compulsive addiction.[68] Gamblers could not stop even when losing, for 'often the dice recall their greedy hands.'[69] Seneca's idea of hell for the inveterate gambler Claudius was for him to be stuck in a room with a dice-box with a hole in it.[70] Gambling could open up other worlds of potential vice to those unable to control themselves. Idleness, sleep, and gambling were thought to open the way to love since they weakened the spirit.[71] Similarly, childhood gambling, as we have seen, was taken as an early sign of later potential problems.[72] In fact, youth was thought to be especially susceptible to the perils of gambling. The following charges were brought against the emperor Didius Julianus, that 'he had been a glutton and a gambler; had exercised with gladiatorial arms; and, moreover, had done all these things when advanced in years', and after escaping the stain of these vices in his youth.[73] In a similar fashion, Apollonius of Tyana explained to the emperor Vespasian: 'About dice and drink and dissipation and the necessity of abhorring these vices, why need I tender you any advice, who, they say, never approved of them even in youth.'[74]

Ammianus Marcellinus, shocked at the gambling mania in all classes of fourth-century Romans, noted that some of the well-to-do objected to being called '*aleatores*' (gamblers) but not to '*tesserarii*' (dicers).[75] For the controlled and pleasant pursuits of play provided images of morality, which contrasted with the recklessness of gambling. The philosopher Canus, sentenced to death by Caligula, was playing *latrunculi* with a fellow prisoner when the centurion came to take him for his execution. He insisted that his guard check the state of the game, in which he was a point in front, in case his opponent should later claim to have won it. Such was his Stoic self-control that life came to mean less than a game.[76] Another such image was drawn from the game of *micatio* (modern Italian *morra*), in which each player raised the fingers of the right hand, varying each time the number, and called aloud the total of fingers raised by both players until one or the other had won by guessing correctly. Thus, a man of integrity was proverbially one with whom 'you could play *micatio* in the dark (*quicum in tenebris mices*)'.[77]

The disdain in which the dominant morality held gambling was reflected in the law. Gambling and betting received continuous attention from the Roman legal system, dating right back to early republican times, though they were not (in the early empire, at least) criminal offences.[78] The *Lex Alearia*, probably of 204 BC,[79] seems to have been the first attempt to legislate against the pleasures of gambling. Other later laws continued this attempt at repression. The *Lex Talaria* prohibited dice-playing except at meal times and during the period of the Saturnalia, and penalties could be as severe as exile, or at least four times the value of the bet.[80] Yet the law seems never to have been enforced seriously, and from the early empire hardly at all. The aediles were entrusted with the surveillance of gaming houses, but they appear to have been incapable of preventing gambling from taking place.[81] A senatorial decree, dating from the republican period,[82] sanctioned betting on athletic contests 'which are done for virtue (*virtutis causa*)', but not on other games. Similar exceptions to the ban on gambling were created by the *Lex Titia de Aleatoribus*, a republican statute which allowed betting on sports in which the bravery (*virtus*) of the competitors was implied,[83] and the *Lex Cornelia de Aleatoribus*, of 81 BC, which declared valid all bets made on athletic games in which competition was considered courageous (*virtus*). It was the exception to wagers laid on contests in which *virtus* was the dominant theme that provided the privilege to racing and the gladiatorial games. *Latrunculi* also remained legal because its skill factor allowed little room for chance to weave its corrupting spell.

Gambling debts, however, remained unrecoverable.[84] Praetors appear to have refused actions to the proprietors of gambling establishments for assault, damage, or theft committed as a result of the excitement of winning, despair at losing, or arguments over alleged cheating.[85] It was only when the Christian emperor Justinian limited betting to a fixed stake on games of skill that the collection of gambling debts was allowed.[86] The Christian stance was, though, tougher in the application of penalties, and gambling became a criminal offence.[87] Whether this worried the gamblers themselves is another matter. The circles of gamblers seem to have had their own socio-moral hierarchy and a code of honour which was unfalteringly obeyed. According to Ambrose, a judgement of the 'Council of Gamblers (*aleonum concilium*)' was more feared than a judicial sentence.[88]

The raising of a deviant activity to the level of a public legal issue was itself a sure sign that its moral status was at stake, and that legitimacy was seen by some as a possibility. The threat to the legitimacy of the moral ideal was the spur to the need for symbolic restatement in legal terms. Thus the legal position was not the enunciator of a consensus within the community. On the contrary, it was when consensus was least attainable that the pressure to establish laws appears to be the greatest, for the laws of gambling need to be understood in terms of the symbols of cultural dominance rather than in the activities of social control. Cultural conflicts were expressed in the symbolic function of the law. For the law represented the public affirmation of social ideals as well as being a means of direct social control. Unlike the instrumental function, the symbolic aspects of law and government did not depend on enforcement for their effect. Hence, the systematic evasion of the Roman laws of gambling was not a result of the inefficiency of the Roman legal system. Instead, the symbolic use of the law functioned to minimize conflicts between the different levels of Roman culture. It achieved this by using the law to proclaim one set of values, while using another in the actual control of behaviour. The existence of the law pacified those cultural leanings which demanded action to support the society's major institutions. It also demonstrated who it was who had legitimacy and domination, and hence enhanced the social status of groups carrying the affirmed culture whilst degrading those condemned as deviant. Prohibition, in this view, became a significant focus for social conflict. Even if the law was broken, it was clear which cultural level was predominant. Juvenal recognized that a double standard was in operation, that 'In men of modest position gaming and adultery are shameful; but when those men of high status do the same things, they are called bright young things and fine gentlemen.'[89]

Society's tensions were relieved by projecting them in the form of an external aleatory menace. The difference between the moral system of the gambler and the dominant morality was used by way of accusation as a means of social definition and control. Hence, accusations of gambling acted as a measure of social strain, an index of difference and temporary lapse from orthodoxy. The gambling laws also reflected the development of a legal sensibility, which saw the world as something to be ordered, and so sought to locate and define each part of society. The dominant view of the gambler was part of this process of defining and delimiting marginal elements of society into negative stereotypes. That gamblers were losers became no more than a commonplace assumption, one which we have seen to be largely false. Quintilian describes this rhetoric of morality in his discussion on commonplaces (*communes loci*): 'As a rule, however, the general character of a commonplace is usually given a special turn: for instance, we make our adulterer blind, our gambler poor, and our profligate old.'[90]

Gambling placed the individual in a new relationship to structures of control and created a feeling of freedom and excitement in so doing. Gambling represented part of the popular culture, which remained outside elite control: it challenged moral and prudent categories, it delighted in a loss of personal control, it placed greater emphasis on chance. However, gambling was such a cross-social activity that it was not linked directly to any lower-class threat. Gamblers were isolated as individuals, they did not represent a group, and so there was no sense of an enemy culture. It is only when a deviant social or political group is formed, with its own system of beliefs, that its difference becomes dangerous. The gambler's deviance represented more of a moral lapse, one which was redeemable by a regaining of personal control. What it did do was threaten dominant cultural sensibilities by suggesting that success could be achieved through luck and not hard graft. Therefore, what came to be condemned as reckless gambling was culturally constituted. If a gaming activity were to avoid such a slur, it would have to be carried out in a manner which did not imperil existing boundaries; it would have to be done in an orderly fashion. But gambling did not pose an actual threat to that order unless it became compulsive. It was only then, when the degree of chance had gone out of the individual's control, that the consequences of gambling could do actual damage to the social hierarchy. Excitement and chance made gambling problematic in a strongly hierarchical society, but gambling required a sense of order to create any effective sense of excitement.

Much of the fun of gambling lay in the knowledge that one was temporarily contradicting society's main structures. It was only the pathological who actually lost control, and it was generally the case that the gambling laws were honoured as much in the breach as in the observance.

The enactment of the gambling laws reflected the growth in popular culture. The new and increasing anxieties of superabundance, the product of empire, had been transposed into the existing moral structure and there was thus a feeling that the vice of gambling had never been so prevalent or excessive.[91] The initial increase in popular gambling activity, that is to say the perceptions of increase, arose with the growth of the city of Rome and the plebs' greater freedom from traditional coercive apparatuses. This resulted initially in an attempt at repression, then in an attempt at controlling the direction of change. So, towards the later republic, concessions were made in order to conciliate popular practice. Certain wagers, based on *virtus*, were allowed in order to channel the development of popular culture into a new hegemony. With the advent of the principate, some of these popular elements were adopted and then adapted to meet new requirements. Augustus was happy to be seen as a keen gambler; but a gambler who remained totally in control. For when Augustus gambled, he supplied the stakes, let people off their losses, and through his generosity hoped to be exalted to 'immortal glory'.[92] It was only when his control had been threatened by military defeat that people had criticized his gambling activities, for during the Sicilian war, this epigram was current:

Having twice been beaten at sea and lost his ships, he gambles all the time in the hope of winning one victory (*Postquam bis classe victus naves perdidit, aliquando ut vincat, ludit assidue aleam*).[93]

The imperial ideology attempted to reach a compromise between the elements of control and chance by emphasizing the importance of victory being achieved through *virtus*. There was an attempt to reconcile two types of power, one which was articulate and self-created, obtained by personal achievement, and another based on prestige and elite patronage. It was, as I have shown, in the imperial games that the gladiators and charioteers, the new heroes, reflected these changing moral relations and power structures. By allowing the plebs the opportunity to bet in an imperially dominated environment, an attempt was made both to accommodate them within a new system of government and to internalize the new values by which they were being governed. This was not only a matter of coercion, it was also a question of enticement, and the plebs did not accept the new morality in its entirety.

9

Sex and the Problematization of Leisure

1 Recreation and Re-creation

Such was the perversity of the boy emperor Heliogabalus that, 'he would act out the story of Paris in his house, and, taking the role of Venus himself, would suddenly drop his clothes to the ground and fall naked on his knees, one hand on his breast, the other before his genitals, and with his buttocks thrust back in front of his partner in depravity.'[1] The purpose of quoting passages such as these appears to be not so much to elucidate but to play with the reader's, and no doubt the author's, prurience, and so successful has the practice been that it is theatrical anecdotes of this type that provide the foundations for most people's knowledge of the Roman world: a world seemingly orgiastic to excess and untempered by any sexual restraint (see plate 8). It should come as no surprise to see Benjamin and Masters conclude that, 'from comparatively staid beginnings Roman sexual history moves toward a crescendo of eroticism such as the world has rarely seen.'[2] But the aim of this chapter is not to examine the hoary old subject of the Romans' sex and sexuality; it is to analyse the precise ways in which problems concerning sexual mores were related to problems concerning leisure.[3] The result will be an examination of the deepest and most long-term historical developments which Roman society was undergoing.

To begin with, it will be useful to define more precisely what is meant by the term 'sexuality'. Whilst sex itself has no history (at least, on anything other than an evolutionary scale), sexuality is a cultural production; 'it represents the *appropriation* of the human body and of its physiological capacities by an ideological discourse.'[4] Hence, the history of sexuality is meaningless unless seen in the context of social struggle. Moving on from this, I hope to show that attitudes to the body, sexuality, family, and reproduction were intimately caught up with attitudes to leisure. For in the Roman world, sex only became a problem when it combined with leisure. It was when sex became leisurely, *otiosus*, that anxieties arose, and this was the result of a fundamental dichotomy which existed between sex as leisure and sex as reproduction. As such, leisurely sex was strongly condemned because it disrupted the proper reproductive order.

I shall begin by looking at the role that sex played in traditional republican society. Traditional Roman society maintained a strong distinction between sex whose primary aim was reproduction and that which was entertainment. Brown considers that in a population 'grazed thin by death . . . only the privileged or the eccentric few could enjoy the freedom to do what they pleased with their sexual drives',[5] but whilst it is probably true to say that the majority's bodies were mobilized for reproduction and were compelled to raise legitimate children, some could still enjoy casual sex, primarily by frequent retreats into the brothel.[6] Cicero was later to emphasize this traditional role:

However, if there is anyone who thinks that youth should be forbidden affairs even with courtesans, he is doubtless eminently austere (I cannot deny it), but his view is contrary not only to the licence of this age, but also to the custom and concession of our ancestors. For when was this not a common practice? When was it blamed? When was it forbidden?[7]

In this period, virtue and vice coexisted in a harmonious and mutually profitable relationship. As in Holland's golden age, 'virtue needed vice as a civic prophylactic, a sponge that could soak up all the loathsomeness that would otherwise seep into the purer body of their community. And virtue needed vice to mark off borders just because its own frontiers were so uncomfortably indefinite.'[8] As the dream-interpreter Artemidorus points out, to dream of 'having sexual intercourse with prostitutes who work in brothels signifies a little disgrace and a small expense.' It was 'a place men had in common'.[9] Harlotry was permitted because it was thought to have a minimizing effect on the extent of adultery engaged in by married women. But it incurred official *infamia*, and prostitutes were legally bound to wear the toga and bleach or dye their hair.[10]

Prostitution cannot be seen in isolation for it was integral to the patriarchal system. In a pre-industrial society like Rome, in which all that many men had to offer was their physical strength, a more 'macho' image of the heterosexual male came to define the normal male culture. The old Romans were a 'manly breed (*mascula proles*)'.[11] A sharp distinction was also drawn between the male and female worlds, one which correlated with conceptions of what constituted public and private: 'it is only right that the female sex has been provided for the care of the home, the male for out-of-doors and open-air activities.'[12] 'A man was a man because he moved effectively in the public world.'[13] A woman's task was to contribute to her male family members' public prestige by her private virtue. The ideal of traditional Roman society was one in which there was, in fact, no private life. 'Private' morality did not exist since individual action was expected to contribute to public prestige. Everything was open to communal access and judgement. Even women were always up for public scrutiny.

Of course, this was an ideal which was never maintained, and people often fell prey to the temptations of pleasure. This was especially galling because pleasure, and its gratification, had strong private connotations. It was the most slothful of vices.[14] In terms of sexuality, 'it is quite mistaken to claim, as does Michel Foucault, that the Romans distinguished between a morally good active sexuality and a morally bad passive sexuality. Sexual pleasure was always passive and as such morally suspect.'[15] For 'all sensual pleasure is opposed to moral rectitude.'[16] Ideally, 'real Romans only had sex with their wives and even then not too often.'[17] Moreover, their intercourse was not undertaken primarily for pleasure but procreation. It was felt that those led astray by pleasure should renounce public office, for the politician must seek pleasure for others, not from others.[18] Only in youth was sexual transgression pardonable, on account of the fact that, being under the influence of youthful *ferocitas*, the young were not fully in control.[19] Such indiscretions became far less excusable when the hot-headedness of youth should have given way to the *gravitas* of maturity.

It was prostitutes who lay on the confines of these conceptual areas of public and private, male and female. Theirs was the public sale of a private act, in as much as they offered leisurely sex openly to any that desired it, and as a result, they lost their own particular gender status, either as a private female or a public male. Female prostitutes became quasi-masculine by having to abandon traditional female codes of dress and decorum and replace them with the toga and personal advertisement. For when a woman entered the enclosed world of officially tolerated prostitution she adopted a state of being rather than a profession, one which not only withdrew her from the proper reproductive order, but actively publicized that withdrawal.

The picture of the traditional strand of Roman culture is clear enough, but there was an increasing amount of interference which disrupted such a view. The growth in urbanism, wealth, and leisure caused certain changes in Roman sexual habits. The spread of urbanization probably created a new demand for prostitution because it created a mass male proletariat in a state of sexual privation. Also, whereas previously only the privileged could do what they wanted with their sex-drives, the breakdown in traditional community structures was reflected in more freely available lower-class sex. As the victim states in pseudo-Quintilian's *The Case of the Call-Girl's Hate Potion*, 'I believe that prostitutes were devised so that there would be someone a poor man would be allowed to make love to.'[20] A growth in popular culture with its greater element of personal autonomy and choice would also have led to an increase in the open enjoyment of leisure sex as the lower classes felt less constrained to abide by traditional codes (which is not to say that it didn't go on before, of course). In Lucian's *Dialogues of the Courtesans*, Corinna's mother consoles her daughter about her having to go on the game to support her family, for as a profession it is well paid and in demand.[21] The expansion of popular culture also created a demand for a greater sexual variety, and this extended as far as the use of infants for fellatio and buggery.[22] What was happening was that the public sphere of Roman life was being invaded by the 'popular', and leisurely sex was part of this challenge to the traditional order.

Attitudes to the distinction between public and private were also transformed. Cicero's claim that, 'the Roman people loathe private luxury, but they love public splendour (*Odit populus Romanus privatam luxuriam, publicam magnificentiam diligit*)'[23] rang increasingly hollow. Not only did many no longer have a problem with marking off an area of their life as private, but within that space they were also prepared to enjoy the pleasures made possible by Rome's success. The whole network of traditional relations was warping under the weight of empire. The hard contrast between male and female images was softened by material prosperity, and this led to a reduction of the cultural gap between the sexes: 'We men have taken over the cosmetics of whores.'[24] Martial tells of one Philaenis, whose clitoris was so pronounced a feature that she played the man with it, exhausting eleven girls in one day and actually sodomizing young men.[25] In satirical terms, it was the advent of a literally unisex culture. According to the Elder Pliny, the things which had 'ruined the morals of the empire (*perdidere imperii mores*)' were 'the practices to which we submit when in health': wrestlers' ointments, broiling baths, drinking on empty stomachs, vomits followed by more heavy drinking, effeminate depilations, and even the pubes of women exposed to public view (*itemque pectines in feminis quidem publicati*).[26] For what was sophisticated, urbane, and elegant could also be seen as effeminate and luxurious.

Sexual desire was the hub and *primum mobile* of the moral order and the frequency of moralizing served to broadcast this fact. Dupont's claim that, 'the less that was said about sex the better',[27] is hardly supported by the mass of texts in which the swelling licentiousness of the Romans is

a prominent theme.[28] Moral discourse of this kind served to mark off the
elite. Astin says:

> the direct and immediate role of the censorial concern with *mores*
> was to be found very largely in its relationship to that small section
> of Roman society which was made up of the senatorial and eques-
> trian orders. So far as can be discerned, it had little direct applica-
> tion to the rest of society; and, despite its ill-defined scope and the
> unfettered discretion of the censors, it was not developed into a
> device for controlling or disciplining the mass of the population.
> Instead, it evolved as a mechanism by which the politically domi-
> nant section of society imposed restraints upon itself and its indi-
> vidual members.[29]

The censors' concern with mores – 'habitual conduct', 'lifestyle' – was
based on a belief that 'laws help towards good morals (*leges quoque
proficiunt ad bonos mores*).'[30] But such concern was felt to be applied to
all Roman citizens, and not just senators and *equites*, because of the
importance attached to the elite's morality. As Cicero says:

> I believe that a transformation takes place in a nation's character
> when the habits and lifestyle of its aristocracy are changed. For that
> reason men of the upper class who do wrong are especially danger-
> ous to the state, because they not only indulge in vicious practices
> themselves, but also infect the whole commonwealth with their
> vices.[31]

As such, elite moralizing was directed mostly at themselves in order to
maintain the traditional gap between them and the lower classes. It is for
this reason that legal hostility towards luxury and extravagance is found
mostly in the laws dating between 180 and 30 BC.

Moralizing also harked back to the idealized relations of traditional
Roman society, and within that discourse the prostitute and the body at
leisure became metaphors for the social decay which was at the root of
the supposed later deterioration. For 'sexual indulgence of all kinds sapped
a man's strength and made him like a woman, unable to take part in
public life.'[32] Prostitution and sexual immorality were seen as responsible
for the declining birth rates, because leisure sex acted as a seminal drain
on Roman life, one which took its virility and left it in the gutter. A
healthy social order was thought to be revealed in healthy bodies, and
anxieties about decline and corruption were expressed in physical
terms. Quintilian notes the possibility of such a physiognomic outlook:
for 'just as blood is the result of a wound, depilation, a voluptuous gait,

or womanish attire may be regarded as indications of effeminacy and unmanliness by anyone who thinks that such symptoms are the result of an immoral character.'[33] This was certainly the prevalent view amongst moralists: 'Just as luxurious banquets and elaborate dress are indications of disease in the state, similarly a lax style, if it be frequent, shows that the mind has lost its balance.'[34] It was also a medical assumption: in ancient times, 'health was generally good because of good morals (*mores*), which neither indolence nor luxury had vitiated ... it is these two which have afflicted the bodies of men, first in Greece, and now amongst us.'[35]

The movement of the body became especially important, and dance was a metaphor for a world being shaken, rattled, and rolled.[36] As Cicero puts it, 'hardly anyone dances unless drunk, either by himself or at any respectable party, unless of course he is mad (*insanit*).'[37] Because of its suggestive properties, and the fact that most tavern dancers were also prostitutes, dance was closely associated with improper sexual activity. Juvenal refers to a Spanish dancing troupe which won applause by 'immodest dance and song, sinking down with quivering thighs to the floor'.[38] Likewise, in the *Priapeia*, the dancer Quinctia prays to Priapus that she may always find favour with her spectators and leave them standing, as it were, like the god himself.[39] This is not to say that dancing was considered to be inherently debauched. Quintilian points out that, 'we are told that the Spartans even regarded a certain form of dance as a useful element in military training. Nor again did the ancient Romans consider such a practice as disgraceful.'[40] But with the advent of empire, dancing acquired a very different style and vastly different connotations. Hence, Scipio Aemilianus criticized the growth in dancing among the young after the Punic wars:

> I swear I saw more than 50 boys and girls, among them – a sight which made me despair of the state – a boy still wearing the bulla, not less than twelve and son of a candidate for the consulship, dancing with castanets. Even the basest slave would shrink from performing such a dance.[41]

Immorality was now seen as being reflected in dance, and tales of wanton cavorting were commonplace. The historian Velleius Paterculus tells of Plancus, who had 'less self-respect than a slave', and did the 'vilest things'.[42] He would do anything for money – he even at a banquet played the role of Glaucus the Nereid, 'performing a dance in which his naked body was painted blue, his head encircled with reeds, at the same time wearing a fish's tail and crawling upon his knees'.

What was written and said about prostitutes and the body was a focus for collective delusion and all manner of concern. Delusion in that it looked back to an idealized and fictitious traditional society, and concern in that prostitutes symbolized disorder, excess, and improvidence. They were associated with instability, loquacity, drink, food, gambling, laziness, and deceit. Above all, prostitutes were seen as a threat to the sexual order. But it was not simply a question of prohibition. The growth of anxiety over prostitution reflected the deep unease aroused in those who believed in the 'moral order' by the social and political transformation then taking place. As such, the concern over prostitution acted as an index of social strain, a function for which prostitutes were well suited on account of their being at the gender crossroads of Roman culture. Moreover, as the old divides between work and leisure were transforming into new, prostitutes were well situated to articulate the resultant tensions. For whilst prostitutes were very much at the centre of anxieties about leisure and the misdirection of the sexual urge, they were also working people. Located on the margins of the traditional divide, they characterized changing attitudes to both leisure and work.

However, moralizing of this kind was a rearguard action, itself an expression of failure. Its purpose had been to act as a tourniquet on the body politic and stem the flow of virile strength from its moral wounds. But, as we shall see, the body politic developed a more regenerative reaction which rendered this curb superfluous. Instead, such restraint became an act of self-mortification, one which was necessary for the psychological survival of Roman culture. As Martial observed, 'this is envy's way: ever to prefer the men of old to those new-born.'[43] Horace's slave Davus told his master, 'you praise the fortunes and manners of the men of old, and yet, if on a sudden some god were for taking you back to those days, you would refuse every time.'[44] With the social development towards the imperial order, moralizing became a cultural topos: not so much a genuine attempt at reactionary change but the continued existence of a mode of thought now incorporated into a new overall system.

What then was this system? The emperors responded to the challenge posed by changing sexual attitudes by attempting to create an image of sex which was workmanlike and productive, believing this to be a return to the original morality of traditional Rome. In the imperial scheme, sex and leisure were incorporated into the family structure, and the family itself into the state's structure. Sex was made acceptable only as a centralizing public benefit, not as a private leisure activity. Through legislation, the emperors tried to stereotype moral relations and generate a subjectivity in which a new morality was created, one based upon an idealization of the Roman *domus*. Legislation was used not only to create and enforce standards, but also to regulate lapses, for this was not an inflexible ideal. This represented an imperial redefinition of government as the public expression of an idealized family, which image was more inclusive both on account of its foundation on a common social group and also its universal message.

The *domus* (household) was one of the basic institutions of Roman life. As Saller says, 'it has perhaps not been sufficiently emphasized that in Roman society, in which wealth and social respectability were closely related, the *domus* was a central symbol of status and honour.'[45] 'Religious, political, and social factors contributed to the value of the *domus* as a symbol for the Romans',[46] and it 'was a focus of honor for Romans: the honor of the *paterfamilias* depended on his ability to protect his household, and in turn the virtue of the household contributed to his prestige.'[47] Cicero thought that, 'the household unit within which everything is shared; that is the element from which a city is made, so to speak the seed-bed of the state (*deinde una domus, communia omnia; id autem est principium urbis et quasi seminarium rei publicae*).'[48] However, as Saller elsewhere points out, 'on account of the age structure of the Roman family the extended patriarchal household must have been unusual.'[49] Moreover, it should not be assumed that the Romans 'had a uniform or self-consistent ideal of the model household.'[50]

Nor should the family be seen as unproblematic, for the family was as much a threat to political order as a constituent feature of it. Mount has gone so far as to claim that, 'the family is a subversive organisation'; it is 'the enduring enemy of all hierarchies, churches and ideologies.'[51] This is probably an exaggeration of what, in theoretical terms, is an institution with a neutral function, but it is true to say that the family does not simply prop up the established order since it can also create a private space for the individual. Loyalty to the family also intervenes and interferes with the relationship between the citizen and the state. During the troubles of the late republic, the state had lost control over the family, so the imperial ideology attempted to replace and enlarge it by fashioning the state, and the relations between society's members, in its image. However, it emphasized an ideal family – a specific type which harked back to the traditional relations between Romans of the past before all these crises had emerged. The state sought to exercise total control over the family in the interests of radical improvement and moral regeneration. Hence, the imperial system of 'home-rule' was not a simple matter of promoting the family, but also of controlling it. As Gardner says, 'Augustan legislation fundamentally undermined the tradition of domestic jurisdiction.'[52]

Leisure, sex, and the family presented related problems, and the emperors' solution was to make an image of recreation which was workmanlike and productive by bringing leisure and sex into an idealized family. This promoted an image of leisure, sex, and the family as positive forces only if properly directed towards the imperial ends. The *domus* encompassed the wider kinship and household group, and this 'central symbol of social status under the Republic was easily adapted to serve a new status symbol in the new political conditions of the Principate.'[53] The imperial family was itself established as an idealized expression of these images: dynastic, properly ordered, and protective. The family image was the focus of the imperial programme in just the same way as the *focus* was the hearth of the house. The state took over some of the traditional roles of the father: 'a good emperor whom you can compare to a good father'.[54] The imperial cult was the public expression of the Genius of the master, the Penates (representing the power which the store-room has to ensure survival), the Vesta (the power of the hearth), and the Lares (who mark off the household).

The emotional bonds of the family required all its members to identify with the master from whom they derived their material and social existence. The *domus* was an ideal of stability and security and the well-managed household produced everything it needed. For the *domus* also signified patrimony. 'Patrimony played as central a role in the ancient economy as the firm or corporation plays in the modern economy.'[55] Hence, the emperors established a public patrimony by translating the local economics of the *domus* to the new political stage. The riches of the empire became the common birthright, but the price was for all its members to be subject to imperial control.

The state claimed the right to intervene 'as if it were the father of everyone'.[56] Augustus became the *pater patriae*, and the 'whole state had become his household.'[57] Pliny observes that, 'everything today, it is true, depends on the will of one man who takes upon himself for the general good all our cares and responsibilities.'[58] The emperor became the 'bond by which the commonwealth is united (*vinculum, per quod res publica cohaeret*)'.[59] Such a bond was based on *patria potestas* (paternal authority), which was the 'fundamental institution underlying Roman institutions', and in consequence, 'public life followed the assumptions of private life, and not vice versa.'[60] This had comprehensive repercussions because the ideal of the family demanded that it should not only produce its own progeny and labour force, but also educate and train them in the proper way. The *paterfamilias* was responsible for the moral welfare of his family, and, for the emperor, to suppress looseness was to rebuild political stability. Seneca explains what this means: that the *pax Romana* will survive and the people be free from danger so long as they 'know how to submit to the rein.' If not, 'this unity and fabric of mightiest empire will fly into many parts, and the end of this city's rule will be one with the end of her obedience.'[61] The return of social and political health demanded a return to the moral health which had made the Romans so successful. The discord of the late republic was thought to have been causally connected to the breakdown of the family, so that if peace was to be re-established, then the family would have to be morally regenerated. *Concordia* was to characterize the empire just as it did the ideal marriage.

This concord was not to be based on any equal partnership. Obedience was one of the main features *patres* were anxious to see in their family. The emperor, as *pater*, had to punish to ensure the efficient functioning of the household unit. It was his moral duty to limit transgression.[62] As such, Augustus' moral legislation needs to be set in relation to his other important policies and be placed 'in the total context of the Augustan programme'.[63] The main target was the 'pleasure-orientated way of life especially of the Roman nobility and the main goal was the restitution of sound family life',[64] but the purpose was neither demographic nor nostalgic; instead, the traditional qualities of *genus* and *nobilitas* were being partly replaced by a *virtus* based upon *industria* and *mobilitas*. 'Even if the special thrust of the laws was aimed at the nobility, the private life of virtually every Roman now became a matter of the state's concerns and regulations.'[65] As Pliny says, 'Even the vulgar crowd can take a lesson from its rulers (*principum disciplinam capere etiam vulgus*).'[66] However, this was not an inflexible ideal, and so the emperor also had to control and regulate lapses. Like a father with his hot-headed sons, the emperor had to allow some rein. McGinn's claim that the aim of the legitimization of prostitution by the state was generally 'neither to safeguard morality nor even to encourage commerce through adjustments in the tax system, but simply to exact as much as possible for the state treasury',[67] is too simplistic, for economics and morality were never separated. Legitimization was not a moral problem since the taxation of prostitutes, begun by Caligula, both added to the common patrimony and increased 'parental' control. It was a 'natural' act for a concerned father to do to protect his family.

The very fact that Augustus and later emperors needed to pass moral legislation reveals that their laws were not entirely successful and that alternative possibilities to their image of order did exist. 'Certainly Augustus wished to be seen as ushering in a Golden Age, and one marked by morality. But only the panegyrist can delude himself that he succeeded.'[68] For 'the more Rome filled up with magnificent images of Augustus and his values, the more overwhelming the impression of his supremacy. But conversely, the more overwhelming the impression, the more oppressive it may have seemed. By the time that Augustus had established a visible monopoly of glory in the city, destroying the pluralist tradition of republican monuments, his pose as simple citizen was wearing very thin.'[69] For, 'images provoked dissent as well as consent',[70] and resistance remained. There was strong elite opinion against the moral legislation.[71] If Pliny's claim was true that, 'it is only the rulers we hate who violate our privacy (*in secreta non inquirant principes nisi quos odimus*)',[72] then there can have been few popular emperors. Popular leisure resisted imperial domination through unlicensed prostitution, dance, and other body 'misuse'. Loose sex also provided an oblique, but powerful, form of social rebellion.[73] Hence, 'the legacy of Augustus was not only peace and problems resolved, but a new set of conflicts and tensions.'[74]

Augustus did not put an end to tensions, but they came to be articulated around the personage of the emperor. The emperors themselves become central to the negotiation of values and to the debate over the remaining problems in Roman society. Uncontrolled leisure was now seen as the problem, and this was expressed in concerns about the actions of the emperor's body. Wicked emperors swam with common prostitutes, dressed up in women's clothing with a protruding bra, appeared before catamites in the garb of a boy exposed for prostitution, and even anticipated Imelda Marcos by never wearing the same shoes twice.[75] Standard tales of immorality became a metaphor for a diseased constitution. For the political constitution and the emperor's own physical constitution were thought to be the same. His body was the body politic, and its actions revealed the moral health of the state. In part, of course, the worst of the emperors could be excused on account of their age, but their very youth was at odds with Roman tradition.[76] What kind of government could you expect with a boy emperor if not one characterized by *ferocitas* (youthful hotheadedness)? Yet this did not represent any resentment of the office of the emperor, only of particular incumbents. The institution of the emperor had become the cultural heart and hearth of Rome, and what made so many of the 'bad' emperors' acts so appalling was that they took place in their *domus*, the place where an emperor's standards should be on show, the focus of their moral pre-eminence.

2 *The Civilizing Process and the Changing Function of Leisure*

Concepts of public and private organized Roman perceptions of morality and how they thought people should be ordered, and because of this fact the distinction between them was very much an ideological issue. Augustus' legislation moved the state further into the private sphere. Sex for the married couple became a civic duty, performed formally for the purposes of re-creation, but also an officially sanctioned recreation. The emperors established a more accessible, and hence more public, morality by making a private concept, the family, public and universal. The potentially inflammatory cocktail of leisure and sex was damped down by the imperial rewriting of public life in the grammar of privacy. However, these new concepts were in contrast with traditional elite images.

The new image was based on the control of the success which had so radically transformed Roman society. Public behaviour had to be appropriate for the grandeur of Rome, and the emperors became the finest exemplars of the image. As Pliny observed, 'one of the chief features of high estate is that it permits no privacy, no concealment, and in the case of princes, it flings open the door not only to their homes but to their private apartments and deepest retreats.'[77] Trajan's home life was seen to be ideal: his family was kept in a state of moral excellence as well; his wife was a supreme model of the ancient virtues; and his sister 'never forgets that she is your sister.'[78] Conversely, for Heliogabalus 'life was nothing but a search for pleasures.'[79] What this meant for the rest of society was that the benefits of wealth and power had to be exhibited in a discreet fashion. They could not be allowed to deprave, and any moral corruption that did result would be publicly revealed in physical perversion. This was especially so for the public figure of the orator: 'Let all finery not suitable to a man's dignity be kept off his person, and let him guard against the like fault in gesture and action.'[80] 'There must be no quick movements of the fingers, no marking time with the finger-tips, but the orator should control himself by the poise of the whole trunk and by a manly inclination of the side.'[81]

This change in the nature of conceptions of what was public and private reflected a deep long-term social shift from a society founded primarily on a public shame culture to one based more on private guilt. Shame cultures are those which 'rely principally on shame as an external sanction for assuring conformity to the cultural norms', guilt cultures those which rely on 'a sense of guilt or "conscience" as an internal sanction'.[82] In the golden age, then, the public realm was dominant and the wish to be private was considered anti-social. For this reason, prostitutes went onto the aediles' list of infamy, 'the normal procedure among our ancestors, who imagined the unchaste to be sufficiently punished by the avowal of their infamy'.[83] But by the late republic public humiliation was no longer such a deterrence. It was not that prostitutes were without any values, for 'even among prostitutes there exists some sort of modesty, and those bodies offered for public pleasure draw over some curtain by which their unhappy submission may be hidden',[84] but their modesty was now more of a personal nature, designed to maintain the privacy of a professional's relationship with a client. What we see reflected in the emperors' extension of public control into the private sphere was an attempt to put the brakes on this slide from shame culture to guilt culture. The breakdown of traditional society had created a sharper division between the public and private worlds, and the emperors were trying to cope with this divide by moving communal problems into the private arena. It was, in other words, a question of how to adapt government to a changing psychological make-up which no longer saw private life as merely an adjunct to the public sphere.

This represented a stage in a process of the internalization of values which found its fullest expression in the rise of Christianity. The appearance of new cults in the Roman world, which was already in full swing by the late republic, had reflected an increase in private religious space in opposition to traditional public religion, and the imperial cult attempted to incorporate this private space into a public framework. A new mode of social relations was in formation, which was characterized by increasing standardization and intensity of regulation. Legislation and moralizing were attempts to regulate and co-opt individuals into the policing of their lives. It was part of a civilizing process, in which Tacitus believed that the 'fetters were tighter' and sentries were set over society.[85]

Elias' concept of the civilizing process describes a process of 'advancing integration'.[86] It is social constraint towards self-constraint, and represents 'an increased consolidation and differentiation of affect controls' both in people's experience (their threshold levels of shame and revulsion) and behaviour (their refinement in manners).[87] Increasing differentiation increases individual regulation and control, so that 'the web of actions grows so complex and extensive, the effort required to behave "correctly" within it becomes so great, that beside the individual's conscious self-control an automatic, blindly functioning apparatus of self-control is firmly established.'[88] The civilizing process, therefore, is characterized by 'centrifugal tendencies', 'more stable central organization', and 'firmer monopolization of physical force'.[89] This is a persuasive thesis in all but one important respect: it assumes that the civilizing process results in a greater degree of actual control. Elias presupposes that the space between public centres and private space always remains the same, when this is not the case. Societies can be thought of as occupying a social space, but the area of that space varies from one to another. A primitive society covers a small area, as if all its members are in the centre circle of a soccer pitch, whereas a more complex society is spread across the whole ground. Hence, primitive societies are not experienced as less complex by their members than our developed ones because it is a question of distance between people and structures. In their world, what to us are tiny acts acquire great significance because of their proximity to other social issues, and can involve a degree of concern which matches any of our life problems. This means that any intensification of power by the centre also acts as a balance to greater distance between the centre itself and the periphery; it does not necessarily involve any greater degree of control. It is a social and cultural attempt to be well balanced – not in a simple functional way, but by adapting its inner play of forces to the changing conditions of its environment.

It would, therefore, be wrong to believe that the Roman process of internalization indicated a change from Romans who were to some extent free to individuals who were bound securely by society. The process of internalization is a change in the nature of the moral structure's relationship to society. The spread of society had created both a sharp division between public and private, and had also left a gap between dominant social structures and society's members. The intensification of government power was therefore necessary in order for its messages to reach those whom it ruled because they now inhabited a far greater social area and were more cut off. That is to say, individuals were situated further from the social centre and for that centre's messages to reach them, the volume had to be increased significantly. This means that if it were ever possible to quantify the total degree of central control, we would find that there was no overall difference between traditional society and the empire.

The dominant view of leisure changed in this transformation from a harmless recreation which supported the system, to an increasingly menacing and perverting danger which had to be mobilized to maintain order. In ideal terms, the attitude towards leisure had been fundamentally positive in traditional Rome, was neutral (in that it was good if directed, bad if not) in the principate, and became negative in the later empire. This represents the problematization of leisure, a process which was linked to the change in the nature of social control. Thus, the function of leisure in Roman history altered as society became more widely spread. In the traditional society, leisure was not part of social control, merely a part of life. It was a positive force of recreation. But in the late republic, leisure became integral to strategies of social control, enabling an elite to maintain its domination in the face of decreasing central authority. Finally, the emperors tried to restore central control by institutionalizing into a public form the elite notion that leisure had to be properly directed for it to be positive. Despite their increasingly intensive efforts, though, leisure remained as a part of private life in addition to its public aspect.

Leisure represented, as it still does, a fundamental problem for the civilizing process because of the freedom it allowed. The question of what people got up to in their leisure epitomized wider issues of social control. The imperial system of government substantially alleviated problems caused by wealth, urbanization, and popular culture, but it never really got to grips with the spread of society and the distance in space between the individual and the state which this entailed. The social space widened still further, distance from the centre increased, and thus a process of peripherization ensued. Religion acquired a crucial role in society because it was well suited to either side of this process: it allowed private space, and it could generate strong centripetal forces by providing a powerful sense of community in an age of disintegration.[90] The later emperors countered the increase in the social area by further centralization. They adapted their government for the guilt culture in which they now lived, and their adoption of Christianity was a part of this movement. Under Christianity, leisure experience was incorporated into religious activity, and this reflected an attempt at the total intensification of power. Leisure outside orthodox religion became sinful: evil, private, and uncontrolled; and because of this conversion of leisure into an inherently negative phenomenon, even when regulated, the later emperors became increasingly worried about collecting the tax on prostitution.[91] In ideal terms, all leisure came to be seen as wicked because it allowed freedom from social control, and whilst some recreation might grudgingly be permitted to revitalize the weak flesh, leisure could not be because it freed the private from the public domain and gave rise to private pleasures. Of course, the emperors did not always see the world in the purist terms of the religious fanatic, and leisure retained a central role in their ideological programme; in fact, Alexander Severus directed the prostitute tax 'to meet the state's expenditures for the restoration of the theatre, the circus, the amphitheatre, and the stadium'. But it was still a case of using the inexcusable to support the excusable. There is, however, no sense in which this process of social diffusion was part of some inevitable decline. For whilst the result in the western empire was fragmentation and decivilization – when the increase in social space had stretched links to breaking point, leaving behind more local, primitive societies – in the east, the imperial settlement flourished for many hundreds of years, and leisure continued to play a fundamental part in its survival.

10

Leisure and the Dialectic of Rome

The preceding chapters have revealed many of the features and tensions of Roman society, but the question remains as to what the place of leisure was in the history of Rome. In this chapter, therefore, I shall try to look at leisure and social change, and shall argue that leisure was nothing less than the synthetic agent which bound together Roman society as it developed from republic to empire. This will allow us to see not only the social conflicts which gave rise to the imperial system, but also the key role that leisure played in Rome's history. As the model for this, I shall take Hegel's view of historical change, a view of history which posits that understanding reality is not understanding a given state of affairs but a dialectical process of change. For every complex situation contains within itself conflicting elements, contradictions that eventually overthrow the original order and lead to the creation of a new society in which these tensions are lessened. As such, it is a move from thesis, to antithesis, to synthesis.

1 *Thesis*

In a sense, the thesis never actually existed, for it stood as the idealized beginning of society when there were no conflicts. In practice, we can see this period as being that of primitive, rustic Rome, which was characterized by a happy division of labour, a lack of private ambition, a strong notion of public responsibility, and a moral strength resistant to the corrupting influence of luxury. This was the golden age to which later writers were romantically to hark back. But romanticism is all that it was.[1]

2 *Antitheses*

However, once we enter the period of Roman history for which we actually possess sources, we are immediately struck by the endless social conflict which filled it. What then were the antitheses in Roman life? What were the contradictions which society as it stood could not solve? Fundamentally, they were the products of anxieties of influx and its control. As Burke observes, new historians 'have done little to challenge the importance of material factors, of the physical environment and its resources, over the long term. It still seems useful to regard these material factors as setting the agenda, the problems to which individuals, groups and, metaphorically speaking, cultures try to adapt or respond.'[2] The acquisition of empire had brought prodigious wealth and power into Roman control, but that very profit brought with it influences which changed the nature of their dominion. The Romans were faced with the total transformation of their material world.

The inundation of Rome with wealth caused the city to balloon in size. Following this phenomenal expansion, the city of Rome came to be recognized as the centre for social problems, and thus acquired 'strong moral resonances'.[3] Many contemporaries believed that it was the city which had destroyed traditional values, and the elite were in no doubt about the potentially demoralizing effects of urban life. As André says, 'à l'époque d'Auguste, l'*otium* populaire urbain est devenu synonyme d'*inertia* et de *luxuria*.'[4] It was the city which interfered with their traditional relationship with the lower classes. For not only was it the city that allowed the plebs the opportunity for greater leisure, both temporally through the corn dole which freed them (at least, in part) from the necessity to work, and experientially through increased leisure provision, but it was the city where traditional morality was most under threat. The rural young were lured by its streets paved with gold, for 'tempted by public and private dole, the young men, who had maintained a wretched existence by manual labour in the country, had come to prefer idleness in the city to their hateful toil (*privatis atque publicis largitionibus excita urbanum otium ingrato labori praetulerat*).'[5] Once in the city, however, the effects could be devastating: 'Giving themselves up to the allurements of the capital and to excesses too shameful to name, the soldiers constantly weakened their physical strength through leisure.'[6] In the past, 'those who spent their time idly within the walls, in the shelter of the city, were looked upon as more sluggish (*desides*) than those who tilled the fields or supervised the labours of the tillers.'[7] Therefore, the city plebs were viewed by the elite as bilgewater (*sentina urbis*)[8] and the dregs of Romulus (*faex Romuli*).[9]

Anxiety was generated by the rise in consumption of material goods

1 Amphitheatre Mosaic. A 3rd-century mosaic from Smirat, Tunisia, shows four named huntsmen fighting four named leopards. In the middle, a page holds a tray with prize money. Inscriptions name the benefactor as Magerius. (Reproduced by permission of Sousse Archaeological Museum, Kasbah)

2 *Lyon Mosaic.* Charioteers race round a clearly shown course. *(Reproduced by permission of Musée de la Civilisation Gallo-Romaine, Lyon)*

3 *Pompeii: 'Scenes de cabaret' I.* Men drinking and gaming in a tavern. (*From M. Collignon, Mélanges Biossier, Paris, 1903, pls I–II*)

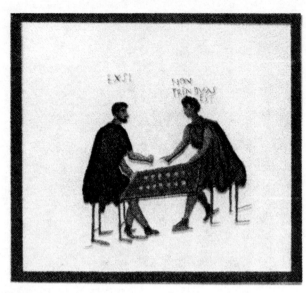

4 *Pompeii: 'Scenes de cabaret' II.* Two men arguing over a tavern game. *(From Prescuhn,* Die neuesten Ausgrabungen, *Leipzig, 1882, pl. 7)*

5 *Pompeii: 'Scenes de cabaret' III.* Men fighting in a tavern. *(From Prescuhn,* Die neuesten Ausgrabungen, *Leipzig, 1882, pl. 7)*

6 *Fighting Cock*. Panel on a pilaster from the cult hall in a bath and palaestra complex at Pergamon. Cockfighting was considered a juvenile sport. *(Reproduced by kind permission of Deutsches Archaeologisches Institut, Istanbul)*

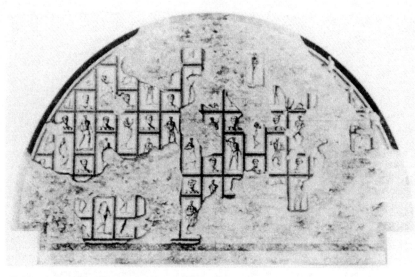

7 *Mosaic from the Thermae of Caracalla.* Athletes, gladiators, and sports equipment, including strigils and lekythoi for oil, are shown in this mosaic from the west palaestra exedra. *(Reproduced by kind permission of Kunstbibliothek, Berlin)*

8 *Pottery Lamp.* An erotic scene on a lamp from the Naples area (3rd century). *(Reproduced by courtesy of the Trustees of the British Museum, London)*

9 *Game Board.* Graffito of a game board on a stadium seat from Aphrodisias. *(Reproduced by kind permission of the Society for the Promotion of Roman Studies; photograph: M. Roueche from Mrs C. M. Roueche,* Performers and Partisans at Aphrodisias)

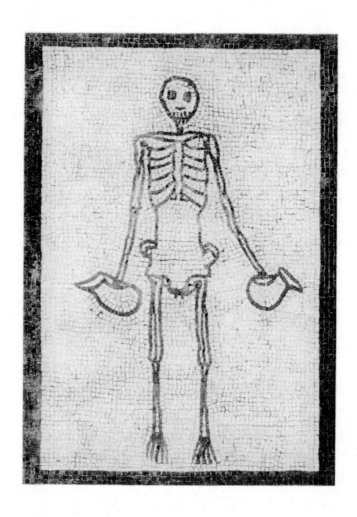

10 *Skeleton Mosaic.* A mosaic from a dining-room (*triclinium*) floor at Pompeii reminds diners to eat well. (*Photograph: Scala, Florence*)

and reflected in moral discourse. According to moralists' analyses, Rome was not merely sinful and vicious but morbidly self-destructive and self-enslaving, for the acquisitive society was also the addictive society. Surplus wealth brought idleness, indolence, and low spirits, which in turn brought cravings for pleasure and stimulus. This led to excess and finery, and under such inordinate stimulation Stoicism yielded to sensuality.[10] Thus the perceived rise in luxury and its concomitant immoralities were causally connected to the growth in leisure: 'luxury came into being simultaneously with the downfall of Carthage, a fatal coincidence that gave us at one and the same time a taste for vices and an opportunity for indulging in them.'[11] It became something of a literary topos to testify to the degeneracy of morals, the result of too much idleness and luxury,[12] and standard tales of immorality became a metaphor for a diseased constitution. This was related to the fact that Romans tended to base their view of the world and its inhabitants on moral terms, and their discussions of immorality are 'often preoccupied with the idea of moral decline'.[13] Contemporaries explained the rise of Rome in terms of moral character, as well as political institutions, military talent, and good fortune,[14] so it was reasonable not only to see any decline in similar terms, but also to see changes in the moral structure, which had brought so much success, as evidence of degeneration itself. For vigilance was thought to have turned to slumber, arms to pleasure, and business to leisure.[15] It became an axiom of Roman culture that what military conquest gave, it could take away. Hence, their fear of being conquered by those whom they had subjugated was exactly counterbalanced by their fear of being overwhelmed by luxury and vice.

Such concerns were also evidenced in the passing of sumptuary laws. Laws can reflect consensus about societal values and so harmonize, regulate, and reconcile; they can also represent interest groups manipulating one another. In these sumptuary laws, which were enacted periodically,[16] luxury entered the political arena, but legislators drew a sharp distinction between the immoral and illegal lust for false station that corrupted men and nations; and the natural and admirable expression of position and self-interest that produced genuine value. We might wonder what was the point of such laws if they could not be upheld, if not even the proliferating terrors of the criminal code could have much deterrent effect. The answer lies in separating the instrumental and symbolic functions of the law.[17] Widely violated and often unenforceable laws persisted in order to emphasize the law's symbolic functions, in contrast to the more instrumental social control functions. These laws did not depend on successful enforcement for their effect, since their very existence symbolized the public affirmation and dominance of ruling social ideals and norms at the expense of others. Even if the law was broken, it was clear whose law it was. This symbolic function served to enhance and glorify the social status and prestige of the traditional elements of Roman life, which held the affirmed values, and to demean and degrade the popular culture, whose moral patterns and lifestyle were condemned as deviant and disreputable. In instances of moralistic crime – gambling, sex, etc. – the criminal law was not a reflection of any consensus within the community. It was when widespread agreement was least attainable that the pressure to legislate the private moral conduct of others became greatest. Hence, the need for symbolic vindication and deference was channelled into political action. For what was at stake was not so much the action of men, whether or not they gambled or procreated, but their ideals and the moralities to which they owed their public allegiance. As such, these were not just struggles over points of law but a confrontation over public symbols of social power and status; and the elevation of deviant activities to the level of a political public issue was thus a sign that its moral status was at stake, that legitimacy was thought possible by others.

The material transformation led to changes in the Romans' social relations, since the old structures were unable to cope with its implications. The principal change in the period of the late republic and early principate was that power became spread down the social ladder more evenly, if not more equally. In the past, traditional culture had always maintained a strong boundary between the elite aristocracy and those beneath them. The influx of wealth had initially increased the degree of social differentiation, and the gap between the elite and the poor grew still wider. But that iron curtain of the social hierarchy became increasingly threatened during the late republic on account of its growing irrelevance in the face of unprecedented wealth and urbanization. The gap between the elite and the masses, which had once separated them so sharply, not only closed, but the borders themselves opened, and this permitted a far greater flow of cultural traffic. The elite culture became partially popularized, that of the plebs gentrified, and nowhere was this more apparent than in their leisure. This development can also be seen in the increasing stratification of Roman society; this was itself a response to the closing of the cultural gap between the vertical limits of Roman life by a strongly hierarchical society seeking to maintain divisions of some kind. For the new interchange between popular and elite, this filling in of the middle ground, created fresh concerns about what such a weakening of the boundaries might mean for traditional identities, and it was 'personality problems' such as these which underlay much of the condemnation which filled their moralizing.

One of the most important features of this social transformation was a development in lower-class choice and a growth in the power of popular culture.[18] The same powerful forces that were transforming the physical environment were acting on the fabric of the popular culture which predominated among the subordinate classes and was associated with them. As the city of Rome developed, traditional rural community standards were breaking down within its walls and a greater element of personal freedom was emerging from the ruins. Urbanization had a 'decisive impact on the kind of traditional communities which had been the focal point of nonwork activity',[19] and individuals became 'far less subject to the controls and obligations of custom'.[20] Therefore, a new tendency arose for people influenced by popular culture to place their own pleasures and needs above the obligations of the community. These people liked to take their pleasures in a new way: noisily, effusively, and in public. The pursuit of pleasure became more respectable, and this conflicted with the conventional private elite pleasures and the old Stoic mentality. The new facilities for self-expression (a vast list, from hairstyles, fashion, jewellery, and entertainment, to ways of dancing, drinking, eating, and different modes of sexual behaviour) explicitly renounced the old community morality, and a new balance was struck between communal obligation and individual freedom. That is not to say that the urban masses became free and autonomous, rather that they became less obligated to local communities than had previously been the case. The matter is one of degree and emphasis, not absolutes. But whatever the exact extent of the change, it undoubtedly jeopardized the control of traditional republican elite morality, and this partial shift away from group subordination along the line towards personal autonomy created a moral crisis.

Nor was this increase in personal freedom merely the result of the removal of external controls by competing aristocrats.[21] There had been a transformation in the internalized beliefs of the lower orders, and a new value-system had been established in contrast to traditional morality. In the same way as the move from republic to empire saw the transformation of a political system from one based on a city-state constitution to a system of government which was monarchy in all but name, so the traditional moral system was forced to adapt, and in places to break, by the weight of forces acting upon it. The fact that a new system had arrived did not mean that there was ever a period of normative void. There was no breakdown, rather 'a switch, a replacement of one set of cultural operating rules with another'.[22] The observers and chroniclers who make up our sources abhorred what this new outlook represented, and even denied that it existed at all. But then it was their morality which was under threat. As such, their attacks on the recreations of popular culture represented an attempt to accommodate the developing circumstances of social and political power and to fashion their moral protest in a style which, as they saw it, met the requirements of maintaining social discipline.

The growth of aristocratic leisure in the republic had been correlated to the influx of wealth. The elite had also come to see *otium* as more exclusively their domain. This increase was coupled with resentment at the lower classes' leisure, but there was no realization that the two went hand-in-hand, nor that such an entrenchment of their attitudes was the result of Roman society's acquiring an egalitarian streak. The adoption of Greek culture was part of this reintegration of the classes. Greek influence, and its corrupting potential on the Roman way of life, was one of the common tensions of Roman life: as Bowersock says, 'The core of a Roman's view of Greek life was *mollitia* [softness] and *otium*.'[23] Yet it was not only some nebulous xenophobic urge which caused the Roman elite to have anxieties about the importation of Greek culture. The emphasis of Greek influence upon arts and pastimes, and skills, such as philosophy and rhetoric, reflected a narrowing of the divide between the traditionally separated sections of Roman society because these attributes could be more equally acquired. In ideal terms, anyone with the talent could acquire such skills or appreciate such art, whereas traditional social power relied almost entirely on a nobility acquired at birth. However, a deep divide still remained because the increase in refined pleasures allowed the elite to adopt new ways of marking themselves off. Even then, though, its accessibility meant that Greek culture could only offer a more inclusive method of differentiation. The gradual establishment of a law code also reflected a new way of seeing the world as a place to be neutrally measured and judged. This is not to say that the Roman empire became a utopian ideal of equality. Far from it, but new currents of impartiality sprang up in the motionless sea of the traditional hierarchy.

It was as if in order to alleviate the tension caused by wealth pouring in, the outer skin of Roman culture at first expanded upwards, but that this left society unbalanced and likely to topple over. Hence, society contracted back to its original height, and this was achieved by using leisure to direct internal forces horizontally outwards. In this process, Roman culture spread outwards, but its internal structure was radically altered, too. This created a more stable base, but society's centres were distanced from the people they governed. That had the twin effect of allowing a greater degree of personal autonomy and also of necessitating stronger central structures (such as emperors) by which to balance such an increase in independence. Roman society was fundamentally transformed, and a new more popular, mass culture emerged.

The problem for the Romans was double-edged in that their new-found power and wealth demanded a more appropriately inclusive high culture, whilst the conventional outlook of their society was fundamentally opposed to its assimilation. To the suburban elite who constituted the moralists, the thesis of traditional rural culture continued to offer a complete solution to the problems concentrated in the city. However, new more sophisticated, more urbane, answers were also available. In reality, there was no single key, but all were part of the Romans' response to the challenge of defining their civilization and their way of life in the face of a wealth which threatened to obliterate the old divides. Attempts were made to shape their environment, through institutions and activities as well as buildings, to meet the potential of the civilized life. Idealized conceptions of the past were important for shaping ideas on what to do to improve society. But all of these ways of discussing the future of Rome, and the implications for their society that were contained within them, served only to reflect the fact that the traditional model by which social life had been ordered was no longer applicable to the urban environment.

3 *Synthesis*

The emperors were on the horns of a dilemma: they had first to solve the problem of gaining control, and then to fashion a method by which they might keep it. In order to do this, they would have to resolve the underlying antitheses which had been racking Roman society. Their response was to steer social developments in their direction, by making a new relationship with those whom they governed which reflected the reduction of the cultural gap between the elite and the lower classes. It was to leisure that this task was assigned. A new mode of citizenship was created, and also a new politics, both of which were more inclusive. But however novel and imaginative the imperial imagery seemed, it was important, for the purposes of legitimacy, to claim that it was, in fact, of great antiquity. Moreover, to discover an archaeology of imperialism must have been reassuring in a world where its novelty must have been as frightening as it was invigorating. The imperial solution represented an attempt both to make power more comprehensive and intensive, and to recover the control lost when new conditions left the old ways antiquated and redundant. As such, the emperors were pioneers in meeting the challenge of the social consequences of mass urbanization, for they were part of a new self-consciousness about urban civilization. The old politics had died because the city had become too large and amorphous to stimulate an individual response any more. The provision of leisure and cultural facilities was the imperial attempt to rescue the city's reputation and make Rome a place fit for the centre of an empire, whilst simultaneously making the city more suited to current social conditions. It was an incorporation of elements of the antitheses into a new social structure, and so an alleviation of social stress.

The growth of a new system of imperial symbols, through which they articulated their government, represented an attempt by the powerful in society to channel the social evolution of the city to their advantage. It was a hegemony, established on the use of power in all its forms – force, coercion, manipulation, bribery, persuasion, and authority, expressed through the symbols of legitimation – but also built upon areas of consensus and cultural agreement.[24] Hegemony represents the struggle for moral, cultural, intellectual, and thereby political leadership over the whole society. However, the leading class becomes hegemonic only to the degree that their ideology is able to accommodate opposing class cultures and values. Hegemony is a mediation of opposing cultures into a negotiated version of ruling class culture and ideology; it is not a question of opposition.[25] Roman hegemony lay between consensus and coercion, and represented a social contract by which the subordinate classes were taught to see society through their rulers' eyes. It was not a simple matter of enforcing domination since the use of force could play only a minimal part. The problem for the elite was that the forces of social change were not easy to control, and the very assets of city life which the empire brought to the lower orders, those of greater choice and greater aggregation of numbers, hindered their effort to control the pattern of development.

In order to compensate for social differences, the system of imperial rule attempted to create a social order based on commonly accepted social values, which was sufficiently definite to allow it to govern the whole populace effectively, and yet flexible enough to allow for group and individual variations. It was not the case that the traditional dominant ideology replaced that of the lower classes. In the empire a new dominant morality arose which incorporated some elements of popular culture, but was mainly still in the hands of the elite. In their provision of leisure, the emperors attempted to market elite ideals in a radically new packaging with the purpose of enticing and training the lower classes into some semblance of aristocratic values; for just as they were to share their pleasures, so they were to share their morals. To achieve that, an audience had to be gathered. Spectacles were held so as to attract the kind of crowds in which the formal distinctions of rank were swallowed up by shared enthusiasms, and this was possible because there were by this period a remarkable number of cultural phenomena in which popular and elite tastes had converged. In the crowds, a process of boundary breaking was achieved and the popular and elite worlds came closer together. Elite traditional morality remained a powerful influence in Roman life, but it is overemphasized by the nature of our sources. For elite hegemony was secured, not by obliterating lower-class culture, but by articulating it to elite culture and ideology so that its political affiliations were altered in the process.

Leisure played a crucial role in these social developments and became the cornerstone of the imperial image of what it meant to be Roman. However, leisure was not so much a catalyst of change but an agent, in that it was itself radically transformed in the reaction. Leisure was no longer the preserve of the elite; instead it became the interface between the various strata of society. The upper levels of Roman society had to use the attractions of leisure in order to entice the plebs into a new hegemony, for a close relation existed between the mechanisms of pleasure and those of consent. New ways of seeing and seeking excitement and pleasure were created, and these quickly established themselves as a more popular prospect of the 'good life'. Relaxation, entertainment, and informal social activities were much more attractive than the austere intellectual demands of elite *otium*. But a delicate balance had to be struck between the desire to keep the plebs busy and the need to provide them with their beloved leisure. So Augustus, 'to prevent the plebs from being called away from their business (*negotiis*) too often because of the corn-distributions, decided to give out tickets for four months' supply three times a year.'[26]

Paternalism of this kind consisted of the art of extending social benefits and alleviating the effects of misfortune while enhancing the prestige and moral worth of the donor. Its essence was tolerance and a disposition towards traditionalism, strongly influenced by an awareness of the methods for maintaining social control. 'Bread and circuses' was an elite attitude founded on the belief that it was all the lower classes were good for, and the suspicion that at the drop of a hat they would revolt. For example, Pylades, the pantomime actor, when reproached by Augustus for deafening Rome with the noise of his quarrels and rivalries, replied, 'it is in your interest Caesar that the people should spend their time on us.'[27] But social control manipulation theories conceal as much as they explain; they ignore the strong urge with which Roman rulers were compelled to honour their good fortune by sharing it with the mass of Romans. For imperial leisure provision was not just suasion or social control, it was also a response to the influx of wealth and the emotions brought on by it. It was impossible to be a member of this hyper-successful society and not pay one's dues.

A new leisure-based pleb politics was created. The plebs were not, as is commonly assumed, depoliticized; nor could they be, for everyone has a politics. The question is not whether the urban plebs were apolitical, but whether their politics were appropriate to their conditions and circumstances. The political aims of the plebs in Rome were two-fold: to obtain sufficient food and to partake of the leisure which marked them out as Romans – bread and circuses. The plebs were not indifferent to dole politics. It is largely irrelevant as to whether the plebs can be characterized as lacking initiative, for whatever their 'true character', they were contained within a highly ritualized political system which was, for the most part, ideologically accepted by both rulers and ruled. The plebs conducted their politics, both during the republic and the empire, within institutions devised by others, and it should not be surprising to see them playing a mainly defensive role. The more important question is whether the plebs extracted anything in return for this hegemony; that is to say, whether their politics were effective.[28]

Pleb politics had developed in accordance with changes in the ruling hierarchy. The switch from republic to empire entailed a restriction of the plebs' traditional political rights, so they altered their politics from one suited to the acquisition of favour from a small but competing aristocracy, into one which best served their interests in a politically centralized regime. The redundant traditional participation of the people was transformed into one focused on the person of the emperor. Bread and circuses thus enabled the common people to participate actively in the new imperial system in which the vote was of no use at all. But that desire did not reflect an ever-increasing demoralization in the face of luxury and indolence. Moreover, bread and circuses were what they wanted, and bread and circuses were what they got.

The result of the imperial programme was that the contradictions of Roman republican culture became less threatening to the survival of Roman society as a whole. But the political change from republic to empire, and the republic's collapse itself, were for a time running sores on the body of Roman life. This allowed some to mine a rich reactionary seam, but the expression of traditional republican sentiments was not incompatible with supporting Augustus, nor did it presuppose a 'republican camp'. People were quite capable of bearing the strains of Roman culture within their individual mental horizons. However, other more persistent difficulties remained. Many areas of popular culture stayed outside imperial control, whilst society itself seemed to be less bound by the rigours of traditional constraints. The advent of empire meant that these tensions were often projected onto the figure of the emperor himself, for, once established, the imperial image became a standard against which both the emperors themselves and society as a whole could be judged. Beliefs became more visual and visible, and the emperor was but the most conspicuous of them. He was the centre of the centre, transformed into an ideal (and sometimes anti-ideal) which stood proxy for the virtues which the gods ordained. The court mirrored the world which the world was to imitate, society would flourish to the degree that it assimilated that fact, and it was the office of the emperor, wielder of the mirror, to ensure that it did.[29]

Disputes over leisure reflected deep concern about status divisions within Roman society, 'and in seeing the solution to it in leisure, it both inflated the importance of leisure and helped in the process of delimiting it.'[30] An enormous burden was placed on leisure for it was to be the means to achieve social reconciliation, as a result of which the whole of Roman society could meet again in a spirit of public concord. The fact that it was to leisure that this tremendous responsibility of improving social relations was assigned gave witness to its new importance and stature. What is more, it succeeded. The dominant culture acquired a degree of control over leisure sufficient for it to be legitimized, so that, whereas in the republic, leisure's legitimacy for the people was denied, it being only for 'the leisured', by the end of our period its legitimacy for all could be accepted. To be sure, the outcome was a compromise, but it was a compromise in which the hegemony was unthreatened.

11

Epilogue: History, Historicism, and Relativism

In the concluding chapter on Rome, I used Hegel's idea of the process of history as a way of describing the transformation which Roman society underwent. However, there is more to Hegel's view of historical change than this process of synthetic development: it also involves the notion of the end of history, which comes when rational truth has triumphed and no better synthesis can be produced. Recently, Fukuyama has gone so far as to suggest that we have now reached that point. In this final section I shall address this question by broadening the discussion to bring together the recurrent problematics of this work – the nature of historical knowledge and historical change. The starting point for this analysis will be to examine the status of my earlier definitions. For one of the principal advantages of writing a history of the leisure of a civilization as ancient as that of the Romans, as opposed to the society from which the term actually stems, is that the different concepts in use chafe, and the friction which this action generates brings to the fore the epistemological problems which bedevil any historical project. The result will, I hope, show the erroneous nature of Fukuyama's claims.

The problems of history are the problems of language, and historical problems arise when language goes on holiday. The fundamental questions for any historian – indeed, anyone studying 'the Other' – are the degree to which it is possible to understand another's mentality and also the terms on which such an understanding might be achieved. There have, as a consequence, been two aspects to this work so far: analysing what can be meant by the term 'leisure', and what the Romans meant by their notion of *otium*; and using the concept of leisure to analyse the society of ancient Rome. But after all that, can we really claim to be any closer to knowing what leisure is or, for that matter, to understanding ancient Rome? The second issue is that any success which the study on Rome may have had results from the fact that it allowed the Romans' culture to express itself on its own hierarchical terms. This method tried not to impose our ideal of equality upon its subject matter; it did not see Roman culture as a straightforward homogeneity. The dilemma which arises from this is that if we are not to maintain even our own egalitarian standards, then what happens to meaning and truth? There is, on the face of it, nothing to stop us falling into simple relativism.

The problem of relativism is of major importance for those who study 'others'.

> The realization that news from elsewhere about ghost marriage, ritual destruction of property, initiatory fellatio, royal immolation, and nonchalent adolescent sex naturally inclines the mind to an 'other beasts other mores' view of things has led to arguments, outraged, desperate, and exultant by turns, designed to persuade us either to resist that inclination in the name of reason, or to embrace it on the same grounds. What looks like a debate about the broader implications of anthropological research is really a debate about how to live with them.[1]

Caught between the Scylla of relativism and the Charybdis of provincialism, Geertz is forced into the self-confessedly lumbering approach of 'anti anti-relativism'. With such an attitude, he feels able to reject anti-relativism without thereby committing himself to the relativism it rejects. There is, however, another, perhaps more deft way through these epistemological straits.

1 *The Status of Definitions*

Wittgenstein was dismissive of definitions: 'What should we gain by a definition, as it can only lead us to other undefined terms?' The question 'What is . . .?' 'is an utterance of unclarity, of mental discomfort, and it is comparable with the question "Why?" as children so often ask it.'[2] Or as Rorty puts it, the desire for a theory of knowledge is a desire for constraint – a desire to find 'foundations to which one might cling, frameworks beyond which one must not stray, objects which impose themselves, representations which cannot be gainsaid.'[3] Wittgenstein did not believe that it was useful to seek the metaphysical essence of concepts such as leisure and *otium*, but rather to try to understand them within their specific language games by bringing the words back to their everyday use. In his opinion, it is a word's use which gives it life and its use can teach us its meaning.

2 *Anthropology, Hermeneutics, and Historicism*

The historian's quandary is that cultures are not self-contained, and the problem of mediation is the starting point of historical analysis. In this work, for example, it was not enough to look at the philology of leisure and *otium*; our concept of leisure had to be used as the analytical tool so that the quality of our understanding of Roman culture might be improved. Unfortunately, the problem of how we are to go about translating from one language game to another and what epistemological status such translations possess are questions about which Wittgenstein was notoriously silent.

Wittgenstein did concede that, 'a definition often clears up the *grammar* of a word.'[4] Words 'have those meanings which we have given them; and we give them meanings by explanations.' In most cases we are not ready to give any explanation of a word, and 'many words in this sense then don't have a strict meaning. But this is not a defect. To think it is would be like saying that the light of my reading lamp is no real light at all because it has no sharp boundary.'[5] Sharp definitions, in other words, belong to the airless world of the vacuum, for once in the atmosphere of real life they blur. A definition doesn't need to be exact. It is a rough approximation and a guide. If I tell you to go over there you don't need the precise area to know where to go. Thus to have understood a definition means to have an idea of the thing defined, but that idea is not an ideal model, it is the shape of the phenomenon in general.[6] When we talk of leisure acts, for example, there is no one thing which makes us use the same word for all. Rather, they are related in many different ways, and it is this complicated network of similarities which Wittgenstein termed 'family resemblance'.[7] For whilst the concept of leisure is not closed by a frontier, nor everywhere circumscribed by rules, such a blurred concept is still a concept.

The earlier interpretive definition of leisure was in accordance with this theory of family resemblances. It highlighted an area to be studied without marking it off too sharply. But since family resemblances depend on genes, the definition also tried to bring out the emotional bases on which the family of leisure acts rests. As such, the definition tries to offer a neutral mode of evaluation, a lowest common denominator, by gaining access to the reality behind phenomena (that is to say, as the real appears to us) by means of our common internal experience of the body. This is in no way a radically new stance; it is rooted in Schopenauer and is now most commonly found in interpretive anthropology, a position whose best-known exponent is Geertz. He takes as his starting point (and I apologize to him for the crass résumé which follows) the view that all humanity shares a common set of emotional responses. We see the world meaningfully through symbols which spark off emotional responses: feelings, moods, and motivations. We organize these responses and symbols into systems which become culturally specific concepts. But as a concept can be broken down into its constituent symbols and emotions, it can be analysed in comparison to the ways in which these same responses are organized in other societies. By accepting that others employ parallel processes of ordering their perceptual universe into something which means something to them, we are able to adapt our culture, our system of signification, to theirs. It is a matter of reshaping categories so that they extend beyond their original context. For if the study of diverse societies tells us anything about what it is to be human, it is that it is a highly adaptive and flexible condition.[8]

This method offers a practical solution to the problem of how we are to understand another's mind-set. It represents an attempt to create neutral ground between us and the Romans and is based on the principles of hermeneutics. 'Hermeneutic understanding is primarily a way of recovering the meaning of the utterances and performances of historical agents.'[9] It is also concerned with transcendental interpretation, and so is about the structure of all human beings. 'The purpose of an hermeneutic inquiry is, thus, twofold: (a) it seeks to understand the other, and (b) by making available the life of the other, it opens up new worlds and possibilities to us.'[10] Gadamer characterizes the process of understanding as the 'fusion of these horizons supposedly existing by themselves',[11] so that earlier frontiers vanish and only one community of thought and action remains. Understanding, therefore, 'is not about "feeling the feelings" or "thinking the thoughts" of others, but about sharing in a form of life. Or in the case of an encounter between hitherto alien forms – *about constructing a form of life of a "higher order", which will incorporate the previous two as its sub-forms.*'[12] Translation is not just a transposition, but an enlargement and expansion of our own language, a taking of our vocabulary into new realms. As such, hermeneutics are an attempt to create a limited hierarchy of knowledge, by which I mean that hermeneutic knowledge claims a higher epistemological status for itself over other knowledge without claiming the properties of ultimate truth.

'Gadamer defines the "central task" of a truly historical hermeneutics as the examination of prejudice and the distinguishing of legitimate from illegitimate prejudices. This task is accomplished through the use of "critical reason"', since reason has 'superior universality'.[13] The fact that the fieldworker has always to report back to a home audience means that anthropologists are also well aware of the need to distinguish between their own analyses and the more homespun philosophies which are the subject of their investigations. Lett has observed that anthropologists, 'as human beings who study other human beings, must be fundamentally concerned with the distinction between the insider's perspective and the outsider's perspective.'[14] The prevalent view is to discriminate between knowledge based on critical reason and that which rests on prejudice alone by adopting the terms 'emic' and 'etic'.[15] 'Emic constructs are accounts, descriptions, and analyses expressed in terms of the conceptual schemes and categories regarded as meaningful and appropriate by the native members of the culture whose beliefs and behaviours are being studied ... Etic constructs are accounts, descriptions, and analyses expressed in terms of the conceptual schemes and categories regarded as meaningful by the community of scientific observers.'[16] All etic constructs must be 'precise, accurate, logical, comprehensive, replicable, falsifiable, and observer-independent', and 'applicable cross-culturally'.[17] The obvious criticism is that etics are merely the emics of a particular scientific subculture, but Lett denies that this is so on the grounds that they can consistently distinguish between true and false empirical claims. The claims are also provisional and subject to relentless scrutiny. Etic knowledge, therefore, is an ideal, but the fact that absolute objectivity is unrealizable is beside the point: etics are more reliable, useful, objective, and self-correcting.

A consequence of this hermeneutical stance is that there is no one correct interpretation. If there were, there would be none, for 'an interpretative way of seeing the past can only be recognized as such in the presence of other ways of seeing the past', and 'paradoxically, the more powerful and authoritative an interpretation, the more writing it generates.'[18] Maximum clarity depends on a proliferation of interpretations, not on a reduction of their number. The implication for history is that it can be practically true provided that it conforms to our standards of using the available evidence.[19] The search is not for truth but for new and better, more interesting and more fruitful ways of speaking. There are obvious criteria for interpretation: not misreading texts, and avoiding mistakes in logic, but beyond that, 'historiography is itself the source of its own interpretative certainties and not the result of the application of some previously given set of certainties.'[20] In this view, historical debate is as much about the crust of interpretation as the past hidden beneath it.

It is at this point, however, that I shall come out of my historicist closet and reveal that I do not consider that we can create any neutral ground between us and the Romans. Nor do I think it possible to create a transcendental epistemological hierarchy. My view is that we are stuck in history and that our very being is historicized – a shared, situated, social way of being – but this historicity of existence and the mediated character of experience are conditions of existence, not obstacles to be overcome. Understanding is a problem in the world, and if it can be solved at all, it is to be solved in the world. For truth and understanding are earthly things, and there is no state of 'understanding', only constant effort against incomprehension.[21] There is no disinterested perception. There is no understanding from 'the native's point of view'. To be sure, we can develop categories which, in accordance with our social ideals, treat all cultures equally and do not impose our very real social divisions, but they are still our categories and our way of thought. Man has no essence, not even as a symbol-builder. That is just our present mode of self-description. For knowledge always has foundations, even hermeneutics, but the foundations are social rather than eternal.

There is no neutral ground between us and the past. Our social ideals create a privileged discourse: eticism, interpretism, hermeneuticism – call it what you will – but its foundations rest on sand. They do not establish a transcendental critical reason, for this is as historicized as any other human mode of thought. Etics are merely our empirical mode of thought, and just because we tend to reduce matters to lowest common denominators that does not give a firmer foundation to our knowledge. Our explanation would still be, not inexplicable, but incompatible with a Roman mentality. Similarly, Geertz's discovery that everyone is in fact a cultural anthropologist reading texts is an imposition. As Crapanzano has put it, 'we must ask: for whom does the cockfight articulate everyday experience . . . and render it more perceptible?' Furthermore, 'we must ask: who is historically positioned to appreciate the construction?'[22] For the Balinese, the cockfights were not fictions to be read but cockfights, whereas for us, they are metaphors. Likewise, Geertz's definition of religion (and, by extension, the definitions in this work) is not a universal or historic definition. It is universally equal, but it is not ahistorical. A universal definition is only universal in that it allows us to look comparatively at all other societies from a consistent standpoint; yet the standpoint is still ours.[23] For whilst it is possible to clear a space of our cultural debris, it is still our space.

The search for any transcendental truth is an attempt to become inhuman. Truth always has a context. Any attempt to create a transcendental objectivity requires that we abandon context, with the result that understanding is diminished. But communication between different cultures is possible without presupposing an Archimedean point of objectivity. Other language games are available to us, and are not entirely closed worlds. The search for historical reality becomes the reconstruction and translation of those games – it is a 'bringing across' into our world knowledge of theirs by means of our mode of explanation. By developing our concepts to their ideal and logical limits (as, following Geertz's lead, I have tried to do in the definitions), outside their everyday use, we can create a combination of general vision looking through polished glass that allows us to improve our perception. If the task of interpretation is to make something that is unfamiliar, distant, and obscure into something real, near, and intelligible, then for us to understand we have to see such abstractions in the life under scrutiny. After all, some degree of abstraction is required for any translation to occur at all, since without it we would be unable even to recognize *otium* as leisure, let alone translate it. The best abstractions in any system of thought are those which explain the most with the least and then allow new details to be understood when encountered, but we should not suppose that those patterns ever actually exist other than in our minds. As such, interpreters and historians are as mediators, but they do not bridge the gap between cultures; they look from afar and report. It is as if they are stood on the Dover cliffs with a telescope pointed at France, not as if they are digging the Chunnel. The implication is that there is no fusion of the horizons, nor transcending of the limitations of both positions; instead, we attempt to extend our view by refining our tools and methods, whilst our own horizon regulates the possibilities of interpretation.

At this point, however, a cry will be raised that I am trying to have my cake and eat it: that I wish to adhere to the practice of interpretism whilst rejecting the principles on which it stands. For the usual objection will be put forward that such historicism sends us plummeting into the standardless morass of relativism.[24] Fukuyama has stated the problem clearly:

> Anyone who accepts the historicist premise – that is, that truth is historically relative – faces the question of the end of history even if he is not aware of it. For unless one posits something like an end of history, it is philosophically impossible to prevent historicism from degenerating into simple relativism, or from undermining any notion of progress. Anyone who believes that earlier thinkers were simply 'products of their times' must, if he is honest and consistent, ask whether he and his own historicism are not also products of their times. The present-day feminist who looks with condescension and disdain at the antiquated views of her grandparents regarding the role of women must ask whether her views are 'absolute,' or whether there are yet more progressive views that will render them just as quaint in the eyes of her granddaughter. And if that is so, why devote one ounce of effort, why argue passionately in favor of today's cause?[25]

There are two solutions to this dilemma: Hegel and the end of history, which posits a victory for rational truth; or the radical historicism of Nietzsche and Heidegger, which denies the existence of any objectivity. As for the latter, Fukuyama says: 'Let me simply suggest that the attempt to work out the political implications of historicism without a concept of an end to history leads to consequences (fascism and the glorification of war) which few of us would be willing to stomach.'

Fukuyama, therefore, has opted for the first solution, the End of History.[26] By this he means that, 'liberal democracy may constitute the "end point of mankind's ideological evolution" and "the final form of human government," and as such constitute the "end of history." '[27] The problems which remain are those of 'incomplete implementation of the twin principles of liberty and equality on which modern democracy is founded, rather than of flaws in the principles themselves.' The ideal cannot be improved on. But what has come to an end is not 'the occurrence of events, even large and grave events, but History; that is, History understood as a single, coherent, evolutionary process, when taking into account the experience of all people at all times.' At the End of History, 'there would be no further progress in the development of underlying principles and institutions, because all of the really big questions had been settled.'[28] We are Nietzsche's 'last men' because we know that our values are culture-specific. Liberal democracy has replaced 'the irrational desire to be recognized as greater than others with a rational desire to be recognized as equal',[29] and therefore represents a victory for reason.

It is not my job to critique Fukuyama here,[30] but if there is an End to History, that will have important historical implications. For if History is an unending dialogue between past and present, as it has become almost trite to say, what happens when History comes to an end? If we have stopped progressing ideologically, then to that extent so has the past. Moreover, if we are at the End of History, then the hermeneutical stance becomes not just our present way of thinking, but the final mode of human thought. As such, Fukuyama offers us a way out of relativism, 'the doctrine that all horizons and values systems are relative to their time and place, and that none are true but reflect the prejudices or interests of those who advance them'.[31]

3 The Impossibility of Relativism

The historicist view can be held without either positing an End of History, or regressing into relativism because of the very impossibility of relativism ever existing. By this I mean that the historicist view necessarily holds that the concept of relativism must always have a social foundation, and so cannot be held in any transcendental form. Hence, for a person to treat all equally requires a set of social ideals which preclude the acceptance of any inegalitarian morality. As such, relativism is only a theoretical construct, and no person can actually be a relativist, for to be one would require an inhuman objectivity.

Let me elaborate on this bold, and rather baldly stated theory by looking at the way in which the dangers of relativism to our moral health are
often raised in connection with cultural history. The complaint is that if
we are to treat all as equal, what happens to right and wrong? Or, to put
it another way, how far can, and should, the historian's sympathies stretch
when faced with the stark brutalities of the Roman gladiatorial combats
and their pantomimic execution of prisoners? By endeavouring to locate
the horror of the arena in the context of its own proseity, the historian is
not, in fact, condoning the fearsome violence which occurred. The very
opposite is nearer the truth. Since history reflects the concerns of the age,
the way of thinking it now reveals is one of pluralism and egalitarianism.
This modern sensibility is quite capable of explaining both Mother Theresa
and Nazis in the same manner, but that does not require that they be
thought of as morally equal. On the contrary, that sensibility, that very
mode of evaluation, could never accept the inequalities and cruelties of
fascism in favour of mercy and compassion, or place those subjects on the
same moral plane. It is not that method and morality have become separated, rather, that moralizing should not be allowed to interfere with the
analysis of the symbol systems and mentalities of cultures, not even those
which gave birth to heinous crimes. As such, ethnography represents an
effort to suspend judgement, to place it outside the sphere of investigation, whilst all the time remaining aware of the moral stance by which it
is informed.

This egalitarianism is not, as so often accused, informed by political
correctness. The desire for historical equality does not necessitate that it
governs our personal and political lives. For the mode of academic analysis is not politically motivated in any narrow sense. The academy allows
the freedom to study societies in conditions of pure equality, when in real
life one's politics have to cope with social, political, and economic realities.[32] This often requires compromise and permits of a wide range of
political responses. By contrast, political correctness enforces equality of
treatment and thought. It is a mutant American hybrid born of interpretive
social ideals and fiercely hierarchical conditions, and whilst its ends are
in accordance with liberal democracy, its means are in opposition to the
very liberalism which spawned it. More importantly for history, political
correctness threatens to invade the object of study, when judgement needs
to be suspended if we are to understand on their terms as well as ours. It
should itself, at least in academic terms, be treated as any other belief
system, and so understood as an intellectualized response by, or more
accurately on behalf of, the powerless and underprivileged, which is aimed
at enforcing equality in a country where the principle is idealized, prom-
ulgated, and promised, but whose systems fail to deliver. In other words,
academics don't all have to be politically alike to be good anthropological

historians, nor does Hitler have to be accepted, nor debate suspended to have an historicist, egalitarian outlook.[33]

The impossibility of relativism ever actually existing in a social form also avoids the relativist impasse that relativism asserts it is 'absolutely true that all truth is relative, thus claiming for the thesis of relativism itself a type of validity this thesis asserts to be impossible.'[34] For the real-life egalitarianism that is confused with relativism is just one of many competing world-views, between which we cannot assign any absolute truth or falsity. Instead, our judgement is seen to be informed by social ideals. The objection might be raised that if you can't escape your preference then what possibility is there of rational thought or action? Two things need to be realized: first, that rational thought is itself the product of egalitarian social ideals, and second, that those social ideals demand the use of rational thought, for that is the only method of judgement left to us.[35]

It has become a commonplace of modern philosophy that truth is an attribute of propositions, and our search for truth, therefore, is a search for 'victory in argument'. 'We shall, in short, be where the Sophists were before Plato brought his principle to bear and invented "philosophical thinking": we shall be looking for an airtight case rather than an unshakable foundation.'[36] However, it will always have to be a case founded on social principles. Our rational certainty represents the idealization of our language game, and if any would wish to change the rules they will have to change the game itself – that is, alter our social ideals. For whatever doubts we may have about the ultimate truth of our world-view, we cannot avoid seeking the truth as we see it. That is to say, we are culturally bound to seek rational certainty, and if we wish our findings to be accepted by the academic community, then we shall have to strive for etic knowledge. It may be that Fukuyama is right and our ideals are beyond development, but whether our etic viewpoint is really the end of the academy is extraneous to its position of dominance.

The ultimate epistemological status of the historian's analyses is lowered by this analysis: they are no more true than the findings of non-reason. Yet, as we have seen, this does not imply any simple relativism. Epistemological doubts are a necessary condition of existence in our egalitarian society and any attempt to rise above them demands a hierarchical view of humanity which is at odds with social equality. This does not mean that reason and non-reason are fundamentally incompatible and that all religious and non-rational views have no place in our society; it means only that truth-claiming, irrational ones do not. In fact, our dominant social ideals and the individualist, spread-out society which spawned them have confined religious, non-rational belief to the personal sphere since faith is emic rather than etic knowledge. Hence, people are, as Russell said, free to believe that a piece of cheese is orbiting Mars if they wish, but this type of thought not only has no social weight, it may even be at odds with egalitarian ideals if it claims to confer special status on its adherents. Some might argue that since one cannot escape from the social foundations of knowledge, religion is redundant in that it acts only as a vehicle for the expression of social ideas, when it would seem more sensible and honest to voice such opinions directly. That would be simplistic; for life is not by its nature rational even if our mentality is, and there is plenty of room and need for the non-rational if we want practical success at understanding. Provided that the non-rational is prevented from becoming irrational there is no conflict with egalitarian ideals. Ultimately, we can never know whose world-view is correct. All we can do is maintain our own earthly ideals as the base on which to build, and the template to which we must always refer.

There is a fundamental tension between our belief in our morality and the knowledge that it is socially founded, our desire not to moralize and the utter impossibility of this ever happening. It is only in the most extreme cases this desire is put to one side – when the analysis seems to threaten the very ideals on which it is based – and moralizing is allowed to interfere. For example, I said above (p. 136) that the Nazi destruction of the Jews could be explained in cultural terms: the Holocaust was exactly how their efficient, regimented, ask-no-questions society would go about the task of genocide. Yet there would be something distasteful, something very un-politically-correct, about this analysis, as if it explained away rather than explained. There have, of course, been myriad massacres throughout history, most of which could be more palatably analysed in cultural terms, but the difference between them and the Holocaust lies in the fact that whereas those other massacres were entirely irrational – in the long tradition of tyrants and dictators – the Germans' was not. Their cultural tradition of rationality somehow came to be based on irrational foundations of the most grotesque kind. The surface effects of reason, expressed in such things as greater efficiency, standardization, and bureaucracy, were perverted towards saving everything save life itself. As such their systematic barbarism bears witness to what can happen to a well-developed rational mentality if it loses touch with its base of social ideals of equality.

The result of this analysis is that we no longer need Hegel's End of History since reason is itself ours and its victory would reflect only our social dominance. We are left only with his notion of the process of history: a never-ending struggle to balance social ideals with changes in material conditions. Roman history has already provided an excellent example of this process at work. In that the establishment of the Roman empire produced a partial decrease in the vertical distance of Roman culture from top to bottom and the introduction of certain meritocratic features, it was, to that extent, a growth in reason. But it was not part of any triumphal rational progress, it was a local response to local problems. The acquisition of empire had caused Roman society to grow vertically and distance the rulers from the ruled. Cut off from society's power structures, the lower orders became ever more threatening to the elite. Society responded with the establishment of the imperial system of government, and this reconnected the different social strata to the central power structures. Roman society regained the horizontal aspects of the early republic, when the plebs had a say (albeit small) in their politics. But it was a new mass society in which the nature of the connection between the elite and the plebs was markedly different from the earlier limited democracy. The lesson for us is that we should not be allowed to fall into the complacent view that our ideals will naturally promote and reproduce themselves. If the material base of our culture were to change, our ideals could alter radically in an attempt to reach a state of balance, even to the extent of coming into conflict with reason. They will only be maintained if individuals struggle to adapt them to changing conditions. For whilst we cannot know whether our ideals are beyond development, we do know that they are neither safe nor secure.

History is becoming more cosmopolitan, and the historian is now philosopher, sociologist, and anthropologist. History is now as a supermarket with a massive array of goods made by the same productive process: variety exists more widely at the surface level, but the single bed on which it rests is as deep as any other. Historicism is no longer seen as the danger, but endism, on account of its intrinsic claim for a triumph of rational thought, which involves an inherent attitude of moral superiority. We cannot know where we stand in any process of history, but whether at the end or not, history is acquiring historical importance: if history has ended, then all well and good – history keeps life different, reminds us how horrible life used to be, and how progressive we now are; if not, if there is only the process, it is not that history teaches us what to be careful of, but the act of history constantly reminds us of our own historicity, and so keeps the ultimate relativity of morals at the forefront of our minds. Otherwise, the result will be a smug and lukewarm condescension which threatens the very ideals from which it stems. The act of history also reminds us of our social ideals at a time when not only are many already exasperated by their less than full implementation, but many more are likely to become so. For their application is becoming ever more difficult in the face of an increasingly hostile economic environment, and some will be attracted by more extreme, and probably extremist, solutions. A more human history is perhaps the best equipped to do this, and at a time when it is problems of life, rather than ideals, that plague us, a more human approach might well be our best way of confronting them. So whilst this might not be the End of History, it could be the dawn of history.

Notes

Chapter 1 *History, Leisure, and Ancient Rome*

1 D. Hume, *An Enquiry Concerning Human Understanding*, section 8.65 in his *Enquiries Concerning Human Understanding and Concerning the Principles of Morals*, Oxford: Clarendon Press, 1975 (first published 1777).
2 S. Schama, *Dead Certainties: (Unwarranted Speculations)*, Granta Books, 1991, p. 319.
3 Quoted by P. Burke in his introduction, p. x, to M. Bloch, *The Historian's Craft*, trans. P. Putnam, Manchester: Manchester University Press, 1992 (first published 1954).
4 R. F. Atkinson, *Knowledge and Explanation in History: An Introduction to the Philosophy of History*, Ithaca, New York: Cornell University Press, 1978, p. 138.
5 As will become clear, this is not an attempt to write a 'total history', as Bloch himself wished to do. For it is impossible to know everything about anything, and such epistemological problems cannot be brushed under a carpet of idealism. Instead, I aim to discover what might be termed the 'key points' in Roman culture, which will build up into a framework of understanding.
6 For a clear and instructive analysis of the whole nature of the 'anthropological attitude' towards the examination of other cultures, see esp., C. Geertz, 'From the Native's Point of View', in his *Local Knowledge: Further Essays in Interpretive Anthropology*, New York: Basic Books, 1983, pp. 55–70, earlier published in K. H. Basso and H. A. Selby (eds), *Meaning in Anthropology*, Albuquerque, New Mexico: University of New Mexico Press, 1976, pp. 221–37; and for a more complete statement, see his *The Interpretation of Cultures*, Hutchinson, 1975. Such an attitude can best be seen in historical action in R. Darnton, *The Great Cat Massacre and Other Episodes in French Cultural History*, New York: Basic Books, 1984.
7 V. Crapanzano, 'Hermes' Dilemma: The Masking of Subversion in Ethnographic Description', in J. Clifford and G. E. Marcus (eds), *Writing Culture: The Poetics and Politics of Ethnography*, Berkeley, California: University of California Press, 1986, p. 74.
8 P. Burke, *History and Social Theory*, Cambridge: Polity, 1992, p. 28.

9 Geertz, 'From the Native's Point of View', p. 57.
10 K. Hopkins, *Conquerors and Slaves*, Cambridge: Cambridge University Press, 1978, p. x.
11 Hopkins, *Conquerors and Slaves*, p. x.
12 K. Hopkins, *Death and Renewal*, Cambridge: Cambridge University Press, 1983, p. 203.
13 Darnton, *The Great Cat Massacre*. A useful discussion of this work, and of the whole concept of historical anthropology, is to be found in R. Chartier, *Cultural History: Between Practices and Representations*, Cambridge: Polity, 1988, ch. 4, 'Text, Symbols and Frenchness: Historical Uses of Symbolic Anthropology', pp. 95–111.
14 E. Griffiths, 'Shuttle Meets Moon Unit', *Sunday Telegraph*, 21 Oct. 1990, p. xi.
15 C. H. Edwards, *Transgression and Control: Studies in Roman Immorality*, unpublished PhD dissertation, Cambridge, 1989, p. 3. On the subject of Roman morality, see now her *The Politics of Immorality in Ancient Rome*, Cambridge: Cambridge University Press, 1993.
16 Griffiths, 'Shuttle Meets Moon Unit'.
17 This sentence is adapted from D. M. Halperin, 'Is There a History of Sexuality?', *H & T*, 28 (1989), p. 273.
18 These questions are adapted versions of those asked by Geertz, 'From the Native's Point of View', p. 70.
19 S. J. Greenblatt, *Shakespearean Negotiations: The Circulation of Social Energy in Renaissance England*, Oxford: Clarendon Press, 1988, p. 1. I am appropriating Greenblatt's comments about Renaissance drama.
20 S. Schama, *The Embarrassment of Riches: An Interpretation of Dutch Culture in the Golden Age*, Collins, 1987, p. xi.
21 The relationship between these cultural levels in the life of a sixteenth-century peasant has been fruitfully explored by C. Ginzburg in his *The Cheese and the Worms: The Cosmos of a Sixteenth-Century Miller*, trans. J. and A. Tedeschi, Routledge and Kegan Paul, 1980. See also, his *Myths, Emblems, Clues*, trans. J. and A. Tedeschi, Hutchinson Radius, 1990.
22 The intentionalist language which appears throughout this work is a historical shorthand. When I say, for example, that 'the emperors dreamt up an ideology' I do not, of course, mean that the imperial committee for propaganda convened and came up with a Roman equivalent of a five-year plan; it is merely a means of explaining a highly complex historical process in a simple, though not I hope simplistic, way that is readily understandable to readers and does not bog them down in the tedious nit-picking in which so many academics delight. Most historical terms involve a level of simplification, and I assume that readers are subtle and intelligent enough to take this into account (not that I am out to flatter you into submission, you understand).
23 It should also be pointed out that when studying a mentality it is frequently irrelevant whether particular events really happened or not; what matters is the attitudes that are revealed in the accusation. This does not, of course, mean that historical accuracy can be thrown out of the window, only that at times it is not the focus of the inquiry.
24 This does not mean that a harsh divide should be raised between rural and urban evidence which would confine provincial people to a primitive conceptual cage.

Whilst there is no doubt that the rural population, which included most people in antiquity, had a less sophisticated outlook than their urban contemporaries, it should also be realized that it was not completely cut off from more cosmopolitan attitudes. In fact, a high degree of contact would seem to be the norm, especially amongst the elite who wrote our literary sources. Therefore, although this book is mainly about urban practices, it would be misleading to separate the town from the country in any exclusive way. Both were part of a common Roman culture.

Chapter 2 *Leisure*

1 August. *Confessions* 11.28.
2 J. Wilson, *Politics and Leisure*, Allen and Unwin, 1988, p. 1. The sociological literature on leisure is enormous, and I therefore review only its more important documents. For those interested in more specific leisure literature, the following are sources which I have found useful: R. Meyersohn, 'A Comprehensive Bibliography on Leisure 1900–1958', in E. Larrabee and R. Meyersohn (eds), *Mass Leisure*, Glencoe, Illinois: The Free Press, 1961; R. Crandall et al., 'A General Bibliography of Leisure Publications', *JLR*, 9 (1977), 15–54; P. Bailey, 'Leisure, Culture and the Historian: Reviewing the First Generation of Leisure Historiography in Britain', *JLS*, 8 (1989), 107–27; N. C. A. Parry, 'Sociological Contributions to the Study of Leisure', *JLS*, 2 (1983), 57–81; and A. W. Bacon, 'Leisure and Research: A Critical Review of the Main Concepts Employed in Contemporary Research', *Society and Leisure*, 2 (1972), 83–92. Leisure studies have also been the focus of much interdisciplinary research, of which the more interesting results are J. T. Coppock, 'Geographical Contributions to the Study of Leisure', *JLS*, 1 (1982), 1–27; R. Ingham, 'Psychological Contributions to the Study of Leisure – Part 1', *JLS*, 5 (1986), 255–79; and R. W. Vickerman, 'The Contributions of Economics to the Study of Leisure: A Review', *JLS*, 2 (1983), 345–64.
3 For an excellent overview of the various definitions of leisure, see M. Kaplan, *Leisure: Theory and Policy*, J. Wiley, 1975, esp. pp. 18–19.
4 Wilson, *Politics and Leisure*, p. 2.
5 For an analysis of the Greek concept of *schole*, see J. L. Stocks, '*Schole*', *CQ*, 30 (1936), 177–87. The passages in which *schole* is central to their philosophical thought are Plato, *Theaetetus* 172–7, Aristotle, *Politics* 7 and 8, esp. 7.13.8–22, and *Nicomachean Ethics* 10. For the place in Roman thought of this philosophical way of thinking about leisure, see J.-M. André, *L'Otium dans la Vie Morale et Intellectuelle Romaine*, Paris: Presses Universitaires de France, 1966.
6 S. DeGrazia, *Of Time, Work, and Leisure*, New York: The Twentieth Century Fund, 1962, p. 14.
7 T. L. Goodale and G. C. Godbey, *The Evolution of Leisure: Historical and Philosophical Perspectives*, State College, PA: Venture, 1988, p. xiii.
8 Goodale and Godbey, *The Evolution of Leisure*, p. xiv.
9 See esp., J. Horne, D. Jary, and A. Tomlinson (eds), *Sport, Leisure and Social Relations*, Routledge and Kegan Paul, 1987, p. 3.
10 See esp., J. Pieper, *Leisure the Basis of Culture*, New York: New American Library, 1963 (first published 1952).

11 It might be useful for those especially interested in this area if I briefly discuss some of the other main contributors to the leisure debate. DeGrazia, in his highly influential work on the subject, attempted to combine the qualitative and quantitative approaches by differentiating between work, free time, and leisure, whilst simultaneously imposing an idealistic conception of leisure:

> Work is the antonym of free time. But not of leisure. Leisure and free time live in two different worlds. We have got into the habit of thinking them the same. Anybody can have free time. Free time is a realizable idea of democracy. Leisure is not fully realizable, and hence an ideal not alone an idea. Free time refers to a special way of calculating a special kind of time. Leisure refers to a state of being, a condition of man, which few desire and fewer achieve. (*Of Time, Work, and Leisure*, pp. 7–8)

The French sociologist, Dumazedier, defined leisure in a way that leaned towards the idealistic, though it had a far lower level of prescription than that of DeGrazia:

> Leisure is activity – apart from the obligations of work, family, and society – to which the individual turns at will, for either relaxation, diversion, or broadening his knowledge and his spontaneous social participation, the free exercise of his creative capacity. (*Toward a Society of Leisure*, Collier-Macmillan, 1967, pp. 16–17)

Leisure is perceived as being a style of behaviour, which may occur in any activity outside of obligations, rather than a definite category. Dumazedier could then establish a typology of leisure activities, ranging from the physical and practical to the social, artistic, and intellectual. To choose one's leisure is to choose one's life. Incidentally, the International Study Group on Leisure and Social Sciences adopted a revised version of this definition (quoted in I. Cosgrove and R. Jackson, *The Geography of Recreation and Leisure*, Hutchinson University Library, 1972, p. 13): 'Leisure consists of a number of occupations in which the individual may indulge of his own free will – either to rest, to amuse himself, to add to his knowledge and improve his skills disinterestedly, or to increase his voluntary participation in the life of the community – after discharging his professional, family and social duties.'

Kelly has contributed much to the leisure debate, and has offered several theories in his works. They are greatly influenced by the humanistic position, but attempt to reduce leisure to a single freedom. One definition is that, 'leisure is activity that is chosen primarily for its own sake' (J. R. Kelly, *Leisure Identities and Interactions*, Allen and Unwin, 1983, p. 15); another more recent one is that, 'leisure is the freedom to be' (J. R. Kelly, *Freedom To Be: A New Sociology of Leisure*, New York: Macmillan, 1987, p. 238). Though simple and easily comprehended, both are highly problematic. If leisure is to be seen as autotelic activity it becomes possible to classify any work as leisure, provided that the workers perceive that their primary reason for undertaking their tasks is intrinsic reward. It does not seem satisfactory for a definition of one concept to encompass its polar opposite. Similarly, if leisure is the freedom to be, not only are there the problems as to how we are to gauge it without recourse to moralizing about what constitutes 'real' existence, but there is the fact that self-actualization of this kind is also possible in other activities, such as family and work.

Roberts avoided these problems by delineating leisure as 'relatively self-determined non-work activity' (K. Roberts, *Contemporary Society and the Growth of Leisure*, Longman, 1978, p. 3). This is a far more neutral definition, and one which has some applicability to the ancient world. He neatly side-steps the problems of how free a person is to choose by incorporating the concept of relativity, whilst avoiding the challenges posed by Kelly's definitions based upon experience only. However, it is not clear that what has been defined can actually be discerned as leisure. For if leisure comes to mean everything outside work which an individual decides to do, it covers an enormous array of activities, from religion to household routines. Moreover, it is not obvious what is meant by 'non-work', and by fastening leisure to work in this way, Roberts has, in effect, said only that leisure is not work and vice versa. Thus, the only way in which we can discover what leisure is is to discover what work is, and we are back to square one.

12 B. B. Linder, *The Harried Leisure Class*, Columbia University Press, 1970, p. 16.
13 T. Veblen, *The Theory of the Leisure Class*, Unwin Books, 1970 (first published 1898).
14 As N. Elias and E. Dunning point out: 'In the present sociological literature, one can notice a tendency to regard leisure merely as an adjunct to work' (*Quest for Excitement: Sport and Leisure in the Civilizing Process*, Oxford: Basil Blackwell, 1986, p. 91).
15 A. Giddens, 'Notes on the Concepts of Play and Leisure', *The Sociological Review*, ns 12 (1964), 73–89.
16 On the problems of residual definitions see, for example, J. T. Haworth and M. A. Smith, *Work and Leisure*, Lepus Books, 1975.
17 B. M. Berger, 'The Sociology of Leisure', in E. O. Smigel (ed.), *Work and Leisure*, New Haven, Connecticut: College and University Press, 1963, p. 29.
18 C. Rojek *Leisure for Leisure: Critical Essays*, Basingstoke: Macmillan Press, 1989, p. 1.
19 Ibid. p. 9.
20 Ibid. p. 203.
21 S. Parker, *Leisure and Work*, Allen and Unwin, 1983, p. 21. For a discussion of the ways in which work and leisure are closely intertwined in primitive societies, and still partially overlapping in pre-industrial ones, see K. Thomas, 'Work and Leisure in Pre-Industrial Society', *P & P*, 29 (1964), 50–66.
22 For this view, see M. A. Smith, S. Porter, and C. S. Smith (eds), *Leisure and Society in Britain*, Allen Lane, 1973, esp. p. 1.
23 For an expansion of this position, see C. N. Bull, 'Comparative Methods in Leisure Research', *Society and Leisure*, 2 (1972), 93–104.
24 Kaplan, *Leisure: Theory and Policy*, p. 26.
25 Wilson, *Politics and Leisure*, p. 4.
26 The more important examples are discussed below, but it has been a near orthodoxy in leisure studies. See for example, E. Shorter, 'Towards a History of La Vie Intime', in M. R. Marrus (ed.), *The Emergence of Leisure*, New York: Harper and

Row, 1974, p. 38 (leisure is a 'modern phenomenon'); and T. M. Kando, *Leisure and Popular Culture in Transition*, St Louis, Missouri: C. V. Mosby, 1975, p. xi ('leisure is a modern sociological problem').

27 J. Dumazedier, *Sociology of Leisure*, Oxford: Elsevier, 1974, pp. 13 and 14.
28 Ibid. p. 14.
29 Marrus, *The Emergence of Leisure*, p. 6.
30 DeGrazia, 'Of Time, Work, and Leisure', in Marrus, *The Emergence of Leisure*, p. 79.
31 H. Cunningham, *Leisure in the Industrial Revolution c.1780–c.1880*, Croom Helm, 1980, p. 57.
32 Marrus, *The Emergence of Leisure*, p. 7. A similar view is also expressed by Touraine: 'the question of leisure activities arises as soon as the members of a society come under cultural influences that are no longer connected with the organized activities of a concrete socioeconomic group. As a result, these cultural experiences are no longer understandable on the basis of the individual's professional and social experience' ('Leisure Activities and Social Participation', in Marrus, *The Emergence of Leisure*, p. 102). This is a dangerous position. Not only is it highly questionable whether we are ever free from social experience, but this view also tends to reduce leisure to a level of individual freedom, separated from the rest of life.
33 In fact, Dumazedier disagrees with him, but only because he allows any leisure to the pre-industrial world at all. He is 'not convinced that the *idleness* of philosophers in ancient Greece . . . can be described as leisure', and he prefers to see it as merely a substitute for work (*Sociology of Leisure*, p. 15).
34 Marrus, *The Emergence of Leisure*, p. 5. There has been general agreement with this position. Veal states that, 'for the vast majority of the world's inhabitants leisure has not been a significant phenomenon, let alone a problem'; but, he continues, 'minorities such as members of royal or aristocratic families and the merely wealthy have frequently enjoyed lives of leisure; they have been faced with decisions about what to do with their leisure time . . . and there is the historical quirk of certain periods in the history of Rome when its citizens are said to have enjoyed no less than 175 days' holiday a year' (A. J. Veal, *Leisure and the Future*, Allen and Unwin, 1987, p. 1). This view is as rare as it is simplistic. There is more to leisure than holidays and economic position, but at least Veal opens the door for a non-elite pre-industrial form of leisure.
35 See K. Roberts, *Leisure*, Longmans, 1970, pp. 41–62.
36 M. Featherstone, 'Leisure, Symbolic Power and the Life Course', in Horne, Jary, and Tomlinson, *Sport, Leisure and Social Relations*, p. 113.

Chapter 3 *Definitions*

1 C. Geertz, 'Religion as a cultural system', in his *The Interpretation of Cultures*, p. 90. His definition of religion is: 'a religion is a system of symbols which acts to establish powerful, pervasive, and long-lasting moods and motivations in men by formulating conceptions of a general order of existence and clothing these conceptions with such an aura of factuality that the moods and motivations seem uniquely realistic.'

2 A point, of course, which Foucault made throughout his *The History of Sexuality*, 3 vols, New York: Pantheon, 1985.

3 I have refrained from reviewing the literature on the subject of work both for reasons of space, and because this is a book about leisure. However, much sociological work has treated the two concepts simultaneously, and there is no doubt that for many in the modern world it is difficult to conceive of the two separately. The following are therefore suggested as starting places for those interested in acquiring a deeper knowledge of this the most laborious of literatures: N. Anderson, *Work and Leisure,* Routledge and Kegan Paul, 1961; DeGrazia, *Of Time, Work, and Leisure*; Parker, *Leisure and Work.*

4 As with work, I will not attempt to review the research on play, but will give pointers to those who are interested in digging deeper. The two primary works are those of J. Huizinga, *Homo Ludens,* Routledge and Kegan Paul, 1949, and R. Caillois, *Man, Play, and Games,* trans. M. Barank, Thames and Hudson, 1962. More recent works that I have found useful are D. F. Lancy and B. A. Tindall (eds), *The Study of Play: Problems and Prospects,* West Point, New York: Leisure Press, 1977; P. Stevens (ed.), *Studies in the Anthropology of Play,* West Point, New York: Leisure Press, 1977; and M. A. Salter (ed.), *Play: Anthropological Perspectives,* West Point, New York: Leisure Press, 1978.

Chapter 4 *Leisure and* Otium

1 P. Veyne (ed.), *A History of Private Life,* trans. A. Goldhammer, Cambridge, Mass.: Bellknap Press of Harvard University, 1987, pp. 118–19. The original French reads: 'Et pourtant, si nous étions sincères, nous trouverions en nous une des clés de cette énigme. Oui, le travail nous semble respectable et nous n'oserions faire profession d'oisiveté, n'empêche que nous sommes très sensibles aux distinctions de classe et, sans nous l'avouer, tenons les ouvriers ou les boutiquiers pour gens de peu: nous ne voudrions pas que nous et nos enfants retombions à leur niveau, tout en ayant un peu honte de ce sentiment.'

2 Matters have also not been helped by the fact that the 'Classics mentality' sometimes seems to have the character of a dodo cross-bred with an ostrich: not only lifeless, but wilfully oblivious to the world around it.

3 Veyne has attempted to break free from the bonds of elite conceptions. He rightly points out that 'historians have too often studied the ancients' ideas about labor as though these were doctrines elaborated by jurists and philosophers. In fact, they were confused collective notions, as well as class ideologies' (ibid. p. 121). He adds that 'workers were reviled not because they worked, but because they belonged to this inferior class . . . Thus, "the ancients' ideas about labor" were not so much ideas as evaluations, positive for the powerful, negative for the humble' (ibid. p. 122). Veyne even includes a section on the definition of *labor*; he points out that 'in this society no one was a worker; all social relations were conceived in terms of friendship or authority' (ibid. p. 125). But no definition is forthcoming; he is content to reject ancient practice as being what we moderns think of as work. Nor does Veyne attempt a definition of leisure. He notes that 'in a period in which

idleness was an ideal, no contrast was drawn between pleasure and work' (ibid. p. 201). The closest he comes to analysing *otium* is in his discussion of the public games: 'Public spectacles were not dependent on individual tastes (as opposed to policy), nor were they leisure activities (as opposed to more serious and laborious parts of life)' (ibid). He seems to be labouring under the same romantic misconceptions as Marrus was seen to be in the previous chapter.

Most other classicists have restricted their attention to the elite conception of *otium* largely because the term itself has not seemed problematic. To illustrate this, perhaps a little unfairly, I would refer the reader to the indexes of the principal classical works of relevance: H. A. Harris, *Sport in Greece and Rome*, Thames and Hudson, 1972, has no entry under leisure or *otium*; likewise, H. H. Scullard, *Festivals and Ceremonies of the Roman Republic*, Thames and Hudson, 1981, has no entries; U. E. Paoli, *Rome: Its People, Life and Customs*, trans. R. D. Macnaughten, Longmans, 1963, does one better. His single entry under *otium* reads: 'What the Romans called *otium*, the time left free from the conduct of public affairs (*negotia*), was a laborious leisure in which many rolls of paper were annually consumed,' and so it is clear that his concern is only with the elite. J. Carcopino, *Daily Life in Ancient Rome*, trans. E. O. Lorimer, Routledge and Kegan Paul, 1973 (first published 1941), contains a section entitled 'The Employment of Leisure', pp. 206–12, but this is purely descriptive. J. P. V. D. Balsdon, *Life and Leisure in Ancient Rome*, Bodley Head, 1969, p. 15, claims that his book is an attempt 'to look at the Romans and their manner of living in the way in which sociologists and others are now concerning themselves with the significance of work and with the employment of leisure in the lives of present-day men and women'. Yet his entry under leisure reads see *otium*, which suggests that he was unaware of the conceptual problems involved. Moreover, for him the life of *otium* was 'life in the shade' (p. 136) an elite life of the pursuit of high culture, literature, and philosophy. He does concede (p. 141) that *otium* could have another dimension: 'Life in the shade could, of course, be a very discreditable existence indeed if it was devoted to nothing better than self-indulgence, in particular lust and the satisfaction of the belly.' But in general (p. 146) he considers the leisure of the underemployed reveals that 'frenzied attempts to kill boredom were indications of a neurosis to which the educated man falls victim more easily than the uneducated.' Consequently, his work is mainly a descriptive list of particular activities. Similarly, J. F. Gardner, *Women in Roman Law and Society*, Croom Helm, 1986, in her chapter on 'Women at Work' contains a subsection on 'Leisure and Pleasure', pp. 245–53; but this too is mainly descriptive. Ch. Wirszubski, 'Cicero's Cum Dignitate Otium: A Reconsideration', *JRS*, 44 (1954), p. 1, asks, 'Is *otium* private leisure or public tranquillity?'; and a more complete answer was given by P. Veyne, *Le Pain et Le Cirque: Sociologie Historique d'un Pluralisme Politique*, Paris: Editions du Seuil, 1976. No entries, however, are contained under *otium*, whilst his view of leisure is primarily economic: 'Loisir voulant dire indépendence économique' (p. 121). Finally, but importantly, André, *L'Otium dans la Vie Morale*, contains no entry under 'loisir'. His work is what it says it is: a study of the intellectual ideal of an educated elite.

4 Edwards, *The Politics of Immorality*, p. 24.
5 Cato *Agr.* 76.4.8.

6 Apul. *Met.* 8.7.

7 Gaius *Inst.* 3.156 'money lying idly at home (*otiosam pecuniam domi*)'; cf. *Dig.* 22.1.13.1 '*otiosa pecunia*'.

8 Fron. *Aq.* 16.1.

9 Man. 2.145–148.

10 Ibid. 4.155.

11 Plin. *Ep.* 9.32.

12 Cic. *Agr.* 2.9.

13 Sen. *Ep.* 55.3.

14 Sal. *Cat.* 37.7.

15 Mart. 5.20.

16 Ter. *Ad.* 863ff.

17 Apul. *Met.* 9.11.

18 Ibid. 7.14.

19 All of these examples are taken from Plin. *Nat.* 7.180–6.

20 Plin. *Ep.* 9.6.4.

21 Sal. *Cat.* 4.1.4.

22 Gell. 11.3.1.

23 Sen. *Ep.* 87.19.

24 Cic. *Rep.* 1.52.

25 Wirszubski, 'Cicero's Cum Dignitate Otium'.

26 André, *L'Otium dans la Vie Morale*, p. 276.

27 Sen. *Ep.* 16.3.

28 Cic. *Tusc.* 3.83.

29 Cic. *Off.* 3.6.

30 Plin. *Ep.* 1.3.3.

31 J. Matthews, *Western Aristocracies and Imperial Court AD 364–425*, Oxford: Clarendon Press, 1975, pp. 1–31. It is, of course, possible that the elite of the late republic and early empire spent more time in office, but it would still seem likely that for most long periods of *otium* were frequent, if not the norm.

32 Cic. *Planc.* 66.

33 Cic. *Off.* 1.150.

34 Sen. *Ep.* 31.4–5.

35 Ibid. 31.7.

36 Sen. *Dial.* 1.5.4.

37 Ovid *Pont.* 1.4.21–2.

38 V. Max. 8.8.1.

39 Stat. *Silv.* 4.4.33–4.

40 P. Oxy. 4.725.35ff. Provision is made for twenty days' holiday.

41 Ovid *Pont.* 1.5.43–4 '*non sum, qui segnia ducam otia: mors nobis tempus habetur iners*'.

42 Hor. *S.* 2.3.14–15.

43 Plin. *Ep.* 3.1.12.

44 Cic. *Tusc.* 5.78.

45 Catul. 51.13–16.

46 Sen. *Ep.* 78.26.

47 Sen. *Con.* 1.pr.3.
48 Cels. 1.1.1; cf. Ovid *Pont.* 1.5.5–6 'You see how leisure corrupts an idle body, how water acquires a taint unless it is in motion.'
49 Luc. 4.704.
50 [Quint.] *Decl.* 19.9; translation from L. A. Sussman, *The Major Declamations Ascribed to Quintilian: A Translation*, New York: P. Lang, 1987. This is, of course, a rhetorical exercise, but as such it represents an exaggeration of a widely held view.
51 Gell. 19.10.12 quoting Ennius' *Iphigenia*.
52 Plin. *Pan.* 82.8–9.
53 Sal. *Cat.* 11.5.
54 Tac. *Ann.* 1.35.
55 Sen. *Ep.* 56.9.
56 Fron. *Str.* 4.1.15.
57 Col. 12.pr.9.
58 Vell. 2.88.2.
59 Plin. *Ep.* 7.24.4–5.
60 Stat. *Silv.* 3.5.60–1.
61 I have dealt only very briefly here with the subject of women's leisure, since it requires a more complete analysis than space allows. Those wishing to pursue this line of inquiry should see Gardner, *Women in Roman Law and Society*, esp. pp. 245–53 on 'Leisure and Pleasure'. For modern comparative material, see R. Deem, 'Women, Leisure and Inequality', *JLS*, 1 (1982), 29–46; S. M. Shaw, 'Gender and Leisure: Inequality in the Distribution of Leisure Time', *JLR*, 17 (1985), 266–82; and J. Hargreaves, 'The Promise and Problems of Women's Leisure and Sport', in Rojek, *Leisure for Leisure*, pp. 130–49.
62 Amm.Marc. 14.6.25.
63 Sen. *Dial.* 7.7.4.
64 Ibid. 7.3.
65 Sen. *Ep.* 72.7.
66 Ibid. 98.1.
67 Ibid. 14.9.
68 Livy 2.28.5 '*otio lascivire plebem*'.
69 Sal. *Jug.* 41.1–41.6.
70 Plin. *Nat.* 36.75.
71 For this view of *otium* as the struggle for the 'good life' through the valleys of sloth, see esp. Seneca's *de Otio*. He, naturally, concludes that it is a struggle worth undertaking, but it is as well to be aware of the risks, for there will be casualties: 'If anyone says that the best life of all is to sail the sea, and then adds that I must not sail upon a sea where shipwrecks are a common occurrence and there are often sudden storms that sweep the helmsmen in an adverse direction, I conclude that this man, although he lauds navigation, really forbids me to launch my ship' (*Dial.* 8.8.4).
72 On the whole issue of luxury, see J. Sekora, *Luxury: The Concept in Western Thought, Eden to Smollett*, Baltimore, Maryland: Johns Hopkins University Press, 1977.

73 For an introduction to the hierarchical nature of Roman society, see esp. P. D. A. Garnsey and R. Saller, *The Roman Empire: Economy, Society and Culture*, Duckworth, 1987, chs. 6–8.

Chapter 5 *Blood, Sweat, and Charioteers: The Imperial Games*

1 C. Geertz, 'Deep Play: Notes on the Balinese Cockfight', in his *The Interpretation of Cultures*, pp. 412–53.
2 Gell. 6.3.31.
3 This notoriety of the games has resulted in numerous books, both academic and popular. The best introduction is still that by L. Friedländer in his *Roman Life and Manners under the Early Empire*, 4 vols, trans. J. H. Freese, L. A. Magnus, and S. B. Gough, Routledge and Kegan Paul, 1908–13 (first published 1863), which provides basic details and information on all of the activities under discussion in this chapter. Of more recent interest is that by M. Clavel-Lévêque, *L'Empire en Jeux: Espace Symbolique et Pratique Sociale dans le Monde Romain*, Paris: Editions du Centre National de la Recherche Scientifique, 1984. Other works of interest are those by T. Wiedemann, *Emperors and Gladiators*, Routledge, 1992; C. A. Barton, *The Sorrows of the Ancient Romans: The Gladiator and the Monster*, Princeton, New Jersey: Princeton University Press, 1993; K. Hopkins, 'Murderous Games', in his *Death and Renewal*, pp. 1–30; M. Wistrand, *Entertainment and Violence in Ancient Rome: The Attitudes of Roman Writers of the First Century AD*, Gothenburg: Acta Universitatis Gothoburgensis, 1992; M. Grant, *Gladiators*, Weidenfeld and Nicolson, 1967; J. Pearson, *Arena: The Story of the Colosseum*, Thames and Hudson, 1973; R. Auguet, *Cruelty and Civilization: The Roman Games*, Allen and Unwin, 1972; M. B. Poliakoff, *Combat Sports in the Ancient World: Competition, Violence and Culture*, Yale University Press, 1987; V. Olivova, *Sports and Games in the Ancient World*, trans, D. Orpington, Orbis, 1984; K. Welch, 'Roman Amphitheatres Revived', *JRA*, 4 (1991), 272–81; A. Guttman, 'Chariot Races, Tournaments and the Civilizing Process', in E. Dunning and C. Rojek (eds), *Sport and Leisure in the Civilizing Process: Critique and Counter-Critique*, Macmillan, 1992, pp. 137–60; and a comparison with the modern television programme, 'Gladiators', by P. Jones, 'Lives, Loves and Deaths of the REAL Gladiators', in *Daily Mail*, 7 Nov. 1992, pp. 22–3. On the staging of executions as episodes from mythology, see K. M. Coleman, 'Fatal Charades: Roman Executions Staged as Mythological Enactments', *JRS*, 80 (1990), 44–73. On horse-racing, see A. Cameron's two works, *Porphyrius the Charioteer*, Oxford: Clarendon Press, 1973, and *Circus Factions: Blues and Greens at Rome and Byzantium*, Oxford: Clarendon Press, 1976; also, A. Hyland, *Equus: The Horse in the Roman World*, Batsford, 1990; and J. H. Humphrey, *Roman Circuses: Arenas for Chariot Racing*, Batsford, 1986. On the *venationes*, see J. M. C. Toynbee, 'Beasts and their Names in the Roman Empire', *PBSR*, 16 (1948), 24–37; and G. Jennison, *Animals for Show and Pleasure in Ancient Rome*, Manchester: Manchester University Press, 1937. On sport in general, see A. J. Butler, *Sport in Classic Times*, E. Benn, 1930; and H. A. Harris, *Sport in Greece and Rome*, Thames and Hudson, 1972.

4 Cic. *Sest.* 124.
5 Epict. *Ench.* 29.3.
6 Suet. *Tib.* 37.2–3.
7 Friedländer, *Roman Life and Manners*, vol. 2, pp. 39–40, based on: Lact. *Div.Inst.* 6.20 and 32; Sen. *Ep.* 83.7; Juv. 11.197; and Rutilius Namatianus *De Reditu Suo* 201.
8 Epict. *Diss.* 1.11.27.
9 See J. G. Gager (ed.), *Curse Tablets and Binding Spells from the Ancient World*, Oxford: Oxford University Press, 1992, pp. 42–77.
10 Hopkins, *Death and Renewal*, p. 29.
11 See ibid. pp. 21–3. On the appeal of charioteers and athletes, see Friedländer, *Roman Life and Manners*, vol. 2, pp. 245–7.
12 Apul. *Met.* 2.15.
13 Hist.Aug. *M.Aurel.* 19.2–6.
14 Artem. 1.5.
15 Ibid. 2.32 trans. R. J. White, *Artemidorus: The Interpretation of Dreams*, Park Ridge, New Jersey: Noyes Press, 1975.
16 Ibid. 4.65 trans. White.
17 Galen *On the Therapeutic Method* 3.5.
18 *Passio SS Felicitatis et Perpetuae* 18.
19 Mart. 10.25; 8.30.
20 Suet. *Nero* 12.2; Mart. *Spect.* 5.
21 Grant, *Gladiators*, p. 8.
22 Jones, 'The Lives, Loves and Deaths of the REAL Gladiators', p. 22.
23 Pearson, *Arena*, p. 153.
24 Welch, 'Roman Amphitheatres Revived', p. 280.
25 Hopkins, *Death and Renewal*, p. 27.
26 Ibid.
27 Ibid. pp. 27–8.
28 Welch, 'Roman Amphitheatres Revived', p. 280.
29 Part of this paragraph is adapted from G. Marvin, *Bullfight*, Oxford: Basil Blackwell, 1988, p. 128, itself a reworking of J. R. Corbin and M. P. Corbin, *Urbane Thought: Culture and Class in an Andalusian City*, Aldershot: Gower Publishing, 1987, although the primary source is Geertz's 'Deep Play'. I am greatly indebted to Marvin's excellent work throughout this chapter.
30 Sen. *Ep.* 22.1.
31 Cic. *de Orat.* 2.317.
32 Plin. *Nat.* 11.144.
33 Sen. *Dial.* 1.3.4.
34 Quint. *Inst.* 2.12.2.
35 Sen. *Dial.* 3.11.2.
36 Cic. *de Orat.* 2.84.
37 Cic. *Orat.* 228.
38 [Quint.] *Decl.* 9.12 '*Quod cotidiana pugnae meditatione tamdiu mori dedici?*'
39 Cic. *Sest.* 80.
40 Cic. *Rosc.* 33.
41 Cic. *Tusc.* 2.41.

42 Sen. *Ep.* 70.20.

43 Ibid. 70.23.

44 Ibid. 70.26.

45 Cic. *Mil.* 92.

46 Sen. *Ep.* 30.8.

47 Sen. *Con.* 9.6.1 and 2.

48 Ibid.

49 On this idea, see J. Urry, *The Tourist Gaze: Leisure and Travel in Contemporary Societies*, Sage, 1990.

50 M. Foucault, *The Birth of the Clinic: An Archaeology of Medical Perception*, trans. A. Sheridan, Tavistock, 1976, p. 89.

51 [Quint.] *Decl.* 9.

52 Ibid. 9.9.

53 Ibid. 9.22.

54 For a fuller analysis of the importance of gambling in the games, see ch. 8 below.

55 Cic. *Rep.* 2.68. fr.5.

56 Artem. 4.56.

57 Plin. *Nat.* 8.160.

58 Sil. 16.303–456.

59 Lib. *Ep.* 199.9.

60 Cic. *Fam.* 7.1.

61 The food was designed to develop muscle, Tac. *Hist.* 2.88, but it was considered to be of poor quality by Juv. 11.20. As [Quint.] *Decl.* 9.5, puts it, 'My gladiator's diet, more obnoxious than any starvation, was fattening up my hated physical body.'

62 Plin. *Nat.* 26.135.

63 *CIL* 6.631.

64 Gell. 12.5.13.

65 Plin. *Nat.* 28.4.

66 Ibid. 35.52.

67 On the notion of *virtus*, see the index entry in D. Earl, *The Moral and Political Tradition of Rome*, Thames and Hudson, 1967.

68 Edwards, *The Politics of Immorality*, p. 20.

69 Tac. *Ann.* 15.48; cf. *Hist.* 1.49.

70 Ibid. 4.17.

71 Ibid. 3.60, 1.15, *Ann.* 6.22, 4.39, 15.5 and 48, *Ger.* 30.2.

72 Vitr. 6.pr.3.

73 Tac. *Hist.* 2.69, 4.73, *Ag.* 33.2.

74 Tac. *Ann.* 15.16.

75 Vitr. 6.pr.2.

76 Sen. *Ben.* 7.1.4 quoting Demetrius the Cynic.

77 Cic. *Tusc.* 2.11.

78 On these concepts, see esp. G. Taylor, *Pride, Shame, and Guilt: Emotions of Self-assessment*, Oxford: Clarendon Press, 1985; and J. G. Peristiany, *Honour and Shame: The Values of Mediterranean Society*, Weidenfeld and Nicolson, 1966.

79 Cyprian, *De Spectaculis* 6.

80 Sen. *Dial.* 1.2.8.

81 '*Si nos coleos haberemus*' was a popular Roman saying; see the entry under '*coleus*' in A. Otto, *Sprichwörter und sprichwörtliche Redensarten der Römer*, Hildesheim: G. Olms, 1968. Cf. Mart. 7.62.6; 12.83.2 *omnes quem modo colei timebant.*

82 This idea is appropriated from Schama's description of Dutch 'water-torture' in the opening chapter of *The Embarrassment of Riches.*

83 For an analysis of the different factors at work in play, see Caillois, *Man, Play, and Games.*

84 These ideas are adapted from P. Brown, 'Sorcery, Demons and the Rise of Christianity: From Late Antiquity into the Middle Ages', in his *Religion and Society in the Age of Saint Augustine*, Faber and Faber, 1972, pp. 119–46.

85 Cic. *Fam.* 7.1.3.

86 Cic. *Tusc.* 2.41.

87 Sen. *Ep.* 7.2ff. trans. Hopkins in his *Death and Renewal*, p. 3.

88 H. Chadwick, 'Augustine and Almachius', *Collection des Etudes Augustiniennes*, Série Antiquité 132 (1992), p. 301. This article also contains basic information on the attitudes of Christians towards the games in the later empire: 'From the Christians criticism was unqualified, whether because of the idolatrous ceremonies associated with the games or because of the inhuman cruelty and the brutalisation of spectators.'

89 Wistrand, *Entertainment and Violence*, pp. 17–18.

90 Sen. *Ep.* 7.2.

91 Hopkins, *Death and Renewal*, pp. 20–1.

92 See, for example: Tac. *Dial.* 10.5; Quint. *Inst.* 2.8.3–4; Plin. *Ep.* 1.20.6; and Sen. *Ep.* 78.16 and 80.2.; on sports in dream interpretation, see Artem. 1.54–63.

93 Suet. *Aug.* 45.2.

94 Ulp. *Dig.* 3.2.4. This was on account of the fact that they competed for the sake of *virtus* (*virtutis enim gratia hoc facere*). This privilege was also extended to the charioteer in the later empire, when his role became more pivotal.

95 Galen, *Exhortation on the Choice of Profession*, 9–11, though Galen had his own axe to grind in that he hated their pseudo-knowledge of the body: see *On Doctors and Gymnasts*, esp. 37 and 46. In Plin. *Nat.* 29.26, 35.168 the gym is immoral as it cultivates the body and not the soul; it also weakens the body for war (Luc. 7.270). The gym was thought by some to be a waste of time (Mart. 7.32). First century AD athletes were generally spoken of disdainfully (Sen. *Ep.* 15.3, 80.2, 88.18; Quint. *Inst.* 12.10.41; Cels. 1.1.3; Plu. *Moralia* 133B–D).

96 The qualities needed by the philosopher were often likened to those possessed by the gladiator; see Barton, *The Sorrows of the Ancient Romans*, pp. 15–21 and 31–4.

Chapter 6 *The Baths*

1 Plin. *Nat.* 26.14.

2 I shall not include a full bathing bibliography as little of it is of interest to the social historian. The best of the recent works are those by J. DeLaine, 'Recent Research on Roman Baths', *JRA*, 1 (1989), 11–32, and 'Roman Baths and Bathing', *JRA*, 6 (1993), 348–58; I. Nielson, *Thermae et Balnea*, Aarhus: Aarhus

University Press, 1990; and F. Yegül, *Baths and Bathing in Classical Antiquity*, Cambridge, Mass.: MIT Press, 1992. A fuller bibliography can be found in the last two of these.

3 Hor. *Ars* 298.
4 DeLaine, 'Recent Research on Roman Baths', p. 11.
5 Nielson, *Thermae et Balnea*, p. 149.
6 DeLaine, 'Recent Research on Roman Baths', p. 11; cf. Tac. *Ag.* 21.
7 Clem.Al. *Paed.* 3.46.
8 Ter. *Ph.* 339–40.
9 Pl. *Mer.* 127.
10 DeLaine, 'Recent Research on Roman Baths', p. 29.
11 Ibid.
12 A. Scobie, 'Slums, Sanitation, and Mortality in the Roman World', *Klio*, 68 (1986), pp. 431–2.
13 Sen. *Dial.* 7.7.3.
14 Galen *On the Therapeutic Method* 13.597.
15 Sen. *Ep.* 86.12.
16 Col. 1.6.19–20.
17 Mart. 12.70; Sen. *Ep.* 122.6; Plin. *Nat.* 14.139; Pers. 3.98.
18 Plin. *Nat.* 14.140; Col. 1.pr.16; Juv. 6.425–9; Sen. *Ep.* 15.3.
19 Hist.Aug. *Pesc.Nig.* 3.10.
20 Philostr. *V.A.* 1.16.
21 B Shabbath 33b; cf. Abodah Zarah 2b. Quoted on p. 268 by N. R. M. de Lange, 'Jewish Attitudes to the Roman Empire', in P. D. A. Garnsey and C. R. Whittaker (eds), *Imperialism in the Ancient World*, Cambridge: Cambridge University Press, 1978.
22 Clem.Al. *Paed.* 3.46.
23 Philostr. *V.A.* 4.42; cf. Plin. *Nat.* 29.26.
24 Livy 23.18.11–12.
25 Juv. 6.425–33.
26 Yegül, *Baths and Bathing in Classical Antiquity*, p. 42. See, for example, Ovid *Ars* 3.639–40.
27 Mart. 1.96 trans. J. Michie, *Martial: The Epigrams*, Penguin, 1978.
28 Sen. *Nat.* 1.16.1–5.
29 Mart. 11.63.
30 Ibid. 11.75.
31 Hist.Aug. *Hel.* 31.7.
32 Juv. 11.156–7.
33 Mart. 6.56, 10.65, 2.62, 2.29, 3.74; Pers. 4.37–40; Juv. 2.9–13, 8.114, 9.13–15; Suet. *Jul.* 45.2; Quint. *Inst.* 1.6; cf. on women Mart. 6.93.
34 Yegül, *Baths and Bathing in Classical Antiquity*, p. 42.
35 Petr. 27; Lucian *Nigr.* 34.
36 Sen. *Dial.* 10.12.7.
37 Juv. 7.130–1.
38 Clem.Al. *Paed.* 3.47 'the bath should be common, on an equal footing to all who bathe there.'

39 Amm.Marc. 28.4.9.
40 Yegül, *Baths and Bathing in Classical Antiquity*, p. 42.
41 S. L. Dyson, *Community and Society in Roman Italy*, Baltimore, Maryland: Johns Hopkins University Press, 1992, p. 174.
42 Mart. 9.33 trans. Michie.
43 Nielson, *Thermae et Balnea*, p. 13.
44 On social outcasts, see E. Goffman, *Stigma: Notes on the Management of Spoiled Identity*, Englewood Cliffs, New Jersey: Prentice-Hall, 1963.
45 Suet. *Aug.* 94.4.
46 Mart. 7.82. Celsus also describes an operation undertaken to conceal the effects of circumcision, *On the Therapeutic Method* 7.25.
47 Artem. 1.64.
48 Amm.Marc. 28.4.19.
49 N. Joseph, *Uniforms and Non-uniforms: Communication through Clothing*, New York: Greenwood Press, 1986, p. 1.
50 For the various types of dress, see L. M. Wilson, *The Clothing of the Ancient Romans*, Baltimore, Maryland: Johns Hopkins University Press, 1938. On the various regulations, see the entries under 'Toga' in A. Berger, 'Encyclopaedic Dictionary of Roman Law', *Transactions of the American Philosophical Society*, 43 (1953), 333–808. Prostitutes, for example, were legally bound to wear the toga; the wearing of the freedom-cap, the *pilleum*, was common at the Saturnalia, being symbolic of the licence of the season. For dress in the later empire, see *Cod.Theod.* 14.10, 15.7.11–12. For the importance of dress in the interpretation of dreams, see Artemidorus' *Oneirocritica* 2.3–2.5.
51 T. D. Biedelman, 'Some Nuer Notions of Nakedness, Nudity, and Sexuality', *Africa*, 38 (1968), 113–32, p. 115.
52 Ibid. p. 114.
53 Cic. *Brut.* 262.
54 Sen. *Ep.* 76.32. Seneca continues, 'let him strip off even his body' to reveal the pure soul beneath.
55 Suet. *Nero* 53; cf. Cic. *Tusc.* 4.70 quoting Ennius, 'The beginning of shame is to strip before fellow-citizens', and Plu. *Moralia* 274A, which states that it used not to be proper for sons to bathe with their fathers.
56 A. Jefferson, 'Bodymatters: Self and Other in Bakhtin, Sartre and Barthes', in K. Hirschkop and D. Shepherd (eds), *Bakhtin and Cultural Theory*, Manchester: Manchester University Press, 1989, p. 152.
57 Juv. 10.356.
58 CIL 6.15258.
59 On the whole subject of body care, see M. Foucault's difficult but often rewarding book, *The Care of the Self*, vol. 3 of *The History of Sexuality*, trans. R. Hurley, Allen Lane, 1986, esp. part 4, 'The Body', pp. 99–144. This quotation is at p. 100.
60 Ibid. p. 101. On the bath environment generally, disease and its noticeability, and the baths' centrality to treatment in Celsus, see Scobie, 'Slums, Sanitation and Mortality in the Roman World'. On the centrality of baths to medical treatment, see also Plin. *Nat.* 20.178, 20.166, 20.161 and 215, 22.100, 22.137, 22.139, 22.155, and 23.29. Baths partly kept Romans clean but, 'It seems probable, then, that

Roman Public Baths might not have been as sanitary as is commonly assumed, and that the risks of becoming infected with a wide range of contagious and infectious diseases in such establishments would have been great' (Scobie, p. 426). It would, however, still seem probable that the baths were cleaner than the rest of Rome (Scobie, pp. 407–24).

61 Celsus *On the Therapeutic Method* 1.1.2.

62 Foucault, *The Care of the Self*, p. 102.

63 P. Brown, *The Body and Society: Men, Women and Sexual Renunciation in Early Christianity*, Faber and Faber, 1988, p. 10.

64 Ibid.

65 Juv. 6.375 trans. P. Green, *Juvenal: The Sixteen Satires*, Penguin, 1967.

66 For a good introduction to the social nature of the body, see B. S. Turner, *The Body and Society*, Oxford: Basil Blackwell, 1984.

67 Brown, *The Body and Society*, p. 11.

68 Ibid. p. 11. This section on the concept of maleness in relation to the body is dealt with more completely by Brown, ch. 1 'Body and City', pp. 5–32. These quotations are at p. 11. On the matter of physiognomy, see Edwards, *Transgression and Control*, ch. 3, 'Mollitia: reading the body', pp. 99–140.

69 F. Dupont, *La Vie Quotidienne du Citoyen Romain sous la République, 509–27 Av.J.-C.*, Paris: Hachette, 1989, p. 272.

70 Sen. *Ep.* 52.12; cf. Macr. 2.4.12.

71 Mart. 12.19.

72 Quint. *Inst.* 1.6.44.

73 This is an adaptation of Schama's description of the Dutch in their golden age, in his *The Embarrassment of Riches*, p. 380.

74 This point is made, in part, by E. W. Merton, in her *Bäder und Badegepflogenheiten in der Darstellung der Historia Augusta*, Bonn: Habelt, 1983. Delaine, 'Recent Research on Roman Baths', p. 28, discusses this: 'Her (Merton's) argument is that the attribution of certain acts to certain emperors reflects 4th c. moral codes rather than historical fact.' However, the twin features of the moral process are not discussed by either author, nor the reasons for the special importance of bath-house acts. On the 'good' emperors' restoring and supporting baths, see Hist.Aug. *Alex.Sev.* 39.3 and 24.5 and *Tac.* 10.4; on free entry, see *Pius* 7.6; on banning mixed bathing, see *Alex.Sev.* 24.2; on their bathing in cool water, see ibid. 30.4; with ordinary people, see ibid. 42.1, Suet. *Titus* 8.2, Hist.Aug. *Hadr.* 17.5. The topos could also be turned on its head, so that the emperor Caracalla's unpopularity was such that he was hated by the people even though he gave them clothes and built them splendid baths, *Sept.Sev.* 21.11. On the frequency of 'bad' emperors' bathing, see *Comm.Ant.* 11.5, *Tyr.Trig.* 29.1; on their hot and perfumed baths, see Suet. *Cal.* 37.1, Philostr. *V.A.* 5.29; on their allowing mixed bathing, see Hist.Aug. *Hel.* 31.7; and on their new excesses, see Suet. *Nero* 31.2, Plin. *Nat.* 11.238, Hist.Aug. *Hel.* 30.7. The hotness of their baths was especially galling in the light of the fact that it was a hot bath which was associated with the great elite suicides of Roman history. See, for example, Tac. *Ann.* 14.64.

75 Ibid. p. 40.

76 Artem. 1.64 trans. White.

Chapter 7 *Goodbye to* Gravitas*: Popular Culture and Leisure*

1 See Ginzburg, *The Cheese and the Worms*; also, J. Sharpe, 'History from Below', in Burke, *New Perspectives*, pp. 24–41.
2 W. H. Beik, 'Searching for Popular Culture in Early Modern France', *JMH*, 49 (1977), p. 266.
3 P. Burke, *Popular Culture in Early Modern Europe*, Temple Smith, 1978, prologue. For Gramsci's writings on popular culture, see D. Forgacs and G. Nowell (eds), *A. Gramsci: Selections from Cultural Writings*, trans. W. Boelhower, Lawrence and Wishart, 1985, and W. L. Adamson, *Hegemony and Revolution: A Study of Antonio Gramsci's Political and Cultural Theory*, Berkeley, California: University of California Press, 1980.
4 T. Brennan, *Public Drinking and Popular Culture in Eighteenth-Century Paris*, Princeton, New Jersey: Princeton University Press, p. 6, quoting Darnton, *The Great Cat Massacre*, pp. 4–6, 77–8.
5 Ginzburg, *The Cheese and the Worms*, pp. xiii–xviii.
6 Ibid. p. xxiv.
7 R. Chartier, 'Culture as Appropriation: Popular Culture Uses in Early Modern France', in S. L. Kaplan (ed.), *Understanding Popular Culture: Europe from the Middle Ages to the Nineteenth Century*, New York: Mouton, 1984, p. 234.
8 Cic. *Pis.* 13 '*ganearum nidore atque fumo*'.
9 Juv. 3.294 '*vervecis labra*'; 11.81 '*vulva*', cf. Hor. *Ep.* 1.15.41 '*nil vulva pulchrius ampla*'.
10 Plin. *Nat.* 9.154.
11 For the different types of bar, see G. Hermansen, *Ostia: Aspects of Roman City Life*, Edmonton, Alberta: University of Alberta Press, 1981, pp. 125–205, 'community centres and trouble spots'; and T. Kleberg, *Hôtels, Restaurants et Cabarets dans L'Antiquité Romaine*, Uppsala: Almqvist and Wiksells, 1957. Also, Gager, *Curse Tablets and Binding Spells from the Ancient World*, pp. 151–74; and L. Casson, *Travel in the Ancient World*, Allen and Unwin, 1974, pp. 197–218. I would like to thank Justin Meggitt for his help in this area; see his 'Meat Consumption and Social Conflict in Corinth', *JThS*, ns 45 (1994), 137–41.
12 On prostitution and sexual dancing, see, for example, Catul. 37.1 and Vergiliana *Copa* 1–4; Ulp. *Dig.* 23.2.43.pr. 'We would say that a woman openly practises prostitution not just where she does so in brothels but also where she is used to showing she has no shame in taverns or other places'; 23.2.43.9 'Where one woman keeps an inn and employs others as prostitutes (as many often do on the pretext that they are servants), she must be classed as a procuress.'
13 Cf. Sen. *Dial.* 7.7.3; cf. Juv. 8.158.
14 Pl. *Poen.* 831–5.
15 Juv. 8.171–6.
16 Artem. 3.57 trans. White.
17 *Cod.Just.* 5.27.1, 8.5.7, 9.9.29.28; Hor. *S.* 1.1.29, 1.5.4; Mart. 3.57.
18 See, for example, Cic. *Pis.* 13, *Phil.* 2.77.
19 Sen. *Ep.* 51.4.

20 Petr. 140.
21 See Cic. *Arch.* 10; Livy 24.24.3; Cic. *Off.* 1.150.
22 Artem. 2.69 trans. White.
23 Tertullian *De Spectaculis* 21; cf. Quint. *Inst.* 1.10.31 'the music which I desire to see taught is not our modern music, which has been emasculated by the lascivious melodies of our effeminate stage and has to no small extent destroyed such manly vigour as we still possessed.'
24 Cic. *Catil.* 2.9.
25 Cic. *Planc.* 30.
26 Wistrand, *Entertainment and Violence*, p. 69.
27 Ibid. p. 32.
28 Ovid *Fast.* 4.946; cf. 5.347 on prostitutes at the Floralia.
29 Cato *Agr.* 57.
30 Mart. 5.84.
31 Lucian *Sat.* 1.2.
32 E. J. Gowers, *The Representation of Food in Roman Literature*, unpublished PhD dissertation, Cambridge, 1989, p. 8. See now *The Loaded Table: Representations of Food in Roman Literature*, Oxford: Clarendon Press, 1993.
33 Ovid *Fast.* 3.523–32.
34 Juv. 10.72–81.
35 Luc. 7.405.
36 E. G. Hardy, *The Satires of Juvenal*, Macmillan, 1891, p. 232.
37 Tac. *Hist.* 2.90.
38 Cic. *Orat.* 173.
39 Quint. *Inst.* 1.12.18.
40 Plin. *Ep.* 13.2 '*Plerique in stationibus sedent tempusque audiendi fabulis conterunt.*'
41 Sen. *Dial.* 9.12.3 '*inquietam inertiam*'.
42 Phaed. 2.5; cf. Mart. 6.78 and Galen *On the Therapeutic Method* 1.2.
43 Lucian *Nigr.* 29.
44 Amm.Marc. 28.4.31.
45 Ibid. 14.6.25.
46 Ibid. 14.6.26.
47 Cic. *Phil.* 11.17.
48 Cic. *Sest.* 119.
49 Cic. *Tusc.* 4.66.
50 Gell. 6.11.1.2.
51 Sen. *Ep.* 99.21.
52 Sen. *Dial.* 9.17.6.
53 Sen. *Ep.* 97.8.
54 Cic. *Tusc.* 3.31.
55 Quint. *Inst.* 10.1.53.
56 Gell. 6.11.4; cf. Cic. *Phil.* 2.77 '*At videte levitatem hominis*'.
57 R. Meiggs, *Roman Ostia*, Oxford: Clarendon Press, 1973, p. 429. On the inn of Helix by the Porta Marina and its lewd pictures, see ibid. p. 430.
58 Paul. *Dig.* 4.4.24.1–2 Inheritances rejected through youthful levity (*iuvenili levitate*)

can sometimes be recovered. Cf. Petr. 110 where Eumolpus, to keep the party going, hurled taunts at the fickleness of women (*muliebrem levitatem*).

59 Apul. *Met.* 4.8.
60 Plin. *Nat.* 8.209.
61 T. A. J. McGinn, 'The Taxation of Roman Prostitutes', *Helios*, 16 (1989), p. 85.
62 Vergiliana *Copa* 37–8.
63 On this subject, see ch. 8 below.
64 Ovid *Pont.* 4.3.31–4; cf. Sen. *Ep.* 98.4 '*levitatem casus*'.
65 Ovid *Tr.* 5.8.18.
66 Apul. *Met.* 8.1.
67 Cic. *Cat.* 2.23.
68 Amm.Marc. 14.6.2. See also T. W. Africa, 'Urban Violence in Imperial Rome', *JIH*, 2 (1971–2), 3–21.
69 Cic. *Flacc.* 18 '*Opifices et tabernarios atque illam omnem faecem civitatum*'. Though see also, *Catil.* 4.17, 'By far the greater part, indeed the whole class – for surely that is the truth – of those who work in shops are the strongest supporters of peace (*amantissimum est oti*).'
70 Hor. *Ep.* 1.19.36 '*ventosae plebis*'; Stat. *Silv.* 2.2.123 '*mobile vulgus*'; Tac. *Hist.* 1.80 '*vulgus, ut mos est, cuiuscumque motus novi cupidum*'; 1.69 'Like all mobs, the common soldiers were given to sudden change (*ut est mos, vulgus mutabile subitis*).'
71 Ovid *Pont.* 2.3.8.
72 Petr. 45.
73 Suet. *Aug.* 45.2.
74 See Juv. 3.278–322 on urban drunks, arguments, and brawls, and burglars as compared to the early Romans and present-day countryside.
75 Marcian. *Dig.* 48.19.11.2 'An offence is committed by design, by impulse, or by accident. Robbers who form a gang offend by design; those who drunkenly resort to fists or swords, by impulse.'
76 Ibid. 11.5.1.2 no redress is given for the manager for assault or loss if gambling is taking place on his premises.
77 Prop. 2.19.5 'No brawl shall arise before thy windows (*nulla neque ante tuas orietur rixa fenestras*).'
78 Plin. *Nat.* 19.59.
79 Prop. 4.8.19 (first line of a couplet alien to its context) 'A noisy brawl broke out in a secret tavern (*turpis in arcana sonuit cum rixa taberna*).'
80 See R. McKibbin, 'The Social Psychology of Unemployment', in his *The Ideologies of Class*, Oxford: Clarendon Press, 1990, pp. 228–58. I am much indebted to this excellent work.
81 Plin. *Ep.* 1.13.2, 2.9.5; Juv. 11.4; Mart. 7.97.11–12.
82 Gell. 3.1.1, although this is specifically *re* the elite.
83 Plin. *Ep.* 5.1.9, on elite members discussing legal business.
84 Mart. 12.proem.; Gell. 5.4.1, 13.31.1.
85 Hor. *S.* 1.7.3.
86 Mart. 11.77.
87 See P. A. Brunt, 'Free Labour and Public Works at Rome', *JRS*, 70 (1980),

81–100, and P. D. A. Garnsey (ed.), *Non-Slave Labour in the Greco-Roman World*, Cambridge Philological Society, suppl. vol. 6 (1980).

88 Cato *Agr.* 1.3.

89 Juv. 10.72.

90 Nep. pr.6.

91 Suet. *Nero* 22.2; cf. 10.2.

92 Dyson, *Community and Society in Roman Italy*, p. 176, although he is talking about Pompeii.

93 Hor. *Ep.* 1.14.21–2.

94 Amm.Marc. 28.4.29.

95 Gell. 1.22.2 refers to 'the street language of the common people (*plebe vulgaria in compitis*)'; cf. Hor. *Ars* 229 'the vulgar speech of a dingy tavern (*obscuras humili sermone tabernas*)'.

96 Amm.Marc. 28.4.30.

97 Plin. *Ep.* 10.34.

98 On the concept of masculinity, see D. D. Gilmore, *Manhood in the Making: Cultural Concepts of Masculinity*, Yale University Press, 1990; J. Hearn and D. Morgan (eds), *Men, Masculinities and Social Theory*, Unwin Hyman, 1990; and A. Brittan, *Masculinity and Power*, Oxford: Basil Blackwell, 1989. On Roman concepts, see J. Walters, *Ancient Roman Concepts of Manhood and their Relation with Other Markers of Social Status*, unpublished PhD dissertation, Cambridge, 1993.

99 For a discussion of these problems, see L. Berkowitz, 'Violence and Rule-Following Behaviour', in P. Marsh and A. Campbell (eds), *Aggression and Violence*, Oxford: Basil Blackwell, 1982, pp. 91–101, and esp. Marvin, *Bullfight*, ch. 9, pp. 143–65.

100 For an incisive analysis of the functions of drinking in eighteenth-century Paris, to which I am much indebted, see Brennan, *Public Drinking and Popular Culture*; also, B. Harrison, *Drink and the Victorians*, Faber and Faber, 1971.

101 Dyson, *Community and Society*, p. 176.

102 On drink, see M. Douglas (ed.), *Constructive Drinking: Perspectives on Drink from Anthropology*, Cambridge: Cambridge University Press, 1987.

103 In part, what I am analysing in this chapter is the Roman form of Huizinga's idea of the play element of culture, but to a greater degree it is a case study in Bakhtin's concept of carnival. In the interests of accessibility and historical accuracy, I have not, however, found it useful to employ these terms directly, but for those keen to know more, see Huizinga, *Homo Ludens*, and Hirschkop and Shepherd, *Bakhtin and Cultural Theory*. The only point I would like to make about Bakhtin's notion that Roman society was characterized by Polyglossia – 'in which different natural languages coexist in a single society' (ibid. p. 17) – as opposed to the Heteroglossia of the modern world – where there is 'unification of the society at the level of language and division at the level of style' (ibid. p. 18) – is that imperial Roman society did have a common language and enormous variations of style. Moreover, the imperial system was an attempt at the creation of a more inclusive language of government, a vernacular of power as it were. To that extent, therefore, the empire had heteroglossic features and the mass

society of the city of Rome once again can be seen to have foreshadowed many of the developments of the later Western world.

104 Tac. *Ann.* 14.20.
105 Quint. *Inst.* 1.2.8.
106 Col. 1.pr.14–17.
107 Hist.Aug. *Gall.* 14.5.
108 *Dig.* 47.22; Philo *Leg.* 311–12.
109 Suet. *Aug.* 32.1.
110 D.C. 60.6.6–7.
111 Gell. 2.24.11; cf. Macr. 3.17.11.
112 Suet. *Jul.* 43.2; D.C. 43.25.2, 54.2.3; Gell. 15.8; Cic. *Fam.* 7.26.2, 9.15.5, 9.26.4.
113 D.C. 39.37.2; Macr. 3.17.14; D.C. 54.2.3; Suet. *Aug.* 34.1; Gell. 2.24.15.
114 Suet. *Tib.* 34, though he did not renew Augustus' legislation; Tac. *Ann.* 3.52–5.
115 D.C. 60.7; cf. Suet. *Claud.* 38.
116 Suet. *Cal.* 40.
117 D.C. 62.14.2, 65.10.3; Suet. *Nero* 16.
118 D.C. 65.10.3.
119 Plin. *Pan.* 46.2.
120 Ibid. 46.5.
121 On actors' high pay, see Cic. *Q.Rosc.* 23; as sex symbols, see Galen *On the Therapeutic Method* 14.630–3K.
122 On food in Rome, see M. Corbier, 'The Ambiguous Status of Meat in Ancient Rome', *Food and Foodways*, 3 (1989), 223–64; Gowers, *The Representation of Food in Roman Literature*, and *The Loaded Table*; N. A. Hudson, 'Food in Roman Satire', in S. H. Braund (ed.), *Satire and Society in Ancient Rome*, Exeter: University of Exeter Press, 1989, pp. 68–87; L. Edmunds, 'Ancient Roman and Modern American Food: A Comparative Sketch of Two Semiological Systems', *Comparative Civilizations Review*, 5 (1986), 52–68; W. J. Slater, *Dining in a Classical Context*, Ann Arbor, Michigan: University of Michigan Press, 1991; O. Murray (ed.), *Sympotica: A Symposium on the Symposion*, Oxford: Clarendon Press, 1990. Of comparative interest are: S. Mennell, *All Manners of Food: Eating and Taste in England and France from the Middle Ages to the Present*, Oxford: Basil Blackwell, 1985; M. Harris, *Good to Eat: Riddles of Food and Culture*, Allen and Unwin, 1985; M. Douglas, 'Deciphering a Meal', in her *Implicit Meanings*, Routledge and Kegan Paul, 1975, pp. 249–75; M. Douglas (ed.), *Food in the Social Order*, New York: Russell Sage, 1984; P. Farb and G. Armelagos, *Consuming Passions: The Anthropology of Eating*, Boston, Mass.: Houghton Mifflin, 1980; and J. Goody, *Cooking, Cuisine and Class*, Cambridge: Cambridge University Press, 1982. On a related topic, readers might also care to note that I have found no evidence for recreational drug abuse; for more information, see J. M. Scott, *The White Poppy: a History of Opium*, Heinemann, 1969, and T. W. Africa, 'The Opium Addiction of Marcus Aurelius', *JHI*, 22 (1961), 97–102.
123 Fron. *Str.* 4.1.2 '*prohibuisset alia carne quam assa elixave milites uti.*' Comment by C. E. Bennett, Loeb edn, p. 268.
124 See C. J. Adams, *The Sexual Politics of Meat*, Cambridge: Polity, 1990.
125 Hor. *Ep.* 1.17.13–14. Cf. D.L. 2.8.68: the cynic Diogenes was cleaning vegetables

for dinner, when Aristippus passed by. Said the former: 'If you had learned to put up with this, you would not be courting princes.' To this gibe Aristippus replied, 'and you, if you knew how to consort with men, would not be cleaning vegetables.'

126 Hor. *S.* 1.6.111–15.

127 See Plin. *Nat.* 19.57 In the traditional society of Cato's day, vegetables were considered to be a luxury for all: 'Nor did people approve very highly of vegetables as they do now, since they condemned delicacies that require another delicacy to help them down.' By the time of the empire, such attitudes survived only as vestiges of the 'golden age', but they were directed against the diets of the lower classes.

128 Hist.Aug. *Did.Iul.* 3.9 '*holeribus leguminibusque contentus sine carne cenaverit.*' Cf. *Comm.Ant.* 11.4 'The various kinds of cooked vegetables he rarely admitted to his banquets, his purpose being to preserve unbroken the succession of dainties (*genera leguminum coctorum ad convivium propter luxuriae continuationem raro vocavit*)'; *Sept.Sev.* 19.8 'He was most sparing in his diet, fond of his native vegetables, liked wine occasionally, and often went without meat (*cibi parcissimus, legumis patrii avidus, vini aliquando cupidus, carnis frequenter ignarus*)'; *Alex.Sev.* 37.2 He was neither 'too sumptuous nor yet too frugal', and (37.4) 'always gave away to his table-servants not only bread but also portions of greens or meat or vegetables.'

129 Hist.Aug. *Max.Duo* 4.1–2.

130 Juv. 11.78–85. Cf. Plin. *Ep.* 10.96.10 on the growth of religious fervour: 'the sacred rites which had been allowed to lapse are being performed again, and flesh of sacrificed victims is on sale everywhere, though up till recently scarcely anyone could be found to buy it.' Presumably, this was because other supplies were readily available.

131 Plin. *Nat.* 19.54.

132 Plin. *Nat.* 19.52 '*ex horto plebei macellum, quanto innocentiore victu!*'

133 Plin. *Nat.* 8.209. See also the literature on the *Testamentum Porcelli*: D. Daube, *Roman Law: Linguistic, Social and Legal Aspects*, Edinburgh: Edinburgh University Press, 1969, pp. 77–91; B. Baldwin, *Studies on Late Roman and Byzantine History, Literature and Language*, Amsterdam: J. Gieben, 1984, pp. 137–52; E. Champlin, 'The Testament of the Piglet', *Phoenix*, 41 (1987), 174–83.

134 On the ancient frugality and early sumptuary laws, see Gell. 2.24.

135 This is not contradicted by the fact that some taverns were owned by the ruling class. In these cases, the elite's desire and need for the profits that accrued from such establishments had merely overcome their ideological hostility towards the lower orders and the uses to which they put tavern space.

136 On the pork supply of the later empire, see *Cod.Theod.* 14.4; Hist.Aug. *Alex.Sev.* 26.1; *Aurel.* 35.2.

137 Hist.Aug. *Hel.* 12.4.

138 Ibid. 19.2.

139 Ibid. 21.7.

140 Ibid. 27.1.

141 Hist.Aug. *Alex.Sev.* 4.3.

142 Ibid. 34.1.
143 Ibid. 37.2.
144 Ibid. 41.5.
145 Cic. *de Orat.* 2.217.
146 For the theory of humour, see M. L. Apte, *Humor and Laughter: An Anthropological Approach*, Ithaca, New York: Cornell University Press, 1985; A. C. Zijderveld, 'The Sociology of Humour and Laughter', *Current Sociology*, 31 (1983), 1–103; S. Freud, *Jokes and their Relation to the Unconscious*, trans. J. Strachey, Routledge and Kegan Paul, 1960 (first published 1905); E. Oring, 'Jokes and their Relation to Sigmund Freud', *Western Folklore*, 43 (1984), 37–48; A. J. Chapman and H. C. Foot (eds), *Humour and Laughter: Theory, Research and Applications*, J. Wiley, 1976; C. P. Wilson, *Jokes: Form, Content, Use and Function*, Academic Press, 1979; R. B. Heilman, *The Ways of the World: Comedy and Society*, Seattle, Washington: University of Washington Press, 1978; M. Mulkay, *On Humour: Its Nature and Its Place in Modern Society*, Cambridge: Polity, 1988; J. Durant and J. Miller (eds), *Laughing Matters: A Serious Look at Humour*, Longman, 1988; M. Douglas, 'The Social Control of Cognition: Some Factors in Joke Perception', *Man*, ns 3 (1968), 361–76; and C. Davies, 'Ethnic Jokes, Moral Values and Social Boundaries', *British Journal of Sociology*, 33 (1982), 383–403.
147 Sen. *Dial.* 2.17.1.
148 Mart. 3.8, 4.65; 2.35; 2.87; 1.19, 2.41, 8.57; 8.60; 12.7; 1.87, 5.4, 3.55, 2.12.
149 Col. 1.8.15.
150 Phaed. 3.pr.33–7.
151 Sen. *Dial.* 2.11.2 and 3.
152 Plin. *Ep.* 4.25.5.
153 Suet. *Aug.* 56.1; Tac. *Ann.* 1.72.
154 Hist.Aug. *Sept.Sev.* 14.12.
155 Suet. *Nero* 39.1–2.
156 On the political use of humour, see G. E. C. Paton and C. Powell (eds), *Humour in Society: Resistance and Control*, Basingstoke: Macmillan, 1988.
157 Macr. 2.4.1.
158 Ibid. 2.4.31. For a collection of jokes, some of them sexual, see 2.2–6.
159 Suet. *Cal.* 24.2.
160 Suet. *Vesp.* 23.4.
161 Hist.Aug. *Hel.* 25.1, 29.3, 32.6.
162 The conclusions of this chapter are inspired by Schama's description of the Dutch in their golden age in his *Embarrassment of Riches*.

Chapter 8 *Gambling*

1 There are no modern secondary works on the Romans' gambling, but many 'everyday life' books contain a page or two, at best, a few stray references, at worst. Of these, the most useful are: Paoli, *Rome: Its People, Life and Customs*, pp. 235–6; Carcopino, *Daily Life in Ancient Rome*, pp. 250–3; and Balsdon, *Life and Leisure in Ancient Rome*, pp. 154–6. A number of books have been written on the

games of the Romans, but have done little to locate them in their social context. The best of these is L. Becq de Fouquières, *Les Jeux des Anciens*, Paris: C. Reinwald, 1873. The modern literature on gambling is large but repetitive. I have included a number in the bibliography, but the following have been the most useful. Psychological analysis has scarcely moved on from Freud; see, for example, J. Halliday and P. Fuller (eds), *The Psychology of Gambling*, Allen Lane, 1974. Sociological literature has been comprehensively reviewed by D. M. Downes et al., *Gambling, Work and Leisure: A Study Across Three Areas*, Routledge and Kegan Paul, 1976. Perhaps the best two recent works are those by R. McKibbin, 'Working-class Gambling in Britain, 1880–1939', in his *The Ideologies of Class*, pp. 101–38, a work to which I am much indebted, and, less specifically on gambling, but with some material that is directly concerned, and much that is closely related, Geertz, 'Deep Play'.

2 In fact, I have not come across a single attempt at definition in the whole of the gambling literature.

3 I would, of course, add that gambling cannot be tied down to a universal set of activities. It is, therefore, quite possible for an individual to earn a living from card-playing or betting, but for these activities to be experienced as work. The professional gambler has more to do with the nine-to-five outlook of an office worker than the pathological leanings of those at Gamblers Anonymous.

4 But Tacitus considered that it was the Germans who had a true passion for games of chance, *Germ.* 24.

5 Juv. 1.88–9, 8.10–11, 14.4–5, 11.132 and 176–7; cf. Pers. 5.57.

6 Cic. *de Orat.* 3.58.

7 Mart. 5.84, 14.18; Pers. 3.44–51.

8 Cic. *Senect.* 58.

9 Ovid *Ars* 2.203–8, 3.353–60; Prop. 2.33b 26.

10 Suet. *Nero* 30.3.

11 Suet. *Claud.* 33.2.

12 M.Ant. 1.5.

13 For more details, see R. Lanciani, 'Gambling and Cheating in Ancient Rome', *North American Review*, 155 (1892), 97–105. Courtesy of Andrew Wilson, I have even seen a photograph of a *tabula lusoria* carved in the middle of the main road in Madaura, North Africa.

14 Hor. *S.* 2.7.15–18; Petr. 33.

15 On the details of particular taverns, see the previous chapter on popular culture and leisure.

16 *PLM* 4.132.

17 *CIL* 8.17938.

18 Matthew 27.35.

19 This was known as *capita aut navim*, referring to the head of Janus and the ship on the two sides of a coin.

20 Ovid *Ars* 3.363–6.

21 *CIL* 13.444; cf. Mart. 7.71.7–8.

22 Suet. *Aug.* 71.2; cf. Pers. 3.48. The approximate probability of throwing a Venus is 25–1, so the pot could become relatively significant even when the stakes per throw were small. The probability of getting a six or three ones though is only

9–1. These odds are based on a rough estimate of the probabilities of the *talus* which I have recreated by actually throwing some knuckle-bones: 9–1 for a throw of both 1 and 6, 2–5 for 3 and 4. 6–1 3344, 10–1 3334/4443, 16–1 3314/3364/ 4413/4463, 25–1 1634 (the Venus), 40–1 3331/3336/4441/4446, 40–1 3333/ 4444, 50–1 1134/6634, 50–1 3316/4416, 100–1 1133/1144/6633/6644, 200–1 1163/1164/6613/6614, 500–1 1113/1114/6663/6664, 1.500–1 1166, 2.500–1 1116/6661, 10.000–1 1111/6666.

23 Mart. 4.66.15–16. For the game of hazard and its numerous variations, see Becq de Fouquières, ch. 14 'Des Petits Jeux de Hasard', pp. 284–301.
24 Pers. 3.50; Mart. 4.14.9; Poll. 9.103.
25 M.Ant. 1.6; Hdn. 3.10.3. See also M. G. Morgan, 'Three Non-Roman Blood Sports', *CQ*, 69 ns 25 (1975), 117–22.
26 Ovid *Nux* 75–6.
27 Mart. 7.91.
28 For more details, see Hopkins, *Death and Renewal*, pp. 25–6.
29 Tac. *Dial.* 29.
30 Juv. 11.201; Tertullian *De Spectaculis* 16.
31 Lucian *Nigr.* 29.
32 Mart. 11.1.9–16.
33 See Cameron, *Circus Factions*, pp. 53–6.
34 Though in the later empire at Constantinople, the pairings seem to have been reversed, reds with greens and blues with whites.
35 Petr. 70.
36 Juv. 11.201–2.
37 *CIL* 6.2.10048.
38 This would seem to be a reasonable assumption since the general impression from the literature is that the two weaker factions, and the stronger pair, performed to a similar standard. This is, of course, an argument *ex silentio*, but there is no hint that the reds were outperforming the whites in any way, which is the important point for this thesis.
39 This is the figure which is currently taken by both the British Totalizer board and the French Pari-Mutuel.
40 Hopkins, *Death and Renewal*, p. 26.
41 For an analysis of the importance of character-contests in modern America, see E. Goffman, 'Where the Action Is', in his *Interaction Ritual: Essays on Face-to-Face Behaviour*, Harmondsworth: Penguin, 1972.
42 Cic. *Catil.* 2.22–3.
43 Pub. 33 '*Aleator quanto in arte est, tanto est nequior.*'
44 Cic. *Catil.* 2.10; cf. 2.23–4 for the full list of the conspirators' vices. For other examples of accusations of gambling, see *Phil.* 8.26, 13.24.
45 Suet. *Jul.* 32 '*iacta alea est*'; Luc. 6.6–8.
46 Hist.Aug. *Comm.Ant.* 9.1; cf. *Ver.* 4.6, 10.8.
47 Suet. *Cal.* 41.2; Sen. *Dial.* 11.17.5.
48 See, for example, Ammianus' description of the *otiosam plebem . . . et desidem*: 'No shoes, cultured names, they live with wine and dice, in haunts, pleasures and games' 28.4.28.
49 Sid.Ap. *Ep.* 1.2.7.

50 Suet. *Aug.* 71.

51 See McKibbin's 'Working-class Gambling in Britain'.

52 For the view of gambling as a decision-making process concerned with the selection of strategies, see R. A. Epstein, *The Theory of Gambling and Statistical Knowledge,* Academic Press, 1967.

53 Galen *On the Therapeutic Method* 16.310.

54 Amm.Marc. 28.4.29.

55 Tertullian *De Spectaculis* 16.

56 For gambling as a popular pastime, see Ovid *Pont.* 4.2.39–42; cf. 1.5.43–6.

57 Suet. *Jul.* 32.

58 Var. *R.* 1.4.3.7–8.

59 Sen. *Ben.* 3.11.1.

60 Sid.Ap. *Ep.* 4.6.1.

61 Cic. *Amic.* 54.

62 Cic. *Parad.* 34.

63 Ulp. *Dig.* 21.1.4.

64 Ibid. 21.1.25.

65 Ps-Cyprian *De Aleatoribus* 6. It is significant that this is one of the earliest extant Christian texts; see S. T. Carroll, 'An Early Church Sermon Against Gambling', *The Second Century,* 8 (1991), 83–95. I have not examined the Christian attitude in this section because it would involve an analysis of the changing ways of thinking about the nature of individual responsibility in relation to social context. However, there also seems to be a strong element of continuity in their attacks on gambling, an inheritance from elite Roman ancestors, and it is this which I wish to emphasize.

66 Cic. *Div.* 2.85.

67 Tac. *Germ.* 24.

68 In the *Digest,* 47.10.26, this is legally recognized: 'If someone makes a mockery of my slave or son, even with their consent, I am regarded as being insulted, as when he takes them into a cook-shop or plays dice with them.'

69 Ovid. *Ars* 1.451–2.

70 Sen. *Apoc.* 14–15.

71 Ovid *Rem.* 145–8; cf. *Met.* 2.203f.

72 Hor. *S.* 2.3.168–75 on the relationship between Aulus' juvenile gambling and his subsequent madness and profligacy.

73 Hist.Aug. *Did.Jul.* 9.1.

74 Philostr. *V.A.* 5.36.

75 Amm.Marc. 28.4.21.

76 Sen. *Dial.* 9.14.7.

77 Cic. *Off.* 3.77; *Fin.* 2.52; Petr. 44; August. *Trin.* 8.5.8.

78 The laws are given in *Dig.* 11.5; Cic. *Phil.* 2.56; and referred to in Hor. *Carm.* 3.24.58; Ovid *Tr.* 2.472. They are listed by J. A. Crook, 'for completeness', in his *Law and Life of Rome,* Thames and Hudson, 1967, p. 271. For Saturnalian examples, see Mart. 11.9. On ancient gaming in general, see *DS* 1.180.

79 The date is that suggested by Berger in his 'Encyclopedic Dictionary of Roman Law'; see also, G. Rotondi, *Leges Publicae Populi Romani,* Milan: Società Editrice Libraria, 1912.

80 Mart. 11.6, 5.84; *Dig.* 11.5.4; Cic. *Phil.* 2.56; Ps.-Asconius *Div.* 24.
81 Mart. 5.84.
82 Paul. *Dig.* 11.5.2.1.
83 The statute is mentioned in Marcian. *Dig.* 11.5.3 together with a *Lex Publicia* and a *Lex Cornelia* the provisions of which are unknown. See also *DAGR* 3.1165.
84 Rotondi, *Leges Publicae Populi Romani*, p. 363; *DAGR* 3.1138.
85 Arguments over honesty arose often enough to make a subject for a Pompeian mosaic. *CIL* 4.581; cf. 4.575.
86 *Cod.Just.* 3.43.
87 Ulp. *Dig.* 11.5.1.4.
88 Amb. *De Tobia* 11.38; cf. Ps.-Cyprian *De Aleatoribus* 5–11.
89 Juv. 11.176–8.
90 Quint. *Inst.* 2.4.22.
91 Juv. 1.88–9 'When was gambling so reckless?'
92 Suet. *Aug.* 71.
93 Ibid. 70.2.

Chapter 9 *Sex and the Problematization of Leisure*

1 Hist.Aug. *Hel.* 5.4.
2 H. Benjamin and R. E. L. Masters, *The Prostitute in Society*, Mayflower-Dell, 1966, p. 42.
3 There seems little point in offering a comprehensive survey of sexual literature since the subject is so vast, but the following are recommended as a start: Foucault, *The History of Sexuality*; F. A. Beach (ed.), *Human Sexuality in Four Perspectives*, Johns Hopkins University Press, 1977; Halperin, 'Is There a History of Sexuality?'; R. A. Padgug, 'Sexual Matters: On Conceptualizing Sexuality in History', *Radical History Review*, 20 (1979), 3–23; A. I. Davidson, 'Sex and the Emergence of Sexuality', *Critical Inquiry*, 14 (1987–8), 16–48; L. Stone, *The Family, Sex and Marriage in England 1500–1800*, Harmondsworth: Penguin, 1979; J. Weeks, *Sex, Politics and Society: The Regulation of Sexuality since 1800*, Longman, 1981. On aspects of Roman sexuality, see J. N. Adams, *The Latin Sexual Vocabulary*, Duckworth, 1982; A. Rousselle, *Porneia: On Desire and the Body in Antiquity*, trans. F. Pheasant, Oxford: Basil Blackwell, 1988; O. Kiefer, *Sexual Life in Ancient Rome*, trans. G. and H. Highet, Panther, 1969; F. Dupont, *Daily Life in Ancient Rome*, trans. C. Woodall, Oxford: Basil Blackwell, 1992; Gardner, *Women in Roman Law and Society*; and Brown, *The Body and Society*.
4 Halperin, 'Is There a History of Sexuality?', p. 257.
5 Brown, *The Body and Society*, p. 6.
6 On prostitution in the ancient world, see H. Herter, 'Die Soziologie der antiken Prostitution', *JbAC*, 3 (1960), 70–111; McGinn, 'The Taxation of Roman Prostitutes'; S. B. Pomeroy, *Goddesses, Whores, Wives, and Slaves: Women in Classical Antiquity*, Robert Hale, 1976. For modern comparative material, see F. Henriques, *Prostitution and Society*, 2 vols, MacGibbon and Kee, 1967; J. F. Decker, *Prostitution: Regulation and Control*, Littleton, Colorado: F. B. Rothman, 1979; A. Corbin, *Women for Hire: Prostitution and Sexuality in France after*

1850, trans. A. Sheridan, Harvard University Press, 1990; G. S. Rousseau and R. Porter (eds), *Sexual Underworlds of the Enlightenment*, Manchester: Manchester University Press, 1987; and W. W. Sanger, *The History of Prostitution*, New York: Medical Publishing, 1913.

7 Cic. *Cael.* 48.
8 Schama, *The Embarrassment of Riches*, p. 480.
9 Artem. 1.78 trans. White; cf. Sen. *Con.* 1.2.5 where a brothel is described as a *communis locus*.
10 Clem.Al. *Paed.* 3.6; cf. Tertullian. *De Cultu Fem.* 2.12 for prostitutes dressed in purple, scarlet, gold, and precious stones.
11 Hor. *Carm.* 3.6.
12 Col. 12.pr.4. On the concepts of public and private, see S. I. Benn and G. F. Gaus (eds), *Public and Private in Social Life*, Croom Helm, 1983; D. Handelman, *Models and Mirrors: Towards an Anthropology of Public Events*, Cambridge: Cambridge University Press, 1990; Veyne, *A History of Private Life*, p. 105, 'the vague distinction between public and private', pp. 95–116 'Where Public Life was Private'; and B. Moore, *Privacy: Studies in Social and Cultural History*, Armonk, New York: M. E. Sharpe, 1984. According to Moore, 'public' has to do with social relations, and is the means by which society organizes such areas of life as involve ascriptions of access, agency, and interest. Physical access is public if anyone is allowed entry. On agency, the basic distinction is between agents acting on their own account or as officers of the state/community. On interest, an act is public if its end is to serve everyone, private if it is to serve a limited group.
13 P. Brown in Veyne, *A History of Private Life*, p. 243.
14 Sen. *Ben.* 4.11.5 '*inertissimum vitium, voluptas*'.
15 Dupont, *Daily Life*, p. 117–18.
16 Cic. *Off.* 3.119 '*omnem voluptatem dicimus honestati esse contrariam.*'
17 Edwards, *The Politics of Immorality*, p. 92.
18 Cic. *Sest.* 138–9.
19 On the *ferocitas* of youth, see Cic. *Senect.* 33, and on youth in general, E. Eyben, *Restless Youth in Ancient Rome*, trans. P. Daly, Routledge, 1993.
20 [Quint.] *Decl.* 14.8.
21 Lucian *D.Meretr.* 6.2.
22 Mart. 9.7.7; Suet. *Tib. 43, Dom.* 8.
23 Cic. *Mur.* 76.
24 Sen. *Nat.* 7.31.2; cf. Col. 12.pr.9.
25 Mart. 7.67.
26 Plin. *Nat.* 29.26.
27 Dupont, *Daily Life*, p. 117.
28 On the increase in literary references to sexual matters, see Edwards, *The Politics of Immorality*.
29 A. E. Astin, 'Regimen Morum', *JRS*, 78 (1988), p. 32.
30 Sen. *Ep.* 94.37.
31 Cic. *Leg.* 3.32.
32 Edwards, *The Politics of Immorality*, p. 86.
33 Quint. *Inst.* 5.9.14.
34 Sen. *Ep.* 114.11.

35 Cels. 1.pr.4–5.
36 Those interested in the social aspects of dance, see A. P. Royce, *The Anthropology of Dance*, Indiana University Press, 1977. On dance in the ancient world, see F. Weege. *Der Tanz in der Antike*, Hildesheim: Olms, 1976.
37 Cic. *Mur* 13. This attitude continued into the Christian era: 'For where there is dancing there is the evil one.' Joh. Chrys. *Hom. in Matth.* 48.5.
38 Juv. 11.162–4.
39 *Priap.* 26; cf. Mart. 14.203, 5.78, 6.71, 11.16; Ovid *Am.* 2.4.29; Hor. *Carm.* 3.6.21–4.
40 Quint. *Inst.* 1.11.18.
41 Macr. 3.14.7.
42 Vell. 2.83.1 '*infra servos; obscenissimarum rerum*'.
43 Mart. 5.10.3–4.
44 Hor. *S.* 2.7.22–4.
45 R. P. Saller, '*Familia, Domus*, and the Roman Conception of the Family', *Phoenix*, 38 (1984), p. 349. On the Roman family, see S. Dixon, *The Roman Mother*, Croom Helm, 1988; K. R. Bradley, *Discovering the Roman Family*, Oxford: Oxford University Press, 1991; B. Rawson (ed.), *The Family in Ancient Rome: New Perspectives*, Croom Helm, 1986; R. Saller, '*Patria Potestas* and the Stereotype of the Roman Family', *Continuity and Change*, 1 (1986), 7–22; S. Treggiari, *Roman Marriage: Iusti Coniuges from the Time of Cicero to the Time of Ulpian*, Oxford: Clarendon Press, 1991; B. Rawson, 'Family Life among the Lower Classes at Rome in the First Two Centuries of the Empire', *CPh*, 61 (1966), 71–83; D. P. Harmon, 'The Family Festivals of Rome', *ANRW*, 2.16.2 (1978), 1592–603; and J. F. Gardner and T. Wiedemann, *The Roman Household: A Sourcebook*, Routledge, 1991. Of more general interest are J. B. Elshtain (ed.), *The Family in Political Thought*, Brighton: Harvester, 1982, and J. G. Peristiany (ed.), *Mediterranean Family Structures*, Cambridge: Cambridge University Press, 1976. For further comparative material, see Saller, '*Patria Potestas*', p. 18.
46 Saller, '*Familia, Domus*, and the Roman Conception of the Family', p. 350.
47 Ibid. p. 353.
48 Cic. *Off.* 1.54.
49 R. Saller, '*Patria Potestas* and the Stereotype of the Roman Family', abstract.
50 Gardner and Wiedemann, *The Roman Household*, p. xiv.
51 F. Mount, *The Subversive Family: An Alternative Reading of Love and Marriage*, Cape, 1982, p. 1.
52 Gardner, *Women in Roman Law and Society*, p. 129.
53 Saller, '*Familia, Domus*, and the Roman Conception of the Family', p. 337.
54 Sen. *Cl.* 1.15.3.
55 Veyne, *A History of Private Life*, p. 139.
56 Tac. *Ann.* 3.28 '*velut parens omnium*'.
57 Edwards, *The Politics of Immorality*, p. 60.
58 Plin. *Ep.* 3.20.12.
59 Sen. *Cl.* 1.4.1.
60 Rawson, *The Family in Ancient Rome*, p. 123.
61 Sen. *Cl.* 1.4.2–3.
62 On imperial moral legislation, see: Suet. *Aug.* 34, *R.G.* 8.5, D.C. 56.1–10, Tac.

Ann. 3.25; Suet. *Claud.* 23.1, *Nero* 10.1, D.C. 54.16.7, Suet. *Tib.* 35, Juv. 9.70–90, Tac. *Ann.* 2.85, Mart. 6.2 and 4, 5.75, 6.7, Juv. 2.29–33, Suet. *Dom.* 8, D.C. 67.12.1. Also, P. Csillag, *The Augustan Laws on Family Relations*, trans. J. Decsényi, Budapest: Akadémiai Kiadó, 1976, and Edwards, *The Politics of Immorality*, pp. 34–62.

63 K. Galinsky, 'Augustus' Legislation on Morals and Marriage', *Philologus*, 125 (1981), p. 127.

64 Ibid. p. 128.

65 Ibid. p. 126.

66 Plin. *Pan.* 46.5.

67 McGinn, 'The Taxation of Roman Prostitutes', p. 99.

68 A. Wallace-Hadrill, 'Rome's Cultural Revolution', *JRS*, 79 (1989), p. 164. This article reviews P. Zanker, *The Power of Images in the Age of Augustus*, trans. A. Shapiro, Ann Arbor, Michigan: University of Michigan Press, 1988.

69 Ibid. p. 163.

70 Ibid. p. 163.

71 Rawson, *The Family in Ancient Rome*, p. 35; Galinsky, 'Augustus' Legislation', p. 126.

72 Plin. *Pan.* 68.6.

73 On Ovid's *Ars Amatoria* and other ambiguous texts, see Wallace-Hadrill, 'Rome's Cultural Revolution', pp. 162–3.

74 Ibid. p. 164.

75 Suet. *Dom.* 22.1; Hist.Aug. *Hel.* 26.5, cf. *Comm.Ant.* 13.4, 'Such was his complete indifference to propriety, that time and again he sat in the theatre and amphitheatre dressed in a woman's garments and drank quite publicly'; *Hel.* 32.1.

76 See Eyben, *Restless Youth in Ancient Rome*, pp. 67–8.

77 Plin. *Pan.* 83.1.

78 Ibid.

79 Hist.Aug. *Hel.* 19.6.

80 Cic. *Off.* 1.130.

81 Quint. *Inst.* 11.3.122 quoting Cic. *Orat.* 59.

82 G. Piers and M. B. Singer, *Shame and Guilt: A Psychoanalytic and a Cultural Study*, New York: W. W. Norton, 1971, p. 59. For the original distinction, see R. Benedict, *The Chrysanthemum and the Sword*, Boston, Mass.: Houghton Miflin, 1946, pp. 222–4. See also Taylor, *Pride, Shame, and Guilt*, and E. R. Dodds, *Pagan and Christian in an Age of Anxiety: Some Aspects of Religious Experience from Marcus Aurelius to Constantine*, Cambridge: Cambridge University Press, 1965.

83 Tac. *Ann.* 2.85.

84 Sen. *Nat.* 1.16.6.

85 Tac. *Ann.* 3.28 'acriora vincla; inditi custodes'. On the civilizing process, see N. Elias, *The Civilizing Process, Vol. 1: The History of Manners*, trans. E. Jephcott, New York: Urizen Books, 1978, and *The Civilizing Process, Vol. 2: State Formation and Civilization*, trans. E. Jephcott, Oxford: Basil Blackwell, 1982.

86 Ibid. vol. 1, p. 224.

87 Ibid. vol. 1, p. 224.

88 Ibid. vol. 2, p. 233.

89 Ibid. vol. 2, p. 235.

90 It is worth noting that the earliest and greatest advances made by Christianity were in the cities, where traditional community ties had most broken down.

91 The tax was reformed by Theodosius in 439, and abolished by Anastasius in 498; see McGinn, 'The Taxation of Roman Prostitutes', pp. 93–4. As he points out (p. 94), Alexander Severus' anxiety 'can be taken to show perhaps that there was some concern in the early third century over the fact that the collection of the tax by the government granted some measure of legitimacy to the practice of prostitution' Hist.Aug. 24.3.

Chapter 10 *Leisure and the Dialectic of Rome*

1 The thesis might be thought of as a state of Bakhtin's concept of Monoglossia.

2 P. Burke, 'Overture: the New History, its Past and its Future', in P. Burke (ed.), *New Perspectives on Historical Writing*, Cambridge: Polity, 1991, p. 18.

3 Edwards, *The Politics of Immorality*, p. 19.

4 André, *L'Otium dans la Vie Morale*, pp. 532–3.

5 Sal. *Cat.* 37.7.

6 Tac. *Hist.* 2.93.

7 Col. 1.pr.17.

8 Cic. *Att.* 1.19.4.

9 Cic. *Qfr.* 2.5.3.

10 Cf. R. Porter, 'Addicted to Modernity: Nervousness in the Early Consumer Society', in J. Melling and J. Barry (eds), *Culture in History: Production, Consumption and Values in Historical Perspective*, Exeter: University of Exeter Press, 1992, p. 185.

11 Plin. *Nat.* 33.150.

12 The most famous is that of the 'bread and circuses' of Juv. 10.72–81; cf. 6.292.

13 Edwards, *Transgression and Control*, p. 11.

14 See Garnsey and Saller, *The Roman Empire: Economy, Society and Culture*, p. 5.

15 Vell. 2.1.1.

16 For the various sumptuary laws, see Gell. 2.24; Macr. 3.17.11f; Tac. *Ann.* 3.52–55; D.C. 61.10.3; Suet. *Aug.* 34. For greater detail and analysis, see ch. 7 above on popular culture and leisure.

17 On the symbolic function of the law, see the excellent article, to which I am greatly indebted, by J. R. Gusfield, 'Moral Passage: The Symbolic Process in Public Designation of Deviance', *Social Problems*, 15 (1967), 175–88; also S. L. Hills, *Crime, Power, and Morality*, Chandler, 1971; and D. Black and M. Mileski (eds), *The Social Organization of Law*, Seminar Press, 1973.

18 For a discussion of the relationship between moral discourse and popular culture, see Shorter, 'Towards a History of La Vie Intime'; also, R. W. Malcolmson, *Popular Recreation in English Society, 1700–1850*, Cambridge: Cambridge University Press, 1973.

19 Shorter, 'Towards a History of La Vie Intime', p. 8.

20 Ibid. p. 9.

21 For an analysis of the elite mentality connected with the display of largesse to the people, or 'euergetism' as he prefers to call it, see P. Veyne, *Bread and Circuses:*

Historical Sociology and Political Pluralism, abridged by O. Murray, trans. B. Pearce, Allen Lane, Penguin, 1990.

22 Shorter, 'Towards a History of La Vie Intime', p. 68.
23 G. W. Bowersock, *Augustus and the Greek World*, Oxford: Clarendon Press, 1965, p. 75.
24 On the various forms of power, see D. H. Wrong, *Power: Its Forms, Bases and Uses*, Oxford: Basil Blackwell, 1979.
25 See Forgacs and Nowell, *A. Gramsci: Selections from Cultural Writings*.
26 Suet. *Aug.* 40.2.
27 D.C. 54.17.4–5.
28 Parts of this section are appropriated from McKibbin's 'The Social Psychology of Unemployment'.
29 This sentence is adapted from C. Geertz, 'Centres, Kings, and Charisma: Symbolics of Power', in his *Local Knowledge*, p. 134.
30 Cunningham, *Leisure in the Industrial Revolution*, p. 137. My conclusions are adapted from his excellent analysis of leisure in the industrial revolution; see esp. pp. 198–9.

Chapter 11　*Epilogue: History, Historicism, and Relativism*

1 C. Geertz, 'Anti Anti-Relativism', *American Anthropologist*, 86 (1984), p. 265.
2 L. Wittgenstein, *The Blue and Brown Books*, Oxford: Basil Blackwell, 1969, p. 26.
3 R. Rorty, *Philosophy and the Mirror of Nature*, Oxford: Basil Blackwell, 1980, p. 315.
4 Wittgenstein, *The Blue and Brown Books*, p. 26.
5 Ibid. p. 27.
6 L. Wittgenstein, *Philosophical Investigations*, trans. G. E. M. Anscombe, Oxford: Basil Blackwell, 1969, p. 34.
7 Ibid. p. 32.
8 Those who have doubts about the merits of the symbolic approach might find comfort in R. Chartier's review of Darnton's *The Great Cat Massacre*, 'Text, Symbols, and Frenchness', *JMH*, 57 (1985), 682–95. Symbolists will find fresh ammunition in Darnton's reply, 'The Symbolic Element in History', *JMH*, 58 (1986), 218–34.
9 G. Mahajan, *Explanation and Understanding in the Human Sciences*, Oxford: Oxford University Press, 1992, p. 50.
10 Ibid. p. 64.
11 H.-G. Gadamer, *Truth and Method*, trans. revised by J. Weinsheimer and D. G. Marshall, Sheed and Ward, 1989, p. 306. Other works on hermeneutics of interest to historians are L. Pompa, *Human Nature and Historical Knowledge: Hume, Hegel, and Vico*, Cambridge: Cambridge University Press, 1990; P. Ricoeur, 'History and Hermeneutics', trans. D. Pellauer, *JPh*, 73 (1976), 683–95; R. J. Howard, *Three Faces of Hermeneutics: An Introduction to Current Theories of Understanding*, Berkeley, California: University of California Press, 1982; G. Nicholson, *Seeing and Reading*, Macmillan, 1984; Z. Bauman, *Hermeneutics and Social*

Science: Approaches to Understanding, Hutchinson, 1978; A. C. Thiselton, *New Horizons in Hermeneutics*, HarperCollins, 1992; S. J. Hekman, *Hermeneutics and the Sociology of Knowledge*, Notre Dame, Indiana: University of Notre Dame Press, 1986; and H. L. Dreyfus and P. Rabinow, *Michel Foucault: Beyond Structuralism and Hermeneutics*, Brighton: Harvester, 1982.

12 Bauman, *Hermeneutics and Social Science*, p. 217.

13 Hekman, *Hermeneutics and the Sociology of Knowledge*, p. 113.

14 J. Lett, 'Emics and Etics: Notes on the Epistemology of Anthropology', in T. N. Headland, K. L. Pike, and M. Harris (eds), *Emics and Etics: The Insider/Outsider Debate*, Newbury Park, California: Sage, 1990, p. 133.

15 Geertz's rather unconvincing solution is to adopt the terms 'experience-near' and 'experience-distant'; see his 'From the Native's Point of View'.

16 Lett, 'Emics and Etics', pp. 130–1.

17 Ibid. p. 133.

18 F. R. Ankersmit, 'The Dilemma of Contemporary Anglo-Saxon Philosophy of History', *H & T*, Beiheft 25 (1986), p. 25.

19 See C. B. McCullagh, 'The Truth of Historical Narratives', *H & T*, Beiheft 25 (1986), 30–46.

20 Ankersmit, 'The Dilemma of Contemporary Anglo-Saxon Philosophy of History', p. 26.

21 For the classic existential position, see M. Heidegger, *Being and Time*, trans. J. Macquarrie and E. Robinson, Oxford: Basil Blackwell, 1967.

22 Crapanzano, 'Hermes' Dilemma: The Masking of Subversion in Ethnographic Description', pp. 72–3.

23 Talal Asad, 'Anthropological Conceptions of Religion: Reflections on Geertz', *Man*, ns 18 (1983), 237–59.

24 For a description of the anti-relativists' vitriolic attack, see Geertz, 'Anti Anti-Relativism', pp. 266–8.

25 F. Fukuyama, 'A Reply to My Critics', *The National Interest*, 18 (1989–90), p. 23.

26 F. Fukuyama, 'The End of History?', *The National Interest*, 16 (1989), 3–18, and now, *The End of History and the Last Man*, Hamish Hamilton, 1992.

27 *The End of History*, p. xi.

28 Ibid. p. xii.

29 Ibid. p. xx.

30 For discussions of Fukuyama's thesis, see 'Responses to Fukuyama', *The National Interest*, 16 (1989), 19–35; S. P. Huntington, 'No Exit: The Errors of Endism', *The National Interest*, 17 (1989), 3–11; L. Wieseltier, 'Spoilers at the Party', *The National Interest*, 17 (1989), 12–16; and K. Minogue, 'Classy But Shaky', *The National Interest*, 26 (1991–2), 71–7.

31 Fukuyama, *The End of History*, pp. 306–7,

32 Democracy has always managed to assuage the internal tensions created by the inability to produce perfect equality by recourse to the more pragmatic principle of freedom – which is, in effect, the freedom to enjoy the advantages of hierarchy. The success of democracy, therefore, has been based upon its having the character of a thermo-couple, a piece of metal made of two strips of different metals which expand at differing rates: any contraction in the ability to apply the principle of equality leads the role of freedom to expand as compensation.

33 Neither, of course, should the counter-accusation of 'political correctness' be allowed to usher in some extremist ideology in its wake.

34 G. Soffer, *Husserl and the Question of Relativism*, Kluwer Academic, 1991, p. 3.

35 In reality, all societies have a mixture of horizontal and vertical modes of measurement, but democracy is the only one which has the horizontal as its fundamental and primary principle.

36 Rorty, *Philosophy and the Mirror of Nature*, pp. 156–7.

Bibliography

The following is a list of books referred to in the notes, or of use as general works of background, reference, or comparative interest. Place of publication is London unless otherwise stated. When there is more than one place of publication, only the London publisher is given.

Abbott, F. F., *The Common People of Ancient Rome*, Routledge, 1912.

Adam, B., *Time and Social Theory*, Cambridge: Polity, 1990.

Adams, C. J., *The Sexual Politics of Meat*, Cambridge: Polity, 1990.

Adams, J. N., *The Latin Sexual Vocabulary*, Duckworth, 1982.

Adams, J. W., 'Anthropology and History in the 1980s', *JIH*, 12 (1981), 253–65.

Adamson, W. L., *Hegemony and Revolution: A Study of Antonio Gramsci's Political and Cultural Theory*, Berkeley, California: University of California Press, 1980.

Africa, T. W., 'The Opium Addiction of Marcus Aurelius', *JHI*, 22 (1961), 97–102.

Africa, T. W., 'Urban Violence in Imperial Rome', *JIH*, 2 (1971), 3–21.

Allan, G. A., *A Sociology of Friendship and Kinship*, Allen and Unwin, 1979.

Allan, G. A., *Friendship: Developing a Sociological Perspective*, Hemel Hempstead: Harvester Wheatsheaf, 1989.

Althusser, L., *Essays on Ideology*, Verso, 1984.

Anderson, J. K., *Hunting in the Ancient World*, Berkeley, California: University of California Press, 1985.

Anderson, N., *Work and Leisure*, Routledge and Kegan Paul, 1961.

André, J.-M., *L'Otium dans la Vie Morale et Intellectuelle Romaine*, Paris: Presses Universitaires de France, 1966.

Ankersmit, F. R., 'The Dilemma of Contemporary Anglo-Saxon Philosophy of History', *H & T*, Beiheft 25 (1986), 1–27.

Appadurai, A. (ed.), *The Social Life of Things: Commodities in Cultural Perspective*, Cambridge: Cambridge University Press, 1986.

Apte, M. L., *Humor and Laughter: An Anthropological Approach*, Ithaca, New York: Cornell University Press, 1985.

Ashton, J., *The History of Gambling in England*, Duckworth, 1898.

Astin, A. E., 'Regimen Morum', *JRS*, 78 (1988), 14–34.

Astin, R. G., 'Roman Board Games I', *G & R*, 10 (1934), 24–34.

Astin, R. G., 'Roman Board Games II', *G & R*, 11 (1935), 76–82.

Atchley, R. C., *The Sociology of Retirement*, New York: J. Wiley, 1976.

Atkinson, R. F., *Knowledge and Explanation in History: An Introduction to the Philosophy of History*, Ithaca, New York: Cornell University Press, 1978.

Auguet, R., *Cruelty and Civilization: The Roman Games*, Allen and Unwin, 1972.

Bacon, A. W., 'Leisure and Research: A Critical Review of the Main Concepts Employed in Contemporary Research', *Society and Leisure*, 2 (1972), 83–92.

Bailey, P., 'Leisure, Culture and the Historian: Reviewing the First Generation of Leisure Historiography in Britain', *JLS*, 8 (1989), 107–27.

Baldwin, B., *Studies on Late Roman and Byzantine History, Literature and Language*, Amsterdam: J. Gieben, 1984.

Balsdon, J. P. V. D., *Life and Leisure in Ancient Rome*, Bodley Head, 1969.

Balsdon, J. P. V. D., *Romans and Aliens*, Duckworth, 1979.

Baron, S. W., *The Contemporary Relevance of History: A Study in Approaches and Methods*, New York: Columbia University Press, 1986.

Barton, C. A., *The Sorrows of the Ancient Romans: The Gladiator and the Monster*, Princeton, New Jersey: Princeton University Press, 1993.

Basso, K. H., and Selby, H. A. (eds), *Meaning in Anthropology*, Albuquerque, New Mexico: University of New Mexico Press, 1976.

Bauman, Z., *Hermeneutics and Social Science: Approaches to Understanding*, Hutchinson, 1978.

Baumeister, R. F., *Identity: Cultural Change and the Struggle for the Self*, Oxford: Oxford University Press, 1986.

Beach, F. A. (ed.), *Human Sexuality in Four Perspectives*, Johns Hopkins University Press, 1977.

Beard, M., and Crawford, M., *Rome in the Late Republic: Problems and Interpretations*, Duckworth, 1985.

Beard, M., et al., *Literacy in the Roman World, JRA*, supplementary series 3 (1991).

Becq de Fouquières, L., *Les Jeux des Anciens*, Paris: C. Reinwald, 1873.

Beik, W. H., 'Searching for Popular Culture in Early Modern France', *JMH*, 49 (1977), 266–81.

Benedict, R., *The Chrysanthemum and the Sword*, Boston, Mass.: Houghton Mifflin, 1946.

Benjamin, H., and Masters, R. E. L., *The Prostitute in Society*, Mayflower-Dell, 1966.

Benn, S. I., and Gaus, G. F. (eds), *Public and Private in Social Life*, Croom Helm, 1983.

Bennett, T., Mercer, C., and Wollacott, J. (eds), *Popular Culture and Social Relations*, Milton Keynes: Open University Press, 1986.

Berger, A., 'Encyclopedic Dictionary of Roman Law', *Transactions of the American Philosophical Society*, 43 (1953), 333–808.

Berger, B. M., 'The Sociology of Leisure', in E. O. Smigel (ed.), *Work and Leisure*, New Haven: College and University Press, 1963, pp. 21–40.

Bergler, E., *The Psychology of Gambling*, New York: International Universities Press, 1985.

Berkowitz, L., 'Violence and Rule-Following Behaviour', in P. Marsh and A. Campbell (eds), *Aggression and Violence*, Oxford: Basil Blackwell, 1982, pp. 91–101.

Bettini, M., *Anthropology and Roman Culture: Kinship, Time, Images of the Soul*, trans. J. Van Sickle, Johns Hopkins University Press, 1991.

Biedelman, T. D., 'Some Nuer Notions of Nakedness, Nudity, and Sexuality', *Africa*, 38 (1968), 113–32.

Biersacke, A., 'Local Knowledge, Local History: Geertz and Beyond', in L. Hunt (ed.), *The New Cultural History*, Berkeley, California: University of California Press, 1989, pp. 72–96.

Black, D., and Mileski, M. (eds), *The Social Organization of Law*, Seminar Press, 1973.

Bloch, H. A., 'The Sociology of Gambling', *American Journal of Sociology*, 57 (1951–2), 215–21.

Bloch, M., *The Historian's Craft*, trans. P. Putnam, Manchester: Manchester University Press, 1992 (first published 1954).

Boatwright, M. T., *Hadrian and the City of Rome*, Princeton, New Jersey: Princeton University Press, 1987.

Bowersock, G. W., *Augustus and the Greek World*, Oxford: Clarendon, 1965.

Boyd, C. E., *Public Libraries and Literary Culture in Ancient Rome*, Chicago, Illinois: University of Chicago Press, 1915.

Bradley, K. R., *Discovering the Roman Family*, Oxford: Oxford University Press, 1991.

Brain, H., 'The Changing Concept of Leisure', *Continuous Learning*, 10 (1971), 79–87.

Bramham, P., et al. (eds), *Leisure and Urban Processes*, Routledge, 1989.

Brantlinger, P., *Bread and Circuses: Theories of Mass Culture as Social Decay*, Ithaca, New York: Cornell University Press, 1983.

Braudel, F., *The Mediterranean and the Mediterranean World in the Age of Philip II*, HarperCollins, 1972 (first published 1947).

Braudel, F., *On History*, trans. S. Matthews, Weidenfeld and Nicolson, 1980.

Brennan, T., *Public Drinking and Popular Culture in Eighteenth-Century Paris*, Princeton, New Jersey: Princeton University Press, 1988.

Brenner, R., and Brenner, G. A., *Gambling and Speculation*, Cambridge: Cambridge University Press, 1990.

Brewster, P. G., 'A Roman Game and its Survival on Four Continents', *CPh*, 38 (1943), 134–7.

Bristol, M. D., *Carnival and Theater: Plebeian Culture and the Structure of Authority in Renaissance England*, Methuen, 1985.

Brittan, A., *Masculinity and Power*, Oxford: Basil Blackwell, 1989.

Brown, P., 'Sorcery, Demons and the Rise of Christianity: From Late Antiquity into the Middle Ages', in his *Religion and Society in the Age of Saint Augustine*, Faber and Faber, 1972, pp. 119–46.

Brown, P., *The Body and Society: Men, Women and Sexual Renunciation in Early Christianity*, Faber and Faber, 1988.

Brunt, P. A, *Social Conflicts in the Roman Republic*, Chatto and Windus, 1971.

Brunt, P. A., 'Free Labour and Public Works at Rome', *JRS*, 70 (1980), 81–100.

Bull, C. N., 'Comparative Methods in Leisure Research,' *Society and Leisure*, 2 (1972), 93–104.

Burke, P., *Popular Culture in Early Modern Europe*, Temple Smith, 1978.

Burke, P., *Sociology and History*, Allen and Unwin, 1980.

Burke, P. (ed.), *New Perspectives on Historical Writing*, Cambridge: Polity, 1991.

Burke, P., *History and Social Theory*, Cambridge: Polity, 1992.

Burke, K., *Permanence and Change: An Anatomy of Purpose*, Berkeley, California: University of California Press, 1984 (first published 1954).

Burke, T., Genn-Bash, A., and Haines, B., *Competition in Theory and Practice*, Croom Helm, 1988.

Bury, J. B., *A History of the Roman Empire from its Foundation to the Death of Marcus Aurelius*, J. Murray, 1904.

Butler, A. J., *Sport in Classic Times*, E. Benn, 1930.

Caillois, R. (sometimes spelt Callois), *Man, Play, and Games*, trans. M. Barank, Thames and Hudson, 1962.

Caillois, R., *The Mask of Medusa*, trans. G. Ordish, Victor Gollancz, 1964.

Cameron, Alan, *Bread and Circuses: The Roman Emperor and his People*, Hertford: Bowman Press, 1973.

Cameron, Alan, *Porphyrius the Charioteer*, Oxford: Clarendon Press, 1973.

Cameron, Alan, *Circus Factions: Blues and Greens at Rome and Byzantium*, Oxford: Clarendon Press, 1976.

Canetti, E., *Crowds and Power*, trans. C. Stewart, V. Gollancz, 1962.

Cannadine, D., and Price, S. (eds), *Rituals of Royalty: Power and Ceremonial in Traditional Societies*, Cambridge: Cambridge University Press, 1987.

Carcopino, J., *Daily Life in Ancient Rome*, trans. E. O. Lorimer, Routledge and Kegan Paul, 1973.

Carroll, S. T., 'An Early Church Sermon Against Gambling,' *The Second Century*, 8 (1991), 83–95.

Casson, L., *Travel in the Ancient World*, Allen and Unwin, 1974.

Chadwick, H., 'Augustine and Almachius', *Collection des Etudes Augustiniennes*, Série Antiquité 132 (1992), 299–303.

Champlin, E., 'The Testament of the Piglet', *Phoenix*, 41 (1987), 174–83.

Chapman, A. J., and Foot, H. C. (eds), *Humour and Laughter: Theory, Research and Applications*, J. Wiley, 1976.

Chartier, R., 'Culture as Appropriation: Popular Culture Uses in Early Modern France', in S. L. Kaplan (ed.), *Understanding Popular Culture: Europe from the Middle Ages to the Nineteenth Century*, New York: Mouton, 1984, pp. 229–53.

Chartier, R., 'Text, Symbols, and Frenchness', *JMH*, 57 (1985), 682–95.

Chartier, R., *Cultural History: Between Practices and Representations*, Cambridge: Polity, 1988.

Cheek, N. H., and Burch, W. R., *The Social Organization of Leisure in Human Society*, Harper and Row, 1976.

Clavel-Lévêque, M., *L'Empire en Jeux: Espace Symbolique et Pratique Sociale dans le Monde Romain*, Paris: Editions du Centre National de la Recherche Scientifique, 1984.

Clayre, A., *Work and Play: Ideas and Experience of Work and Leisure*, Weidenfeld and Nicolson, 1974.

Clegg, S. R., *Frameworks of Power*, Sage, 1989.

Clifford, J., and Marcus, G. E. (eds), *Writing Culture: The Poetics and Politics of Ethnography*, Berkeley, California: University of California Press, 1986.

Cohen, J., *Chance, Skill and Luck*, Baltimore, Maryland: Penguin, 1960.

Cohn, B. S., 'Anthropology and History in the 1980s', *JIH*, 12 (1981), 227–52.

Coleman, K. M., 'Fatal Charades: Roman Executions Staged as Mythological Enactments', *JRS*, 80 (1990), 44–73.

Coppock, J. T., 'Geographical Contributions to the Study of Leisure', *JLS*, 1 (1982), 1–27.

Corbier, M., 'The Ambiguous Status of Meat in Ancient Rome', *Food and Foodways*, 3 (1989), 223–64.

Corbin, A., *Women for Hire: Prostitution and Sexuality in France after 1850*, trans. A. Sheridan, Harvard University Press, 1990.

Corbin, J. R., *Symbolic Deaths*, Milton Keynes: Open University Educational Enterprises, 1982.

Corbin, J. R., and Corbin, M. P., *Urbane Thought: Culture and Class in an Andalusian City*, Aldershot: Gower, 1987.

Cosgrove, I., and Jackson, R., *The Geography of Recreation and Leisure*, Hutchinson University Library, 1972.

Cowell, F. R., *Everyday Life in Ancient Rome*, Batsford, 1961.

Crandall, R., et al., 'A General Bibliography of Leisure Publications', *JLR*, 9 (1977), 15–54.

Crandall, R., 'Social Interaction, Affect and Leisure', *JLR*, 11 (1979), 165–81.

Crapanzano, V., review of C. Geertz, H. Geertz, and L. Rosen, *Meaning and Order in Moroccan Society: Three Essays in Cultural Analysis*, in *Economic Development and Cultural Change*, 29 (1981), 849–60.

Crapanzano, V., 'Hermes' Dilemma: The Masking of Subversion in Ethnographic Description', in J. Clifford and G. E. Marcus (eds), *Writing Culture*, Berkeley, California: University of California Press, 1986, pp. 51–76.

Crapanzano, V., *Hermes' Dilemma and Hamlet's Desire: On the Epistemology of Interpretation*, Cambridge, Mass.: Harvard University Press, 1992.

Crawford, D. W., Jackson, E. L., and Godbey, G., 'A Hierarchical Model of Leisure Constraints', *Journal of Leisure Sciences*, 13 (1991), 309–20.

Crespi, I., 'The Social Significance of Card Playing as a Leisure Time Activity', *American Sociological Review*, 21 (1956), 717–21.

Crone, P., *Pre-industrial Societies*, Oxford: Basil Blackwell, 1989.

Crook, J. A., *Law and Life of Rome*, Thames and Hudson, 1967.

Csikszentmihalyi, M., and Rochberg-Halton, E., *The Meaning of Things: Domestic Symbols and the Self*, Cambridge: Cambridge University Press, 1981.

Csillag, P., *The Augustan Laws on Family Relations*, trans. J. Decsényi, Budapest: Akadémiai Kiadó, 1976.

Cunningham, H., *Leisure in the Industrial Revolution c.1780–c.1880*, Croom Helm, 1980.

Daniels, B. C., 'Did the Puritans Have Fun? Leisure, Recreation and the Concept of Pleasure in Early New England', *Journal of American Studies*, 25 (1991), 7–22.

Darnton, R., *The Great Cat Massacre and Other Episodes in French Cultural History*, New York: Basic Books, 1984.

Darnton, R., 'The Symbolic Element in History', *JMH*, 58 (1986), 218–34.

Darnton, R., *The Kiss of Lamourette: Reflections in Cultural History*, Faber and Faber, 1990.

Daube, D., *Roman Law: Linguistic, Social and Philosophical Aspects*, Edinburgh: Edinburgh University Press, 1969.

David, F. N., *Games, Gods and Gambling*, C. Griffin, 1962.

Davidson, A. I., 'Sex and the Emergence of Sexuality', *Critical Inquiry*, 14 (1987–8), 16–48.

Davies, C., 'Ethnic Jokes, Moral Values and Social Boundaries', *British Journal of Sociology*, 33 (1982), 383–403.

Davis, H. E., *History and Power: The Social Relevance of History*, University Press of America, 1983.

Decker, J. F., *Prostitution: Regulation and Control*, Littleton, Colorado: F. B. Rothman, 1979.

Deem, R., 'Women, Leisure and Inequality', *JLS*, 1 (1982), 29–46.

DeGrazia, S., *Of Time, Work, and Leisure*, New York: The Twentieth Century Fund, 1962.

DeLaine, J., 'Recent Research on Roman Baths', *JRA*, 1 (1989), 11–32.

DeLaine, J., 'Roman Baths and Bathing', *JRA*, 6 (1993), 348–58.

de Robertis, F. M., *Storia delle Corporazioni e del Regime Associativo nel Mondo Romano*, Bari: Adriatica Editrice, 1971.

de Ste Croix, G. E. M., *The Class Struggle in the Ancient Greek World: From the Archaic Age to the Arab Conquests*, Duckworth, 1981.

Dill, S., *Roman Society from Nero to Marcus Aurelius*, Macmillan, 1905.

Dixon, S., *The Roman Mother*, Croom Helm, 1988.

Dodds, E. R., *Pagan and Christian in an Age of Anxiety: Some Aspects of Religious Experience from Marcus Aurelius to Constantine*, Cambridge: Cambridge University Press, 1965.

Donald, M. N., and Havighurst, R. J., 'The Meanings of Leisure', *Social Forces*, 37 (1958–9), 355–60.

Douglas, M., 'The Social Control of Cognition: Some Factors in Joke Perception', *Man*, ns 3 (1968), 361–76.

Douglas, M., *Implicit Meanings*, Routledge and Kegan Paul, 1975.

Douglas, M., *Purity and Danger: An Analysis of the Concept of Pollution and Taboo*, Ark, 1984 (first published 1966).

Douglas, M. (ed.), *Food in the Social Order*, New York: Russell Sage Foundation, 1984.

Douglas, M., *Risk Acceptability According to the Social Sciences*, Routledge and Kegan Paul, 1986.

Douglas, M. (ed.), *Constructive Drinking: Perspectives on Drink from Anthropology*, Cambridge: Cambridge University Press, 1987.

Dowie, J., and Lefrere, P. (eds), *Risk and Chance*, Milton Keynes: Open University Press, 1980.

Downes, D. M., et al., *Gambling, Work and Leisure: A Study Across Three Areas*, Routledge and Kegan Paul, 1976.

Dray, W., *Perspectives on History*, Routledge and Kegan Paul, 1980.

Dreyfus, H. L., and Rabinow, P., *Michel Foucault: Beyond Structuralism and Hermeneutics*, Brighton: Harvester, 1982.

Dumazedier, J., *Toward a Society of Leisure*, trans. S. E. McClure, Collier-Macmillan, 1967.

Dumazedier, J., *Sociology of Leisure*, trans. M. A. Mckenzie, Oxford: Elsevier, 1974.

Duncan-Jones, R. P., *The Economy of the Roman Empire: Quantitative Studies*, Cambridge: Cambridge University Press, 1974.

Dunning, E., and Rojek, C., *Sport and Leisure in the Civilizing Process: Critique and Counter-Critique*, Macmillan, 1992.

Dupont, F., *La Vie Quotidienne du Citoyen Romain sous la République, 509–27 Av.J.-C.*, Paris: Hachette, 1989.

Dupont, F., *Daily Life in Ancient Rome*, trans. C. Woodall, Oxford: Basil Blackwell, 1992.

Durant, J., and Miller, J. (eds), *Laughing Matters: A Serious Look at Humour*, Longman, 1988.

Dyson, S. L., *Community and Society in Roman Italy*, Baltimore, Maryland: Johns Hopkins University Press, 1992.

Earl, D., *The Moral and Political Tradition of Rome*, Thames and Hudson, 1967.

Edmunds, L., 'Ancient Roman and Modern American Food: A Comparative Sketch of Two Semiological Systems', *Comparative Civilizations Review*, 5 (1986), 52–68.

Edwards, C. H., *Transgression and Control: Studies in Ancient Roman Immorality*, unpublished PhD dissertation, Cambridge, 1989.

Edwards, C. H., *The Politics of Immorality in Ancient Rome*, Cambridge: Cambridge University Press, 1993.

Edwards, H., *Sociology of Sport*, Homewood, Illinois: Dersey Press, 1973.

Elias, N., *The Civilizing Process, Vol. 1: The History of Manners*, trans. E. Jephcott, New York: Urizen Books, 1978 (first published 1939).

Elias, N., *The Civilizing Process, Vol. 2: State Formation and Civilization*, trans. E. Jephcott, Oxford: Basil Blackwell, 1982 (first published 1939).

Elias, N., and Dunning, E., *Quest for Excitement: Sport and Leisure in the Civilizing Process*, Oxford: Basil Blackwell, 1986.

Elshtain, J. B. (ed.), *The Family in Political Thought*, Brighton: Harvester, 1982.

Elsner, J. R., *Art and the Roman Viewer: The Transformation of Art from Augustus to Justinian*, unpublished PhD dissertation, Cambridge, 1990.

Epstein, R. A., *The Theory of Gambling and Statistical Knowledge*, Academic Press, 1967.

Etzioni-Halevy, E., and Etzioni, A., *Social Change: Sources, Patterns, and Consequences*, New York: Basic Books, 1973.

Eyben, E., *Restless Youth in Ancient Rome*, trans. P. Daly, Routledge, 1993.

Farb, P., and Armelagos, G., *Consuming Passions: The Anthropology of Eating*, Boston, Mass.: Houghton Mifflin, 1980.

Featherstone, M. (ed.), *Cultural Theory and Cultural Change*, Sage, 1992.

Finkelstein, J., *The Fashioned Self*, Cambridge: Polity, 1991.

Fischer, D. H., *Historians' Fallacies: Toward a Logic of Historical Thought*, Routledge and Kegan Paul, 1970.

Forgacs, D., and Nowell, G. (eds), *A. Gramsci: Selections from Cultural Writings*, trans. W. Boelhower, Lawrence and Wishart, 1985.

Foucault, M., *The Birth of the Clinic: An Archaeology of Medical Perception*, trans. A. Sheridan, Tavistock, 1976.

Foucault, M., *Discipline and Punish: The Birth of the Prison*, trans. A. Sheridan, Allen Lane, 1977.

Foucault, M., *The History of Sexuality*, 3 vols, trans. R. Hurley, New York: Pantheon, 1985.

Foucault, M., *The Archaeology of Knowledge*, trans. A. M. Sheridan Smith, Tavistock, 1992.

Fowler, W. W., *Social Life at Rome in the Age of Cicero*, Macmillan, 1908.

Freud, S., *Jokes and their Relation to the Unconscious*, trans. J. Strachey, Routledge and Kegan Paul, 1960 (first published 1905).

Friedländer, L., *Roman Life and Manners under the Early Empire*, 4 vols, trans. J. H. Freese, L. A. Magnus, and S. B. Gough, Routledge and Kegan Paul, 1908–13 (first published 1863).

Fukuyama, F., 'The End of History?', *The National Interest*, 16 (1989), 3–18.

Fukuyama, F., 'A Reply to My Critics', *The National Interest*, 18 (1989–90), 21–8.

Fukuyama, F., *The End of History and the Last Man*, Hamish Hamilton, 1992.

Gadamer, H.-G., *Truth and Method*, trans. revised by J. Weinsheimer and D. G. Marshall, Sheed and Ward, 1989.

Gager, J. G. (ed.), *Curse Tablets and Binding Spells from the Ancient World*, Oxford: Oxford University Press, 1992.

Galinsky, K., 'Augustus' Legislation on Morals and Marriage', *Philologus*, 125 (1981), 126–44.

Gardiner, J. (ed.), *What is History Today . . .?*, Basingstoke: Macmillan, 1988.

Gardner, J. F., *Women in Roman Law and Society*, Croom Helm, 1986.

Gardner, J. F., and Wiedemann, T., *The Roman Household: A Sourcebook*, Routledge, 1991.

Gardner, J. F., *Being a Roman Citizen*, Routledge, 1993.

Garfinkel, H., 'Conditions of Successful Degradation Ceremonies', *American Journal of Sociology*, 61 (1955–6), 420–4.

Garnsey, P. D. A., and Whittaker, C. R. (eds), *Imperialism in the Ancient World*, Cambridge: Cambridge University Press, 1978.

Garnsey, P. D. A. (ed.), *Non-Slave Labour in the Greco-Roman World*, Cambridge Philological Society, suppl. vol. 6 (1980).

Garnsey, P. D. A., and Saller, R., *The Roman Empire: Economy, Society and Culture*, Duckworth, 1987.

Geertz, C., *The Interpretation of Cultures*, Hutchinson, 1975.

Geertz, C., 'From the Native's Point of View', in K. H. Basso and H. A. Selby (eds), *Meaning in Anthropology*, Albuquerque, New Mexico: University of New Mexico Press, 1976, pp. 221–37.

Geertz, C., *Local Knowledge: Further Essays in Interpretive Anthropology*, New York: Basic Books, 1983.

Geertz, C., 'Anti Anti-Relativism', *American Anthropologist*, 86 (1984), 263–78.

Geertz, C., 'Waddling In', *TLS*, 7 June 1985, p. 2.

Geertz, C., *Works and Lives: The Anthropologist as Author*, Cambridge: Polity, 1988.

Gerard, D. E. (ed.), *Libraries and Leisure*, Diploma Press, 1975.

Giddens, A., 'Notes on the Concepts of Play and Leisure', *The Sociological Review*, ns 12 (1964), 73–89.

Giddens, A., and Turner, J. H., *Social Theory Today*, Cambridge: Polity, 1987.

Giddens, A., *Modernity and Self-Identity: Self and Society in the Late Modern Age*, Cambridge: Polity, 1991.

Gillespie, M. A., *Hegel, Heidegger, and the Ground of History*, Chicago, Illinois: University of Chicago Press, 1984.

Gilmore, D. D., *Manhood in the Making: Cultural Concepts of Masculinity*, Yale University Press, 1990.

Ginzburg, C., *The Cheese and the Worms: The Cosmos of a Sixteenth-Century Miller*, trans. J. and A. Tedeschi, Routledge and Kegan Paul, 1980.

Ginzburg, C., *Myths, Emblems, Clues*, trans. J. and A. Tedeschi, Hutchinson Radius, 1990.

Girard, R., *Violence and the Sacred*, trans. P. Gregory, Baltimore, Maryland: Johns Hopkins University Press, 1977.

Glasser, R., *Leisure: Penalty or Prize?*, Macmillan, 1970.

Goffman, E., *Encounters*, Harmondsworth: Penguin, 1961.

Goffman, E., *Stigma: Notes on the Management of Spoiled Identity*, Englewood Cliffs, New Jersey: Prentice-Hall, 1963.

Goffman, E., 'Where the Action Is', in his *Interaction Ritual: Essays on Face-to-Face Behaviour*, Harmondsworth: Penguin, 1972.

Golvin, J.-C., *L'Amphithéâtre Romain: Essai sur la Théorisation de sa Forme et de ses Fonctions*, 2 vols, Paris: Boccard, 1988.

Goodale, T. L. and Godbey, G. C., *The Evolution of Leisure: Historical and Philosophical Perspectives*, State College, PA: Venture, 1988.

Goody, J., *Cooking, Cuisine and Class*, Cambridge: Cambridge University Press, 1982.

Goudsblom, J., *Nihilism and Culture*, Oxford: Basil Blackwell, 1980.

Gowers, E. J., *The Representation of Food in Roman Literature*, unpublished PhD dissertation, Cambridge, 1989.

Gowers, E. J., *The Loaded Table: Representations of Food in Roman Literature*, Oxford: Clarendon Press, 1993.

Grant, M., *Gladiators*, Weidenfeld and Nicolson, 1967.

Green, P., *Juvenal: The Sixteen Satires*, Harmondsworth: Penguin, 1987.

Green, P., *Classical Bearings: Interpreting Ancient History and Culture*, Thames and Hudson, 1989.

Greenblatt, S. J., *Shakespearean Negotiations: The Circulation of Social Energy in Renaissance England*, Oxford: Clarendon Press, 1988.

Gregory, D., and Urry, J. (eds), *Social Relations and Spatial Structures*, Basingstoke: Macmillan, 1985.

Grieves, J., 'Acquiring a Leisure Identity: Juvenile Jazz Bands and the Moral Universe of "Healthy" Leisure Time', *JLS*, 8 (1989), 1–9.

Griffiths, E., 'Shuttle Meets Moon Unit', *Sunday Telegraph*, 21 Oct. 1990, p. xi.

Gross, E., 'A Functional Approach to Leisure Analysis', *Social Problems*, 9 (1961), 2–8.

Gusfield, J. R., 'Moral Passage: The Symbolic Process in Public Designation of Deviance', *Social Problems*, 15 (1967), 175–88.

Gusman, P., *Pompeii: The City, Its Life and Art*, trans. F. Simmonds and M. Jourdain, Heinemann, 1900.

Guttman, A., 'Sport and Celebration', *Stadion*, 12 (1986), 1–7.

Haan, N., et al., *Social Science as Moral Inquiry*, New York: Columbia University Press, 1983.

Halbwachs, M., *The Collective Memory*, trans. F. J and V. Y. Ditter, Harper and Row, 1980 (first published 1950).

Halliday, J., and Fuller, P. (eds), *The Psychology of Gambling*, Allen Lane, 1974.

Halperin, D. M., 'Is There a History of Sexuality?', *H & T*, 28 (1989), 257–74.

Hamel, G., *Poverty and Charity in Roman Palestine, First Three Centuries C.E.*, Berkeley, California: University of California Press, 1990.

Handelman, D., *Models and Mirrors: Towards an Anthropology of Public Events*, Cambridge: Cambridge University Press, 1990.

Hansel, M., and Cohen, J., *Risk and Gambling: The Study of Subjective Probability*, Longmans, 1956.

Hardy, E. G., *The Satires of Juvenal*, Macmillan, 1891.

Hargreaves, J., *Sport, Power and Culture: A Social and Historical Analysis of Popular Sports in Britain*, Cambridge: Polity, 1986.

Hargreaves, J., 'The Body, Sport and Power Relations', in J. Horne, D. Jary and A. Tomlinson (eds), *Sport, Leisure and Social Relations*, Routledge and Kegan Paul, 1987, pp. 139–59.

Hargreaves, J., 'The Promise and Problems of Women's Leisure and Sport', in C. Rojek (ed.), *Leisure for Leisure: Critical Essays*, Macmillan Press, 1989, pp. 130–49.

Harmon, D. P., 'The Family Festivals of Rome', *ANRW*, 2.16.2 (1978), 1592–1603.

Harre, R., 'Leisure and its varieties', *JLS*, 9 (1990), 187–95.

Harris, H. A., *Sport in Greece and Rome*, Thames and Hudson, 1972.

Harris, M., *Good to Eat: Riddles of Food and Culture*, Allen and Unwin, 1985.

Harris, W. V., *Ancient Literacy*, Cambridge, Mass.: Harvard University Press, 1989.

Harrison, B., *Drink and the Victorians*, Faber and Faber, 1971.

Hartley, J. R., *Fly-fishing in Ancient Rome*, Erewhon: Mendacks Press, 1928.

Haworth, J. T., and Smith, M. A., *Work and Leisure*, Lepus Books, 1975.

Headland, T. N., Pike, K. L., and Harris, M., *Emics and Etics: The Insider/Outsider Debate*, Newbury Park, California: Sage, 1990.

Hearn, J., and Morgan, D. (eds), *Men, Masculinities and Social Theory*, Unwin Hyman, 1990.

Heeley, J., 'Leisure and Moral Reform', *JLS*, 5 (1986), 57–67.

Heidegger, M., *Being and Time*, trans. J. Macquarrie and E. Robinson, Oxford: Basil Blackwell, 1967.

Heilman, R. B., *The Ways of the World: Comedy and Society*, Seattle, Washington: University of Washington Press, 1978.

Hekman, S. J., *Hermeneutics and the Sociology of Knowledge*, Notre Dame, Indiana: University of Notre Dame Press, 1986.

Held, D., and Giddens, A. (eds), *Classes, Power, and Conflict*, Basingstoke: Macmillan, 1982.

Henriques, F., *Prostitution and Society*, 2 vols, MacGibbon and Kee, 1967.

Herman, R. D. (ed.), *Gambling*, New York: Harper and Row, 1967.

Hermansen, G., *Ostia: Aspects of Roman City Life*, Edmonton, Alberta: University of Alberta Press, 1981.

Herter, H., 'Die Soziologie der antiken Prostitution', *JbAC*, 3 (1960), 70–111.

Hill, C., *The World Turned Upside Down*, Maurice Temple Smith, 1972.

Hills, S. L., *Crime, Power, and Morality*, Chandler, 1971.

Hindess, B., *Choice and Rationality in Social Theory*, Unwin Hyman, 1988.

Hirschkop, K., and Shepherd, D., *Bakhtin and Cultural Theory*, Manchester: Manchester University Press, 1989.

Hoberman, J. M., *Sport and Political Ideology*, Heinemann Educational, 1984.

Hopkins, K., *Conquerors and Slaves*, Cambridge: Cambridge University Press, 1978.

Hopkins, K., *Death and Renewal*, Cambridge: Cambridge University Press, 1983.

Hormuth, S. E., *The Ecology of the Self*, Cambridge: Cambridge University Press, 1990.

Horn, M. J., *The Second Skin*, Boston, Mass.: Houghton Mifflin, 1968.

Horne, J., Jary, D., and Tomlinson, A. (eds), *Sport, Leisure and Social Relations*, Routledge and Kegan Paul, 1987.

Howard, R. J., *Three Faces of Hermeneutics: An Introduction to Current Theories of Understanding*, Berkeley, California: University of California Press, 1982.

Hudson, N. A., 'Food in Roman Satire', in S. H. Braund (ed.), *Satire and Society in Ancient Rome*, Exeter: University of Exeter Press, 1989, pp. 68–87.

Huizinga, J., *Homo Ludens*, Routledge and Kegan Paul, 1949.

Hume, D., *Enquiries Concerning Human Understanding and Concerning the Principles of Morals*, Oxford: Clarendon Press, 1975 (first published 1777).

Humphrey, J. H., *Roman Circuses: Arenas for Chariot Racing*, Batsford, 1986.

Hunnicut, B. K., 'Leisure and Play in Plato's Teaching and Philosophy of Learning', *Journal of Leisure Sciences*, 12 (1990), 211–27.

Hunt, L. (ed.), *The New Cultural History*, Berkeley, California: University of California Press, 1989.

Huntington, S. P., 'No Exit: The Errors of Endism', *The National Interest*, 17 (1989), 3–11.

Huttunen, P., *The Social Strata in the Imperial City of Rome*, Oulu: University of Oulu Press, 1974.

Hyland, A., *Equus: The Horse in the Roman World*, Batsford, 1990.

Ingham, R., 'Psychological Contributions to the Study of Leisure – Part 1', *JLS*, 5 (1986), 255–79.

Jansen-Verbeke, M., 'Women, Shopping and Leisure', *JLS*, 6 (1987), 71–86.

Jefferson, A., 'Bodymatters: Self and Other in Bakhtin, Sartre and Barthes', in K. Hirschkop and D. Shepherd, *Bakhtin and Cultural Theory*, Manchester: Manchester University Press, 1989, pp. 152–77.

Jennison, G., *Animals for Show and Pleasure in Ancient Rome*, Manchester: Manchester University Press, 1937.

Jones, A. H. M., *The Later Roman Empire, 284–602: A Social, Economic and Administrative Survey*, 3 vols, Oxford: Basil Blackwell, 1964.

Jones, J. P., *Gambling Yesterday and Today*, Newton Abbott: David and Charles, 1973.

Jones, P., 'Lives, Loves and Deaths of the REAL Gladiators', in *Daily Mail*, 7 Nov. 1992, pp. 22–3.

Joseph, N., *Uniforms and Non-uniforms: Communication through Clothing*, New York: Greenwood Press, 1986.

Kando, T. M., *Leisure and Popular Culture in Transition*, St Louis, Missouri: C. V. Mosby, 1975.

Kaplan, M., *Leisure: Theory and Policy*, J. Wiley, 1975.

Kaplan, S. L. (ed.), *Understanding Popular Culture: Europe from the Middle Ages to the Nineteenth Century*, New York: Mouton, 1984.

Kelly, J. R., *Leisure Identities and Interactions*, Allen and Unwin, 1983.

Kelly, J. R., *Freedom To Be: A New Sociology of Leisure*, New York: Macmillan, 1987.

Kendrick, S., Straw, P., and McCrore, D. (eds), *Interpreting the Past, Understanding the Present*, Macmillan, 1990.

Kenyon, F. G., *Books and Readers in Ancient Greece and Rome*, Oxford: Clarendon Press, 1951.

Kiefer, O., *Sexual Life in Ancient Rome*, trans. G. and H. Highet, Panther, 1969.

Kleberg, T., *Hôtels, Restaurants et Cabarets dans L'Antiquité Romaine*, Uppsala: Almqvist and Wiksells, 1957.

Knapp, A. B. (ed.), *Archaeology, Annales, and Ethnohistory*, Cambridge: Cambridge University Press, 1992.

Kolenda, K., *Rorty's Humanistic Pragmatism: Philosophy Democratized*, Tampa, Florida: University of South Florida Press, 1990.

LaCapra, D., *History and Criticism*, Ithaca, New York: Cornell University Press, 1985.

Lamb, H. A. J., 'Sanitation, an Historical Survey', *The Architects' Journal*, 4 March 1937.

Lanciani, R., 'Gambling and Cheating in Ancient Rome,' *North American Review*, 155 (1892), 97–105.

Lancy, D. F., and Tindall, B. A. (eds), *The Study of Play: Problems and Prospects*, West Point, New York: Leisure Press, 1977.

Landman, L., 'Jewish Attitudes Towards Gambling: The Professional and Compulsive Gambler', *JQR*, 57 (1966–7), 298–318, and 58 (1967–8), 34–62.

Larrabee, E., and Meyersohn, R. (eds), *Mass Leisure*, Glencoe, Illinois: Free Press, 1961.

Le Goff, J., and Nora, P. (eds), *Constructing the Past: Essays in Historical Methodology*, Cambridge: Cambridge University Press, 1985.

Lemert, C. C., and Gillan, G., *Michel Foucault: Social Theory and Transgression*, New York: Columbia University Press, 1982.

Le Roy Ladurie, E., *The Mind and Method of the Historian*, trans. S. and B. Reynolds, Brighton: Harvester, 1981.

Lett, J. 'Emics and Etics: Notes on the Epistemology of Anthropology', in T. N. Headland, K. L. Pike, and M. Harris (eds), *Emics and Etics: The Insider/Outsider Debate*, Newbury Park, California: Sage, 1990, pp. 127–42.

Lewis, G. H., *The Sociology of Popular Culture, Current Sociology*, 26 (3) (1978).

Lewis, N., and Reinhold, M., *Roman Civilization*, 2 vols, New York: Columbia University Press, 1963.

Linder, B. B., *The Harried Leisure Class*, New York: Columbia University Press, 1970.

Lintott, A. W., *Violence in Republican Rome*, Oxford: Clarendon Press, 1968.

Liversidge, J., *Everyday Life in the Roman Empire*, Batsford, 1976.

Lloyd, G. E. R., *Demystifying Mentalities*, Cambridge: Cambridge University Press, 1990.

Lovett, E., 'The Ancient and Modern Game of Astragals', *FL*, 12 (1901), 280–293.

Lukacs, J., 'Poker and American Character', *Horizon*, 5 (1963), 56–62.

Lukes, S. (ed.), *Power*, Oxford: Basil Blackwell, 1986.

Macfarlane, L. J., *Violence and the State*, Nelson, 1974.

Maertens, J.-T., *Dans la Peau des Autres*, Paris: Aubier Montaigne, 1978.

Magoulias, H. J., 'Bathhouse, Inn, Tavern, Prostitution and the Stage as Seen in the Lives of the Saints of the Sixth and Seventh Centuries', *Annuaire de la Société des Etudes Byzantines*, 38 (1971), 233–52.

Maguire, J., 'Image of Manliness and Competing Ways of Living in Late Victorian and Edwardian Britain', *British Journal of Sports History*, 3 (1986), 265–87.

Mahajan, G., *Explanation and Understanding in the Human Sciences*, Oxford: Oxford University Press, 1992.

Malachowski, A. R. (ed.), *Reading Rorty: Critical Responses to Philosophy and the Mirror of Nature (and Beyond)*, Oxford: Basil Blackwell, 1990.

Malcolmson, R. W., *Popular Recreation in English Society, 1700–1850*, Cambridge: Cambridge University Press, 1973.

Mandelbaum, M., *Philosophy, History and the Sciences*, Johns Hopkins University Press, 1984.

Marger, M. N., *Elites and Masses: An Introduction to Political Sociology*, New York: Van Nostrand, 1981.

Marrus, M. R. (ed.), *The Emergence of Leisure*, New York: Harper and Row, 1974.

Marsh, P., and Campbell, A. (eds), *Aggression and Violence*, Oxford: Basil Blackwell, 1982.

Marshall, A. J., 'Library Resources and Creative Writing at Rome', *Phoenix*, 30 (1976), 252–64.

Martin, W., and Mason, S., 'Leisure and Shopping', *JLS*, 6 (1987), 93–8.

Marvin, G., 'Honour, Integrity and the Problem of Violence in the Spanish Bullfight', in D. Riches (ed.), *The Anthropology of Violence*, Oxford: Basil Blackwell, 1986, pp. 118–35.

Marvin, G., *Bullfight*, Oxford: Basil Blackwell, 1988.

Marwick, A., *The Nature of History*, Macmillan, 1970.

Marx, E., *The Social Context of Violent Behaviour*, Routledge and Kegan Paul, 1976.

Matthews, J., *Western Aristocracies and Imperial Court AD 364–425*, Oxford: Clarendon Press, 1975.

Mattingly, H., *The Man in the Roman Street*, New York: Numismatic Review, 1947.

Mazzolani, L. S., *The Idea of the City in Roman Thought*, trans. S. O'Donnell, Indiana University Press, 1970.

McCullagh, C. B., 'The Truth of Historical Narratives', *H & T*, Beiheft 25 (1986), 30–46.

McGinn, T. A. J., 'The Taxation of Roman Prostitutes', *Helios*, 16 (1989), 79–110.

McKibbin, R., *The Ideologies of Class: Social Relations in Britain, 1880–1950*, Oxford: Clarendon Press, 1990.

Meadow, A., and Zurcher, L. A., 'On Bullfights and Baseball: An Example of Interaction of Social Institutions', in E. Dunning (ed.), *The Sociology of Sport*, Frank Cass, 1971, pp. 175–97.

Meiggs, R., *Roman Ostia*, Oxford: Clarendon Press, 1973.

Meggitt, J. J., 'Meat Consumption and Social Conflict in Corinth', *JThS*, ns 45 (1994), 137–41.

Meller, H. E., *Leisure and the Changing City*, 1870–1914, Routledge and Kegan Paul, 1976.

Melling, J., and Barry, J. (eds), *Culture in History: Production, Consumption and Values in Historical Perspective*, Exeter: University of Exeter Press, 1992.

Mennell, S., *All Manners of Food: Eating and Taste in England and France from the Middle Ages to the Present*, Oxford: Basil Blackwell, 1985.

Merton, E. W., *Bäder und Badegepflogenheiten in der Darstellung der Historia Augusta*, Bonn: Habelt, 1983.

Merton, R. K., *Social Theory and Social Structure*, Glencoe, Illinois: The Free Press, 1954.

Meyersohn, R., 'A Comprehensive Bibliography on Leisure 1900–1958', in E. Larrabee and R. Meyersohn (eds), *Mass Leisure*, Glencoe, Illinois: The Free Press, 1961.

Michie, J., *Martial: The Epigrams*, Harmondsworth: Penguin, 1978.

Millar, F., *The Emperor in the Roman World, 31 BC–337 AD*, Duckworth, 1977.

Millar, F., and Segal, E. (eds), *Caesar Augustus: Seven Aspects*, Oxford: Clarendon Press, 1984.

Minogue, K., 'Classy But Shaky', *The National Interest*, 26 (1991–2), 71–7.

Mitchell, J., *Betting*, Pelham, 1972.

Moeller, W., 'The Riot of AD 59 at Pompeii', *Historia*, 19 (1970), 84–95.

Mommsen, T., *The History of Rome*, 4 vols, trans. W. P. Dickinson, R. Bentley, 1880–1.

Moore, B., *Privacy: Studies in Social and Cultural History*, Armonk, New York: M. E. Sharpe, 1984.

Moore, P. G., *The Business of Risk*, Cambridge: Cambridge University Press, 1983.

Moore, S. F., and Myerhoff, B. G. (eds), *Secular Ritual*, Assen, Amsterdam: Van Gorcum, 1977.

Moore, S. F., and Myerhoff, B. G. (eds), *Symbol and Politics in Communal Ideology: Cases and Questions*, Ithaca, New York: Cornell University Press, 1975.

Morgan, M. G., 'Three Non-Roman Blood Sports', *CQ*, 69, ns 25 (1975), 117–22.

Morris, M., and Patton, P. (eds), *Foucault: Power, Truth, Strategy*, Sydney: Feral, 1979.

Mount, F., *The Subversive Family: An Alternative Reading of Love and Marriage*, Cape, 1982.

Mulkay, M., *On Humour: Its Nature and Its Place in Modern Society*, Cambridge: Polity, 1988.

Murra, J. V., Wachtel, N., and Revel, J. (eds), *Anthropological History of Andean Polities*, Cambridge: Cambridge University Press, 1986.

Murray, O. (ed.), *Sympotica: A Symposium on the Symposion*, Oxford: Clarendon Press, 1990.

Newman, O., *Gambling: Hazard and Reward*, Athlone Press, 1972.

Nicholson, G., *Seeing and Reading*, Macmillan, 1984.

Nicolet, C., *The World of the Citizen in Republican Rome*, trans. P. S. Falla, Berkeley, California: University of California Press, 1980.

Nielson, I., *Thermae et Balnea*, Aarhus: Aarhus University Press, 1990.

Olivova, V., *Sports and Games in the Ancient World*, trans. D. Orpington, Orbis, 1984.

Olszewska, A., and Roberts, K. (eds), *Leisure and Lifestyle*, Sage, 1989.

Oring, E., 'Jokes and their Relation to Sigmund Freud', *Western Folklore*, 43 (1984), 37–48.

Otto, A., *Sprichtwörter und sprichtwörtliche Redensarten der Römer*, Hildesheim: G. Olms, 1968.

Overholt, W. H., *Political Risk*, Euromoney, 1982.

Padgug, R. A., 'Sexual Matters: On Conceptualizing Sexuality in History', *Radical History Review*, 20 (1979), 3–23.

Paoli, U. E., *Rome: Its People, Life and Customs*, trans. R. D. Macnaughten, Longmans, 1963.

Parker, S., *The Sociology of Leisure*, Allen and Unwin, 1976.

Parker, S., *Leisure and Work*, Allen and Unwin, 1983.

Parry, N. C. A., 'Sociological Contributions to the Study of Leisure', *JLS*, 2 (1983), 57–81.

Pasquinucci, M., *Terme Romane e Vita Quotidiana*, Rome: Edizioni Panini, 1986.

Paton, G. E. C., and Powell, C. (eds), *Humour in Society: Resistance and Control*, Basingstoke: Macmillan, 1988.

Patterson, J., 'The City of Rome: From Republic to Empire', *JRS*, 82 (1992), 186–215.

Pattison, R., *On Literacy: The Politics of the Word from Homer to the Age of Rock*, Oxford: Oxford University Press, 1982.

Pearson, J., *Arena: The Story of the Colosseum*, Thames and Hudson, 1973.

Peristiany, J. G., *Honour and Shame: The Values of Mediterranean Society*, Weidenfeld and Nicolson, 1966.

Peristiany, J. G. (ed.), *Mediterranean Family Structures*, Cambridge: Cambridge University Press, 1976.

Pieper, J., *Leisure the Basis of Culture*, New York: New American Library, 1963 (first published 1952).

Piers, G., and Singer, M. B., *Shame and Guilt: A Psychoanalytic and a Cultural Study*, New York: W. W. Norton, 1971.

Pittock, J. H., and Wear, A. (eds), *Interpretation and Cultural History*, Basingstoke: Macmillan, 1991.

Plummer, K., *Sexual Stigma: An Interactionist Account*, Routledge and Kegan Paul, 1975.

Podilchak, W., 'Distinctions of Fun, Enjoyment and Leisure', *JLS*, 10 (1991), 133–48.

Poliakoff, M. B., *Combat Sports in the Ancient World: Competition, Violence and Culture*, Yale University Press, 1987.

Pomeroy, S. B., *Goddesses, Whores, Wives, and Slaves: Women in Classical Antiquity*, Robert Hale, 1976.

Pompa, L., *Human Nature and Historical Knowledge: Hume, Hegel, and Vico*, Cambridge: Cambridge University Press, 1990.

Porter, D. H., *The Emergence of the Past: A Theory of Historical Explanation*, Chicago, Illinois: University of Chicago Press, 1981.

Porter, R., *English Society in the Eighteenth Century*, Allen Lane, 1982.

Porter, R., and Tomaselli, S., *The Dialectics of Friendship*, Routledge, 1989.

Porter, R., 'Addicted to Modernity: Nervousness in the Early Consumer Society', in J. Melling and J. Barry (eds), *Culture in History: Production, Consumption, and*

Values in Historical Perspective, Exeter: University of Exeter Press, 1992, pp. 180–94.

Price, S. R. F., *Rituals and Power: The Roman Imperial Cult in Asia Minor*, Cambridge: Cambridge University Press, 1984.

Raaflaub, K. A., and Toher, M. (eds), *Between Republic and Empire: Interpretations of Augustus and his Principate*, Berkeley, California: University of California Press, 1990.

Rader, M., *Marx's Interpretation of History*, New York: Oxford University Press, 1979.

Radcliffe, W., *Fishing from the Earliest Times*, J. Murray, 1921.

Rawson, B., 'Family Life among the Lower Classes at Rome in the First Two Centuries of the Empire', *CPh*, 61 (1966), 71–83.

Rawson, B. (ed.), *The Family in Ancient Rome: New Perspectives*, Croom Helm, 1986.

Rawson, E., 'Chariot-Racing in the Roman Republic', *PBSR*, 49 (1981), 1–16.

Riches, D. (ed.), *The Anthropology of Violence*, Oxford: Basil Blackwell, 1986.

Ricoeur, P., 'History and Hermeneutics', trans. D. Pellauer, *JPh*, 73 (1976), 683–95.

Ricoeur, P., *The Reality of the Historical Past*, Milwaukee, Wisconsin: Marquette University Press, 1984.

Roach, M. E., and Eicher, J. B. (eds), *Dress, Adornment, and the Social Order*, J. Wiley, 1965.

Robbins, F. G., *The Sociology of Play, Recreation and Leisure Time*, Dubuque, Iowa: Brown, 1955.

Robert, K., *Les Gladiateurs dans l'Orient Grec*, Amsterdam: Hakkert, 1971.

Roberts, J. M., Arth, M. J., and Bush, R. R., 'Games in Culture', *American Anthropologist*, 61 (1959), 597–605.

Roberts, K., *Leisure*, Longman, 1970.

Roberts, K., *Contemporary Society and the Growth of Leisure*, Longman, 1978.

Roberts, K., *Youth and Leisure*, Allen and Unwin, 1983.

Rogers, M., 'Caillois' Classification of Games', *JLS*, 1 (1982), 225–31.

Rojek, C., 'Did Marx Have a Theory of Leisure?', *JLS*, 3 (1984), 163–74.

Rojek, C. (ed.), *Leisure for Leisure: Critical Essays*, Basingstoke: Macmillan Press, 1989.

Rorty, R., *Philosophy and the Mirror of Nature*, Oxford: Basil Blackwell, 1980.

Rotondi, G., *Leges Publicae Populi Romani*, Milan: Società Editrice Libraria, 1912.

Rousseau, G. S., and Porter, R. (eds), *Sexual Underworlds of the Enlightenment*, Manchester: Manchester University Press, 1987.

Rousselle, A., *Porneia: On Desire and the Body in Antiquity*, trans. F. Pheasant, Oxford: Basil Blackwell, 1988.

Royce, A. P., *The Anthropology of Dance*, Indiana University Press, 1977.

Rubner, A., *The Economics of Gambling*, Macmillan, 1966.

Sagarin, E., and Birenbaum, A. (eds), *People in Places: The Sociology of the Familiar*, Nelson, 1973.

Sahlins, M., *Islands of History*, Chicago, Illinois: University of Chicago Press, 1985.

Sallares, R., *The Ecology of the Ancient Greek World*, Duckworth, 1991.

Saller, R. P., *Personal Patronage under the Early Empire*, Cambridge: Cambridge University Press, 1982.

Saller, R. P., 'Familia, Domus, and the Roman Conception of the Family', *Phoenix*, 38 (1984), 336–55.

Saller, R. P., '*Patria Potestas* and the Stereotype of the Roman Family', *Continuity and Change*, 1 (1986), 7–22.

Salter, M. A. (ed.), *Play: Anthropological Perspectives*, West Point, New York: Leisure Press, 1978.

Salzman, M. R., *On Roman Time: The Codex-calendar of 354 and the Rhythms of Urban Life in Late Antiquity*, Berkeley, California: University of California Press, 1990.

Samuel, R., and Jones, G. S. (eds), *Culture, Ideology and Politics*, Routledge and Kegan Paul, 1983.

Sanger, W. W., *The History of Prostitution*, New York: Medical Publishing, 1913.

Saunders, D. M., and Turner, D. E., 'Gambling and Leisure: The Case of Racing', *JLS*, 6 (1987), 281–99.

Schama, S., *The Embarrassment of Riches: An Interpretation of Dutch Culture in the Golden Age*, Collins, 1987.

Schama, S., *Citizens: A Chronicle of the French Revolution*, New York: A. Knopf, 1989.

Schama, S., *Dead Certainties: (Unwarranted Speculations)*, Granta Books, 1991.

Schrift, A. D., *Nietzsche and the Question of Interpretation: Between Hermeneutics and Deconstruction*, Routledge, 1990.

Scobie, A., 'Slums, Sanitation, and Mortality in the Roman World', *Klio*, 68 (1986), 399–433.

Scott, J. M., *The White Poppy: A History of Opium*, Heinemann, 1969.

Scullard, H. H., *Festivals and Ceremonies of the Roman Republic*, Thames and Hudson, 1981.

Seabrook, J., *The Leisure Society*, Oxford: Basil Blackwell, 1988.

Segal, E., 'To Win or to Die of Shame: A Taxonomy of Values', *Journal of Sport History*, 11 (1984), 25–31.

Sekora, J., *Luxury; The Concept in Western Thought, Eden to Smollett*, Johns Hopkins University Press, 1977.

Shaw, S. M., 'Gender and Leisure: Inequality in the Distribution of Leisure Time', *JLR*, 17 (1985), 266–82.

Shelton, J.-A., *As the Romans Did: A Source Book in Roman Social History*, Oxford: Oxford University Press, 1988.

Short, J. F., and Wolfgang, M. E. (eds), *Collective Violence*, New York: Aldine, 1972.

Shorter, E., 'Towards a History of La Vie Intime: The Evidence of Cultural Criticism in Nineteenth Century Bavaria', in M. R. Marrus (ed.), *The Emergence of Leisure*, New York: Harper and Row, 1974, pp. 38–68.

Showerman, G., *Rome and the Romans*, New York: The MacMillan Co., 1931.

Sjoberg, L. (ed.), *Risk and Society*, Allen and Unwin, 1987.

Skinner, Q. (ed.), *The Return of Grand Theory in the Human Sciences*, Cambridge: Cambridge University Press, 1985.

Slater, N. W., *Reading Petronius*, Baltimore, Maryland: Johns Hopkins University Press, 1990.

Slater, W. J., *Dining in a Classical Context*, Ann Arbor, Michigan: University of Michigan Press, 1991.

Smigel, E. O. (ed.), *Work and Leisure*, New Haven, Connecticut: College and University Press, 1963.

Smith, M. A., Porter, S., and Smith, C. S. (eds), *Leisure and Society in Britain*, Allen Lane, 1973.

Soffer, G., *Husserl and the Question of Relativism*, Kluwer Academic, 1991.

Sorabji, R., *Time, Creation and the Continuum: Theories in Antiquity and the Early Middle Ages*, Duckworth, 1983.

Spruill, C. R., *Power Paradigms in the Social Sciences*, University Press of America, 1983.

Stearns, P. N., 'Social History Update: Encountering Postmodernism', *Journal of Social History*, 24 (1990), 449–52.

Steffenhagen, R. A., and Burns, J. D., *The Social Dynamics of Self-esteem*, New York: Praeger, 1987.

Steinmetz, A., *The Gaming Table: Its Votaries and Victims*, 2 vols, Tinsley, 1870.

Stevens, P. (ed.), *Studies in the Anthropology of Play*, West Point, New York: Leisure Press, 1977.

Stocks, J. L., 'Schole', *CQ*, 30 (1936), 177–87.

Stokes, G., 'Work, Unemployment and Leisure', *JLS*, 2 (1983), 269–86.

Stone, L., *The Family, Sex and Marriage in England 1500–1800*, Harmondsworth: Penguin, 1979.

Stone, L., 'The Revival of Narrative', *P & P*, 85 (1979), 3–24.

Stone, L., *The Past and the Present*, Routledge and Kegan Paul, 1981.

Stormann, W., 'Work: True Leisure's Home?', *JLS*, 8 (1989), 25–33.

Street, B., 'Orality and Literacy as Ideological Constructions: Some Problems in Cross-cultural Studies', *Culture and History*, 2 (1987), 7–30.

Sussman, L. A., *The Major Declamations Ascribed to Quintilian: A Translation*, New York: P. Lang, 1987.

Sussman, L. S., 'Workers and Drones: Labor, Idleness and Gender Definition in Hesiod's Beehive', *Arethusa*, 11 (1978), 27–41.

Syme, R., *The Roman Revolution*, Oxford: Oxford University Press, 1939.

Talal Asad, 'Anthropological Conceptions of Religion: Reflections on Geertz', *Man*, ns 18 (1983), 237–59.

Tanzer, H. H., *The Common People of Pompeii*, Baltimore, Maryland: Johns Hopkins University Press, 1939.

Taylor, G., *Pride, Shame, and Guilt: Emotions of Self-assessment*, Oxford: Clarendon Press, 1985.

Tec, N., *Gambling in Sweden*, Totowa, New Jersey: The Bedminster Press, 1964.

Therborn, G., *The Ideology of Power and the Power of Ideology*, Verso, 1980.

Thiselton, A. C., *New Horizons in Hermeneutics*, HarperCollins, 1992.

Thomas, K., 'Work and Leisure in Pre-Industrial Society', *P & P*, 29 (1964), 50–66.

Thompson, J. B., *Studies in the Theory of Ideology*, Cambridge: Polity, 1984.

Thompson, J. B., *Ideology and Modern Culture*, Cambridge: Polity, 1990.

Thompson, D. W., 'Games and Playthings', *G & R*, 2 (1933), 71–9.

Thorne, C., *Ideology and Power*, Macmillan, 1965.

Touraine, A., 'Leisure Activities and Social Participation', in M. R. Marrus (ed.), *The Emergence of Leisure*, New York: Harper and Row, 1974, pp. 101–15.

Toynbee, J. M. C., 'Beasts and their Names in the Roman Empire', *PBSR*, 16 (1948), 24–37.

Treggiari, S., *Roman Marriage: Iusti Coniuges from the Time of Cicero to the Time of Ulpian*, Oxford: Clarendon Press, 1991.

Turner, B. S., *The Body and Society*, Oxford: Basil Blackwell, 1984.

Turner, V., *From Ritual to Theatre: The Human Seriousness of Play*, New York: Performing Arts Journal Publications, 1982.

Unger, P., *Identity, Consciousness and Value*, Oxford: Oxford University Press, 1990.

Urry, J., *The Tourist Gaze: Leisure and Travel in Contemporary Societies*, Sage, 1990.

van der Dussen, W. J., and Rubinoff, L. (eds), *Objectivity, Method and Point of View: Essays in the Philosophy of History*, Leiden: E. J. Brill, 1991.

Van Moorst, H., 'Leisure and Social Theory', *JLS*, 1 (1982), 157–69.

Vattimo, G., *The End of Modernity: Nihilism and Hermeneutics in Post-modern Culture*, trans. J. R. Snyder, Cambridge: Polity, 1988.

Veal, A. J., *Leisure and the Future*, Allen and Unwin, 1987.

Veblen, T., *The Theory of the Leisure Class*, Unwin Books, 1970 (first published 1898).

Veyne, P., *Le Pain et Le Cirque: Sociologie Historique d'un Pluralisme Politique*, Paris: Editions du Seuil, 1976. Translated as *Bread and Circuses: Historical Sociology and Political Pluralism*, abridged by O. Murray, trans. B. Pearce, Allen Lane, Penguin, 1990.

Veyne, P. (ed.), *A History of Private Life*, trans. A. Goldhammer, Cambridge, Mass.: Bellknap Press of Harvard University, 1987.

Vickerman, R. W., 'The Contributions of Economics to the Study of Leisure: A Review', *JLS*, 2 (1983), 345–64.

Vogel, L., 'Circus Race Scenes', *ABull*, 51 (1969), 155–60.

Von Furstenberg, G. M., *Acting under Uncertainty*, Kluwer Academic, 1990.

Vovelle, M., *Ideologies and Mentalities*, trans. E. O'Flaherty, Cambridge: Polity, 1990.

Wagenaar, W. A., *Paradoxes of Gambling Behaviour*, Hove: Erlbaum, 1988.

Walker, J. A., 'Death as Recreation: Armchair Mountaineering', *JLS*, 3 (1984), 67–76.

Wallace, A. F. C., et al. (eds), *Perspectives on Anthropology 1976*, Washington D.C.: American Anthropological Association (no. 10), 1977.

Wallace-Hadrill, A., 'Rome's Cultural Revolution', *JRS*, 79 (1989), 157–64.

Walters, J., *Ancient Roman Concepts of Manhood and their Relation with Other Markers of Social Status*, unpublished PhD dissertation, Cambridge, 1993.

Waltzing, J.-P., *Etude Historique sur les Corporations Professionnelles chez les Romains*, 4 vols, New York: Georg Olms, 1970 (first published 1895–1900).

Walvin, J., and Mangan, J. A. (eds), *Manliness and Morality: Middle-class Masculinity in Britain and America, 1880–1940*, Manchester: Manchester University Press, 1987.

Warde-Fowler, W., *Social Life at Rome in the Age of Cicero*, Macmillan, 1908.

Weber, M., *The Protestant Ethic and the Spirit of Capitalism*, trans. T. Parsons, Allen and Unwin, 1976.

Weege. F., *Der Tanz in der Antike*, Hildersheim: Olms, 1976.

Weeks, J., *Sex, Politics and Society: The Regulation of Sexuality Since 1800*, Longman, 1981.

Welch, K., 'Roman Amphitheatres Revived', *JRA*, 4 (1991), 272–81.
White, H., *Metahistory*, Baltimore, Maryland: Johns Hopkins University Press, 1973.
White, H., and Manuel, F. E., *Theories of History*, Los Angeles, California: William Andrews Clark Memorial Library, 1978.
White, R. J., *Artemidorus: The Interpretation of Dreams*, Park Ridge, New Jersey: Noyes Press, 1975.
Wiedemann, T., *Emperors and Gladiators*, Routledge, 1992.
Wieseltier, L., 'Spoilers at the Party', *The National Interest*, 17 (1989), 12–16.
Wilson, C. P., *Jokes: Form, Content, Use and Function*, Academic Press, 1979.
Wilson, J., *Politics and Leisure*, Allen and Unwin, 1988.
Wilson, L. M., T*he Clothing of the Ancient Romans*, Baltimore, Maryland: Johns Hopkins University Press, 1938.
Wirszubski, Ch. *Libertas as a Political Idea at Rome During the Late Republic and Early Principate*, Cambridge: Cambridge University Press, 1960.
Wirszubski, Ch., 'Cicero's Cum Dignitate Otium: A Reconsideration', *JRS*, 44 (1954), 1–13. Reprinted in R. Seager, *The Crisis of the Roman Republic*, Cambridge: Heffer, 1969, pp. 183–95.
Wistrand, M., *Entertainment and Violence in Ancient Rome: The Attitudes of Roman Writers of the First Century AD*, Gothenburg: Acta Universitatis Gothoburgensis, 1992.
Wittgenstein, L., *Philosophical Investigations*, trans. G. E. M. Anscombe, Oxford: Basil Blackwell, 1969.
Wittgenstein, L., *The Blue and Brown Books*, Oxford: Basil Blackwell, 1969.
Wittgenstein, L., *Culture and Value*, ed. G. H. Von Wright in collaboration with H. Nyman, trans. P. Winch, Oxford: Basil Blackwell, 1980.
Wright, L., *Clean and Decent: The History of the Bath and Loo*, Routledge and Kegan Paul, 1980.
Wrong, D. H., *Power: Its Forms, Bases and Uses*, Oxford: Basil Blackwell, 1979.
Wykes, A., *Gambling*, Aldus, 1964.
Wynne, D., 'Leisure, Lifestyle and the Construction of Social Position', *JLS*, 9 (1990), 21–34.
Yardley, K., and Honess, T. (eds), *Self and Identity: Psychosocial Perspectives*, Chichester: Wiley, 1987.
Yavetz, Z., *Plebs and Princeps*, Oxford: Clarendon Press, 1969.
Yavetz, Z., *Julius Caesar and his Public Image*, Thames and Hudson, 1983.
Yegül, F., *Baths and Bathing in Classical Antiquity*, Cambridge, Mass: MIT Press, 1992.
Yeo, E., and Yeo, S. (eds), *Popular Culture and Class Conflict 1590–1914*, Brighton: Harvester, 1981.
York, M., *The Roman Festival Calendar of Numa Pompilius*, New York: P. Lang, 1986.
Yovel, Y., *Kant and the Philosophy of History*, Princeton, New Jersey: Princeton University Press, 1980.
Zanker, P., *The Power of Images in the Age of Augustus*, trans. A. Shapiro, Ann Arbor, Michigan: University of Michigan Press, 1988.
Zijderveld, A. C., 'The Sociology of Humour and Laughter', *Current Sociology*, 31 (1983), 1–103.

Zola, I. K., 'Observations on Gambling in a Lower-Class Setting', *Social Problems*, 10 (1962), 353–61.

Zuzanek, J., and Mannell, R., 'Work–Leisure Relationships from a Sociological and Social Psychological Perspective', *JLS*, 2 (1983), 327–44.

Index